3/10

Crossing
the Gods

Crossing the Gods

World Religions and Worldly Politics

N. J. Demerath III

Rutgers University Press

New Brunswick, New Jersey, and London

Library of Congress Cataloging-in-Publication Data

Demerath, N.J. (Nicholas Jay), 1936–
    Crossing the gods : world religions and wordly politics/N.J. Demerath III.
      p. cm.
    Includes bibliographical references and index.
    ISBN 0-8135-2924-7 (alk. paper)
    1. Religion and politics—United States. I. Title.

BL65.P7 D46 2001
291.1'77—dc21

                                               00-045747

British Cataloging-in-Publication data for this book is available from the British Library.

Manufactured in the United States of America

To Helen,
spirit for us all

Contents

Preface

In the sprawling metropolis of Apocrypha, there is a tale of two deranged blind men—one who has spent his life wandering in his backyard convinced he has traversed the world, another who has spent his life traversing the world convinced that he has never left his backyard. I can identify with both. Over the past decade, I have paid research visits to fourteen countries around the globe. In moving between Brazil, Guatemala, Poland, Northern Ireland, Sweden, Egypt, Turkey, Pakistan, Indonesia, Israel, India, Thailand, Japan, and China, I have been struck by both similarities and differences with the United States, but I have always had the sense of remaining close to my own backyard.

In looking at different patterns of religion, violence, politics, and the state within these different cultures, I have also been constantly aware of comparing the incomparable. One particular image seems to symbolize my mission. In the fall of 1993 in New Delhi, India, I happened to glimpse a television report on a man setting a world record for tightrope walking at altitude. He was walking between two hot-air balloons at five thousand feet without a net, taking one very cautious step after another, with the help of a long balancing pole in a whistling wind. I realized that I had been doing much the same thing—at least metaphorically.

It wasn't that I had defied death or pursued a world's record, but there was something about the daredevil's adventure that symbolized cross-cultural research. A hot-air balloon is not a bad representation for any culture, and in moving between more than a dozen countries, I often had the sense of tiptoeing across a void with nothing to catch me and with spectators more likely to wonder at my foolishness than my skill. I have been periodically encouraged by realizing that at least the fellow on television completed his task successfully.

But if cross-cultural comparisons may seem misbegotten, there was a time when many social scientists viewed any scholarship on religion as suspect. As recently as twenty years ago, any Western social scientist focusing on religion was likely to be regarded in the same way that the social sciences had come to regard religion itself: anachronistic and irrelevant. Suddenly, however, these perceptions began to change. In 1979 a series of events called new attention to religion's power and pertinence.

In 1979 the United States was still reeling from Jonestown and its 914 deaths in the jungle of British Guyana. This was a numbing climax to the growing cult phenomenon, that had spread sufficiently into the middle class to constitute not only a threat to established churches but a commentary on the inadequacies of families, schools, and mental health agencies. Some of us were even approached to counsel those who were touched by it. Nineteen seventy-nine was also the year that Jerry Falwell's Moral Majority moved into high gear as part of Ronald Reagan's 1980 presidential campaign. Traditional American religion seemed to be overspilling its traditional boundaries. Evangelicalism was no longer just otherworldly escapist fare for the disadvantaged; at least one strain had taken this-worldly political form in pressing for a social agenda on the right. Liberal Protestantism had long been taken for granted even by those secularists who disdained it, but it was now in decline. As religious conservatism surged, secularists were not only perplexed but challenged.

Even more important than domestic religious developments of 1979 were four developments elsewhere. First, in that year Pope John Paul II attended the Puebla Conference of Latin American Bishops in Mexico, addressed the indigenous denizens of Oaxaca and Chiapas, and gave at least ambiguous imprimatur to the gathering strains of Liberation Theology and its "preferential option for the poor." Second, in 1979 the same pope returned to his native Poland and provided symbolic blessing for the link between the Polish Catholic Church and the trade union Solidarity in a movement that would take over the country a decade later. Third, 1979 was the year of the famed Camp David Accords in which President Jimmy Carter secured a negotiated Middle East agreement between Egypt's Islamic president, Anwar Sadat, and Israel's Jewish prime minister, Menachem Begin, for which both of the latter shared a Nobel Prize. Finally, it was also in 1979 that the Ayatollah Khomeini returned to Iran from Paris to assume the combined roles of spiritual leader and de facto chief of state; that same year the U.S. embassy in Tehran was seized and sixty-six Americans taken hostage, fifty-three not to be released until the eve of Reagan's presidential inauguration fourteen months later.

Religion seemed no longer down and out but up and in. Scholars of religion began to reflect the change and ceased to be the wallflower waifs of the local social scene. Now, instead of leaving us behind in the search for more interesting cocktail party conversation, folks began to seek us out. In the years that have elapsed since 1979, it is not clear that we have fully captured the truth, though we have certainly assaulted it from different perspectives. Especially where power is concerned, religion is neither the wimp of past deprecations nor the bully of more recent journalistic accounts. Religion seemed in dire need of enhanced cross-national and cross-cultural international perspectives.

Yet I was not an obvious candidate to provide it. After more than thirty years of writing and teaching about American religion and culture, I had become embarrassed by my provincialism. I began to worry that some of the things I assumed to be universals were absent in other societies. Does every country require some form of civil religious common denominator? Must every effective religion have an organizational embodiment akin to the Western church? Conversely, I also began to suspect that some of the traits I presumed uniquely American were also present elsewhere. Is the "separation of church and state" as singular as we sometimes suppose? Is this the only country where liberal religion is in decline while conservative religion grows?

Meanwhile, my classroom experiences suggested that I was not alone in my provincialism. My courses on the sociology of religion had become increasingly global in their content, but most of the students shared my backyard confinement. I found it difficult to teach about other religions purely in their own terms or as an exercise in academic abstraction. Students' eyes glazed over at one more cerebral summary of another foreign religion's history and practices.

Nonetheless, there was something compelling about religion's involvement in the turbulence of politics. Isolated accounts of the doctrines and rituals of non-Christian faiths such as Judaism, Islam, Hinduism, or Buddhism can be numbingly pedantic—especially when they are cast in terms of some hypothetical individual adherent with little regard for religion's varying social contexts. Although I shall provide brief primers on each of these world religions at the appropriate junctures, I do so with full awareness that accounts floating in a contextual limbo with no appreciation for historical and national settings can be both highly misleading and not a little soporific. I saw time and again how students who had slept through textbook exegeses suddenly awakened to analyses of a religion's role in the hurly-burly world of societal change and conflict. When any religion is implicated in tragic violence and political conflict, it can take on new and compelling urgency, and religion has been implicated in violence in almost every one of the countries we shall be considering. As just one example, it is hard not to respond to estimates of more than five hundred thousand deaths that resulted from the mutual Hindu-Muslim carnage following the partition of India and Pakistan in 1947 and the mounting toll of the continuing violence. Religion seems to come most alive in the midst of death.

As these realizations dawned, I was involved in a study of religion and politics in Springfield, Massachusetts. That project and its resulting book were as intensively local as this one has been extensively global. As I repeatedly drove the twenty-five miles to Springfield from my home in Amherst, I began to think of that drive as a kind of intellectual treadmill. The more I learned about my own immediate area, the more eager I became for direct experience with other peoples, other societies, and other religious traditions, and the more I suspected that the real secret to religion's social significance and vitality required an appreciation of some very non-American dynamics.

Reconnoitering the Book

Because this book has a geographical flavor, its basic thesis is briefly introduced in an initial reconnaissance. The thesis involves three related paradoxes concerning the relations between religion and politics, sacred and secular, and canon and context. Religious purists have stressed each of these distinctions and sought to keep the twain apart; but religious vitality and understanding depend upon bridging the distinctions and benefiting from the mix. Yet the bridging contains risks as well as gains, as we shall see repeatedly.

There are two main parts to what follows. The first involves "Circling the Globe" and might be termed a "travelography" because it combines two well-established genres. It reports on a tourist's odyssey around the world, and it offers a bit of the anthropologist's field ethnography. Here I want to share my experiences and perceptions in each country to provide a sense of how religion and politics have been involved in the past and how they are interacting now.

The object in the first half of the book is to introduce some of the global religious and political variations that can be so elusive and confusing. Rather than leap into deeper analysis, it seems only fair to begin with some basic description. How do these places feel to a visitor? What are the basic fault lines along which current tensions and conflicts have formed? What are the trajectories of change from past to present and possibly into the future?

The book's second part is called "Coming Home" because it returns our focus to the United States and seeks explanations for what was observed in our world tour. If the first half involved travelography, this one offers a more conceptual and comparative "travelology" that combines travel and ethnology to explore the causes and consequences of religiously inflamed political conflict at several different levels. The issues include culture wars, religion as a cause and construct of violence, and the problems of separating religion from politics versus the imperatives of separating religion from the state. Finally, the book probes behind America's status and self-image as the world's most religious nation. It places that claim in comparative context and argues that America is not more religious but "differently religious" as a result of its once distinctive patterns of congregational religion, religious pluralism, diverse forms of religious identity, and civil religion—all seen in the perspective of a world that is simultaneously undergoing globalization, on the one hand, and witnessing assertions of very localized forms of nationalism and "culturism," on the other.

A major objective in all of this is to examine the United States through the cross-cultural kaleidoscope formed by the fourteen cases. Concepts that have become major staples in understanding American religion take on different meanings in other settings. Once the concepts are enriched and critiqued through exposure abroad, they offer fresh perspectives here at home.

A word about the book's title. The most obvious connotation of "Crossing the Gods" refers to the project's cross-national comparisons across the world. But it has several other semioses. It suggests somewhat impishly that religious violence may reflect a crossing or betrayal of gods who become angry or cross as a result. It also implies at least the possibility of a syncretic, hybridizing crossing of the gods as religions reveal increasingly similar dynamics in the global mix. One of these dynamics involves the crossing of religion into politics and vice versa—patterns that often seem to involve a double cross. And insofar as the book is the work of someone whose home culture is Christian, the title is a warning that its depictions of other gods may reflect the cross of at least a culturally Christian bias, however wayward. In the final analysis, our backyards are never far from view.

Acknowledgments

Any project that involves a lone scholar wandering the world is apt to incur far more than the unusual indebtedness. I am especially grateful to the Lilly Endowment for providing the basic grant that made these trips possible. But Lilly's former vice president for religion, Robert Lynn, and his successor, Craig Dykstra, have provided much more than funds. They have offered patient support and gentle responsiveness at every turn.

In addition to Lilly's support, I was also an appreciative recipient of a Fulbright Award for study in India in 1993. Moreover, my shoestring travel budget was critically augmented from time to time by lecture fees at various universities in the countries I was visiting.

Certainly the single largest source of support and assistance involved the many individuals who guided me, tutored me, entertained me, befriended me, and endured me in country after country around the globe. Limitations of both style and space preclude an adequate expression of my gratitude to the entire roster of social science colleagues, religionists, politicians, government officials, and journalists who gave this project life and meaning. They were universally generous with their time, their knowledge, their patience, and their humor.

In each country, however, a few key individuals went beyond the pale. Before singling them out for appreciation, it should be well understood that I am not singling them out as responsible for any of the project's deficiencies. This volume would never have lifted off without boosts from the following persons in various settings: Brazil: Madeleine Cousineau, Luiz Alberto Gomez de Souza, Ivo Lasbaupin, and Cecelia Mariz; Guatemala: Rick and Betty Adams, John A. Nelson, Douglas Sullivan-Gonsalez, Daniel Saxon; Poland: Halina Gryzmala-Moszczynska, Miraslawa Grabowska, Krzysztof Kosela, Shawn Landres; Northern Ireland: John Fulton, David Livingston, Liam O'Dowd, Sister Geraldine Smyth; Sweden: Lennart Ejerfelt, Goran Goranssen, Krister Stendahl; Egypt: Ahmed Abdallah, Raymond W. Baker, Donna Divine, Saad Ibrahim; Turkey: Akile Gursoy, Tony Greenwood, Metin Heper, Binnaz Toprak, Ilter Turan; Pakistan: Peter Dobbs, Anwar Syed, Aslam Syed, Anita Weiss; Indonesia: Arief Budiman, Jaard Hommes, Anna Hommes, Saraswati Sunindyo, Bak Wirawan, Lian Wirawan; Israel: Gideon Aran, Menachem Friedman, Charles Liebman, Karen Loeb, Shalom Schwartz; India: Dipankar Gupta, Mala Gupta, Mushiral Hasan, Zoya Hasan, Milton Israel, T. N. Madan, John Mansfield, and Romila Thapar; Thailand: Samboon Suksamran, Prasert Yamklingfung; Japan: Yoshiya Abe, Koya Azumi, Richard Gardner, Naoki Onishi, and Susumu Shimazono; China: Andrew Abel, Chen Zemin, Albert Cohen, Xu Xiao Niam, and a number of scholars who would perhaps prefer anonymity in China's ever-changing political climate.

I am grateful to the many students and colleagues who have listened dutifully to my lectures and seminars on the book's developing themes over the past decade. I am even more grateful to those who have talked back. Karen Straight served as my able bibliographic alter ego in the local library while I was on the road and in the air. Karen Mason lent me her superb secretarial skills and "can-do" competence as the volume hobbled down the home stretch. Mark Silk provided invaluable feedback on the manuscript at several stages. David Myers, my editor at Rutgers University Press, did what every good editor should do in alternating praise and well-deserved criticism. This book's shortcomings were considerably longer when he first saw it. Robert Burchfield was an exemplary copyeditor whose once-over-heavily was both informed and gentle.

My wife, Judy, has been a wonderful travel companion on several of the trips required for this project. Otherwise, she has been a model of support and patience when I have been either out of the country or out of touch in a world wholly my own. Finally, this book is dedicated to my mother, who continues to bless her children, grandchildren, and great-grandchildren with her wisdom, wit, and abiding love.

Revised Reprintings

Several portions of this book represent revised versions of previously published articles. I am grateful to a number of journals and their editors for granting access to following articles:

"Religious Capital and Capital Religions: Cross-Cultural and Non-Legal Factors in the Separation of Church and State," *Daedalus* 120 (summer 1991): 21–40.

"The Moth and the Flame: Religion and Power in Comparative Blur," Furfee Lecture, Association for the Sociology of Religion, August 1993, *Sociology of Religion* 55 (winter 1994):105–117.

"Religion, Politics, and the State: Cross-Cultural Observations," *Cross-Currents* (spring 1997):43–58; Karen Straight, coauthor.

"Lions among the Lambs: America's 'Culture Wars' in Cross-Cultural Perspective," in *Culture Wars in American Politics: Critical Views of a Popular Thesis*, ed. Rhys Williams (Chicago: Aldine de Gruyter, 1997); Karen Straight, coauthor.

"Excepting American Exceptionalism: Is the U.S. the World's Most Religious Nation?" *The Annals* 558 (July 1998):28–37.

"The Rise of 'Cultural Religion' in European Christianity: Learning from Poland, Northern Ireland, and Sweden," *Social Compass* 47 (June 2000):127–139.

Crossing
the Gods

Introduction

Moths and Flames

The image of a moth circling a flame is virtually universal. Moths everywhere are drawn to the warmth and light of a flame, and moths everywhere risk an igniting fate similar to the mythical Greek Icarus who perished when flying too close to the sun. The moral here involves a cautionary paradox. The object is to fly near enough to the heat to receive its benefits without flying so near as to suffer its costs. The optimal course is difficult to calculate and maintain. Increasing benefits also entail increasing risks.

Religion offers a worldwide case in point. Like the moth, religion often ventures out of its safe orbit to experience the light and heat of a flame. When religion keeps its distance, it maintains purity at the risk of a precious but often irrelevant marginality; when religion approaches the flame, it experiences relevance at the risk of being consumed.

Consider religion's relation to politics. To many Western ears, the very phrase "religion and politics" means trouble. It is a volatile combination that suggests something is wrong. After all, religion involves otherworldly beliefs and rituals that need to be nurtured in their own sacred garden. Politics, on the other hand, involves all-too-worldly concerns pursued within a secular weed patch of compromise and corruption. Religion seems at its best when it is farthest from politics. Politics may appear to be at its best when it involves religion, but such appearances are treacherously deceiving. Surely the best relationship between these two realms is no relationship at all.

Or is it? As we shall see, there is truth in this view—a view that is part of the dual legacy of Protestant Christianity and the American "separation of church and state." But in other ways, this perspective confuses two distinctions and draws the wrong line in the wrong sand. There is a critical distinction between religion's relationship to politics and religion's relationship to the state. Politics involves processes of power seeking

1

and policy shaping; states involve governing structures that generally derive from some form of charter or constitution. One without the other is rare. Politics without states can amount to an anarchic free-for-all; states without politics are the dictatorial regimes of despots and oligarchies.

John F. Kennedy's campaign in 1960 for the U.S. presidency illustrates religion's different relation to each. As a Roman Catholic, Kennedy revived old concerns among Protestants that a Catholic president would be a stalking horse for the Pope, who would soon take over the U.S. government and make it a Vatican stable. Kennedy's appearance before a group of largely Baptist clergy in Houston, Texas, was a critical turning point in his presidential campaign. Basically, he affirmed religion in politics but attacked religion in the state by noting the difference between a Catholic politician and a Catholic president. The former could certainly pursue his private convictions, Catholic or otherwise, but the latter is sworn to uphold and work within the laws of the land and especially its constitutional framework.

The Baptists nodded approvingly as members of a denomination that had been an early advocate of separating church and state in seventeenth-century Rhode Island. By now the distinction is commonly acknowledged, if not always implemented. But cleaving religion from politics is a very different matter. Separating religion from the state is both possible and desirable; separating religion from politics is frequently neither possible nor desirable.

Clergy and other religious officials often address such religiously sensitive political issues as conscientious objector status in the military, nuclear disarmament, abortion, contraception, capital punishment, gay and lesbian rights, family values, and questions of poverty and inequality. But they know and generally accept that, even if their positions resonate, they must work within a state structure where some things may be changed by law but others must endure because they involve basic constitutional rights protected by the courts. Such rights generally include some version of the freedom of—and possibly from—religion.

It is true that not all religion is socially engulfed. Some forms offer meaning and belonging to individuals and to small communities of adherents that do not require political involvement and where retreat into a private sanctum is in order. Some religious groups take such extreme positions in avoiding wider social entanglements that these become political positions in their own right when they involve, for example, aberrant patterns of communal living, home schooling, or preventing their severely ill children from receiving standard medical care.

What attracts religion to the political arena? The answer is similar to the infamous Willy Sutton's explanation of why he robbed banks:

"Because that's where the money is." From a religious perspective, politics is where a good deal of the moral and ethical payoff resides. If some religion is privatized and inward looking and other religion is in aggressive and aloof retreat from its surrounding community, clearly there is another, more socially active pattern. Most religions have a social agenda not only for themselves and their members but for the society around them. Many religions define their very rationale in the mission to confront sin and sloth in the world beyond their sanctuaries.

It is by virtue of this impulse that religion is implicated in both the best of times and the worst of times. Religious conflict may be a low point for the surrounding society but a high point for the religions themselves. Any religion's vision of a better world or world to come may be as chilling to the unconverted as it is uplifting to the faithful. The more zealous the vision, the more alienating its potential. Passionate convictions are always jealous masters. As militant, even terrorist, movements around the world attest, the strength of one's own commitments is often measured by one's intolerance of others' commitments.

A religion without a crisis can be a religion with a crisis. Religions must be wary of easy routinization and "lazy monopolies." Lassitude is an archenemy of faith, and there is nothing like a crisis to supply the requisite fire. The sense of a looming threat helps to mobilize the faithful and concentrate resources. Just as incumbent politicians are sometimes accused of war mongering for the sake of reelection, so are religious leaders sometimes thought of as hypersensitive to evil and moral decline. Even when crises are real and disabling in the short run, they can lead the resulting remnants to new opportunities and new fulfillments.

Here religious prophets are the great exemplars, and in the pages to follow, we shall meet many around the world who resemble the Americans Martin Luther King Jr. and Malcolm X. Religious movements in American politics range from the Christian Coalition of evangelical Protestantism to the Catholic bishops' stance on behalf of a "consistent ethic" that favors life when threatened by nuclear weapons, capital punishment, poverty, or abortion. Nor are these exclusively the work of entrepreneurial activists. Such movements reach deep into the churches and temples of America to mobilize both direct and indirect support among the faithful.

But like the moth, religion increases both its possible gains and possible losses by approaching the political flame too closely. The assassinations of Martin Luther King Jr. and Malcolm X represent the most tragic outcome shared by many others around the world, including Catholic proponents of Liberation Theology in Latin America, Protestants and Catholics on both sides of the violence in Northern Ireland, Muslim clerics and activists from Nigeria to Indonesia, Sikh devotees in India, and leaders of unofficial "house" churches in China, to name but a few.

There are also losses short of death. The cultural power of religion in deploying moral suasion can win dramatic victories against overwhelming odds, as illustrated by King and the nonviolent civil rights movement in the U.S. South during the 1960s. But over the long haul, the political establishment's greater access to money, media control, and coercion takes its toll. Religion may experience both direct and indirect losses. The direct losses of legislative inaction or government suppression are painfully obvious, and fighting uphill political battles can be momentarily exciting but ultimately draining for any religious group or movement. In the United States, this is well illustrated by both the conservative Moral Majority and the Christian Coalition on the right and by the liberal National Council of Churches on the left.

Indirect losses may be more severe. Religion in politics can sometimes not only turn apparent defeat into a martyr's victory but turn apparent victory into a co-opted defeat. When any religion is welcomed into the halls of power, assured that it is "preaching to the converted," and given a well-upholstered seat at the right hand of power, there are almost inevitable problems ahead. This is the road to apathy, laxity, and the universal threat to religion that comes in the form of complacency. I shall examine several countries that are officially religious—whether Christian, Islamic, or Buddhist. But if the designation suggests a religious state, the reality is more often a state religion. With few exceptions, the powers of national governments far outstrip the powers of religious bodies. States frequently align themselves with religion in order to control it. They even provide funds for religion as long as it conforms to state rules and regulations.

For many religions, politics offers alluring bait, but state establishment represents a barbed hook. In fact, establishment status confers only marginal advantages on those religious majorities most likely to gain such standing. In yet another irony of religion's relation to power, establishment may be more of a problem than a triumph for both religion and the state. In country after country, a religion's capital is often most effective when it is not a capital religion. This is nowhere more apparent than in the United States, where the First Amendment's prohibition of the state establishment of religion leveled the playing field for a highly competitive form of denominational vitality as the state by and large stayed out of the contest.

So far I have concentrated on religious moths and political flames. There are, however, also political moths seeking religious flames. If anything, this may be the more dangerous syndrome. Consider the assassinations of such leading political figures as Egypt's Anwar Sadat, Israel's

Yitzhak Rabin, and India's Mohandas Gandhi, not to mention his unrelated namesake, Indira Gandhi. All of these political leaders were drawn into religious conflicts they were unable to resolve.

Many politicians seek out religion voluntarily as a basic component of their strategies to gain or retain office. Once again, the question is why should the political moth approach the religious flame? The possible benefits are several. First, just as politics can energize religion, religion can energize politics. Second, religion and its cultural power can provide legitimacy and moral leverage—a kind of innocence by association. Third, politicians may seek direct access to a particularly important or troublesome religious community as a way of pacifying problems before they erupt.

American politicians are scarcely unique in cloaking themselves in religious garments on the hustings. Politicians all over the world don religious garbs. But here, too, maximizing gains may involve maximizing risks. All of the politicians just mentioned were assassinated by members of their own religion or by religious groups they had gone out of their way to befriend.

In the passionate world of religious activism, there is sometimes a fine line between loyalty and betrayal. As already noted, it is one thing to woo religion as a politician but quite another to do so as a state official, and the risks are different in each case. Politicking may suffer when religious ties to one community cut the candidate off from other communities. Religious politicking may also build up high expectations that even successful candidates will be unwilling or unable to fulfill as state officeholders—one more version of what might be called pie-in-the-sky rhetoric running afoul of pie-in-the-face reality.

The risks of establishing religion are even greater for the society. The American founders sensed the risk, hence the very first item of the First Amendment's religion clause: "Congress shall make no law respecting an establishment of religion, or prohibiting the free exercise thereof." At the time, there was concern about getting a fledgling federal government off the ground without having it captured by one religious denomination at the expense of others. As we shall see repeatedly around the world, state anointment of any one religion in the midst of religious diversity is a sure-fire recipe for conflict and possibly for violence. Guatemala, Northern Ireland, Israel, and India are only a few of the nations where religious strife over state power has had bloody consequences.

Sacred and Secular

Religion's relationships with politics are in many ways only special cases of a larger distinction between the worlds of the sacred and the secular and the sometimes paradoxical relations between them. Again the moth and the flame are instructive.

Sacred things are things set apart that inspire special awe and veneration, that excite moments of self-transcendence and confer a measure of collective identity, and that generally involve some form of ritual and the odd leap of faith. By contrast, the secular is experienced as ordinary, everyday, and uninspiring. The secular may involve powerful forces that need to be confronted, but they are perceived as external realities rather than internal bonds.

Religion and the sacred are not synonymous. Although religion offers a rich array of sacred examples, religion does not have the exclusive sacred franchise, nor is it exclusively sacred. Music, sports, and politics are only a few alternative sources of the sacred, and religion sometimes fades to the point of seeing its sacred core succumb to its secular trappings.

Much of this may seem like the kind of idle word play that angels are reputed to inscribe on the heads of pins. The words become more significant, however, when the historical dimension is added. Instead of merely parsing the sacred as an idealized abstraction, there is now considerable dispute about whether societies have experienced secularization. over time. "Secularization" refers to the process by which the sacred is either taken for granted or is no longer taken at all. Secularized religion declines through the demystification and disenchantment of its message and the disengagement and displacement of its social standing.

But this is not necessarily an "all-to-nothing" trend that is linear, inevitable, and irreversible. It is important to avoid the mythological poles of early religious omnipotence, on the one extreme, and later religious demise, on the other. Nor is religious persistence itself a rebuttal to secularization, for the real question is persistence in what form. Every version of today's religion—whether liberal or conservative, mainstream or militant—differs from its previous incarnations. Moreover, it is hard to characterize any single country in terms of a single trend. A surging religion in one part of society may be accompanied by a sagging religion in another part. There are subtle dynamics and seemingly inconsistent trends between the exaggerated extremes of a totally religious and a totally secularized culture.

One reason why secularization never reaches the nadir of religious death involves the countervailing process of sacralization. Just as old forms of religion may lose their salience, new forms of religion may emerge in their stead. Just as the sacred may become secular, so may the secular become sacred and qualify as at least quasi-religions—for example, science and technology, Communism, or various forms of classical and pop art with their devotees. Without arguing some cultural version of Newton's third law that for every force in the direction of secularization there must be an equal and opposite force on behalf of sacralization, the two processes are as symbiotic in the long run as they are conflicting over the shorter haul. As secularization provides room for new forms of sacralization, the two trends work together in producing continued religious vitality through change rather than continued religious decline through changelessness in a changing world.

In all of this, one hears again the faint flutter of moth wings approaching a candle. Just as religion is drawn to politics, so is the sacred drawn to the secular. While there are some forms of the sacred that maintain their isolation in monasteries, convents, and communal retreats, most sacred moths circle the secular flames in the world at large because this is not only where the action is but where the potential adherents are located. The secular can offer real advantages to the sacred. It is by now a commonplace that even religious fundamentalists use new modes of communication and on occasion new forms of weaponry. Contact with the secular also leads to new adaptations of the sacred that keep it relevant. But as with the moth that approaches the flame too closely, the warmth of one moment can become very hot the next—and then very cold.

Moths of each generation succeed each other, and there is a cycling to the circling. "Cult-ure" gone "too secular" may leave a void to be filled by new cults pursuing new or resurgent conceptions of the sacred. Since even the most perfervid religions are subject to some degree of secularization as an accompaniment to social change, there is some form of sacralization waiting to emerge. After all, attracting secular moths to sacred flames is also a recurring theme in religion.

Canons and Contexts

All of the foregoing helps to explain how this book differs from many others on world religions. Much of this rich literature tends to present religions within their own traditional canons of belief and practice, as if these remained somehow fixed and invariant across time and space. Of course, there is a timelessness to religion, and there are moments and aspects of religion that span major social and societal differences. I shall provide brief accounts of the classical components of each world religion as we encounter them. But this is not the side of religion emphasized here.

Instead, this book stresses context more than canon. If the comparative materials here demonstrate anything, it is that any given religion is best understood—perhaps only really understood—in its myriad social and political settings. One reason for examining as many countries as I do is that comparative religion is not solely a matter of comparing the great faiths themselves. There are gaping differences between Christianity in Latin America and Europe. Judaism varies between the United States and Israel. Islam is not the same in Turkey as it is in Egypt, Pakistan, or Indonesia. Hinduism varies between north and south India, let alone Nepal or Indonesia's Bali. There are both canonical and contextual distinctions between the Buddhism of Thailand, Japan, and China. And within all of these contexts, differences of region, race, class, gender, and generation matter greatly.

Yet there is a persistent tendency to analyze religion in its own pure terms. When we discover that religious action does not always live up to religious doctrine, we are inclined to blame some idiosyncratic perversion of religion alone rather than seek an explanation in religion's social milieu. Focusing on traditional religious doctrine, ritual, and ethics may make sense theologically but not sociologically. When religion goes awry, the fault is apt to lie more in its external context than in any internally generated pathologies. Religious aberrations are more likely to arise from pulls rather than from pushes.

Religious dynamics are also more likely to stem from religion's surroundings than from its inspired virtuosos alone. The history of religion is often portrayed as a parade of religious prophets and saints occasionally interrupted by knaves and fools. There is a heroic version of every religion that stresses its charismatic visionaries, as opposed to the faithful flock. But while entrepreneurial leadership is a factor in almost every religious movement, such leaders are socially molded. Whether one is a Christian, a Muslim, a Hindu, or a Buddhist, different contexts determine whether one's faith is actively engaged in the public arena or in virtuous retreat from it. The kind of religion one believes in and practices is deeply affected by the choices available.

This is why the well-intended efforts of the saintly who seek to reform their faiths from within so often fall short. Most reforms only occur when religion confronts its context instead of turning its back upon it. Religion at its best is neither immaculate nor virginal in its wider relationships. Just as sexual contact is necessary to biological vitality, so is secular contact necessary to ethical vitality.

Because different contexts produce different religious scenarios, many conceptions of religion that fit snugly in one area are procrustean in another. For example, in America "religious pluralism" suggests tolerantly coexisting but distinctly demarcated religious communities; by contrast, in many Asian countries, "religious pluralism" involves several different faiths coexisting within the same individual. This difference between external and internal pluralism both reflects and reflects back upon the very different religious scenes involved.

In the midst of religious diversity, one often hears of a "civil religion" that represents a society's common religious denominator and binds a nation together through a shared faith, such as America's own "Judeo-Christian heritage." But sometimes civil religion emerges spontaneously from the grassroots, and sometimes it is manufactured and imposed by national leaders. Sometimes civil religion is less religious in the narrow sense and more sacred in its broader connotations. Instead of reflecting Buddhism, Christianity, Hinduism, or Islam, it may involve a quasi-religious ideological commitment to the welfare state or to a Communist system. It may even involve more of a "religion of the civil" than a civil religion as such.

Even different religious identities may vary by context. Within any single faith, labeling oneself a "believer" may mean different things in different settings. This is all the more so because religious belief is generally less a matter of intellectual conviction than a form of social affiliation and cultural identification, which helps to explain why it is possible for an individual to be either culturally religious at one end of the religious continuum or a religious fundamentalist at the other end without partaking of any of the faith's explicit belief or ritual practices. As we shall see, religious labels are dangerous to apply, especially the often misleading shibboleth of fundamentalism. In some settings, the most extreme religionists are pursuing new visions rather than returning to older litanies. And just as the great majority of religionists in every faith are not extreme, so are significant minorities within the extremist camps not primarily religious as they pursue essentially secular agendas by using religion strategically. Some religions like Islam are plagued as much by the absence of a codified and institutionalized liberal faction as by the presence of a reactionary phalanx.

Because canons come to life only in specific contexts, I shall describe each of the fourteen countries to follow by moving inward from the society to religion rather than by moving outward from religion to society. The intention is to supply readers less with textbook exegeses of world religions than with casebook accounts of how these religions have found very different orbits around their very different flames.

Part One

Circling

the Globe

1

Religion in

Oppression,

Liberation, and

Competition in

Brazil and

Guatemala

Religion's relationship to politics and the state has a long and checkered history in Latin America. Religion has been both a political contestant and a political arena, both a state ally and a state victim. Brazil and Guatemala hardly exhaust the Latin American scene, but they do illuminate many of its highs and lows.

The early histories of both countries illustrate the compounded colonialism of European states working with and through the Catholic Church. Both countries have also witnessed subsequent changes in Catholicism—beginning with its formal disestablishment from state officialdom in the late nineteenth century and continuing into its more combative movement against the state with the rise of Liberation Theology in the second half of the twentieth century. Liberation Theology has been marked by soaring progressive hopes and sometimes sadly unfulfilled realities. In Brazil, the movement has traversed a full institutional cycle, whereas in Guatemala it is still in midstage. Meanwhile, both countries also host other religions, including Afro-Brazilian spiritism, Guatemala's indigenous Mayan worship, and a surging evangelical Protestantism.

Encapsulating Christianity

Later accounts of Jewish, Islamic, Hindu, Buddhist, Shinto, and Confucian societies will begin with brief sociological accounts of these religious canons and their histories. At least a cursory orientation to Christianity seems appropriate here, since it is the primary religion in these first two chapters on Latin America and Europe, respectively. And before ethnographers try to describe someone else's culture, it seems only fair for them to face the challenge of describing their own.

Like all religions, Christianity lies at the vortex of a series of tensions that provide short-run dilemmas in search of long-range resolutions. Theologically, Christianity pursues this-worldly change by offering otherworldly salvation through the grace of a monotheistic God whose intervention is alternately judgmental and forgiving. Christianity depends upon sin and the sinner as the targets for its blessings. By the same token, it depends upon life's sometimes cruel vicissitudes as a test of faith in a God who is simultaneously all-knowing and unprovable. All of this is reflected in a wide array of institutionally sanctified regimens that combine deep love and seemingly arbitrary power in ways that are both complementary and conflicting.

Christian history also follows a dialectical pattern. At some points, the gaps between religion and power, sacred and secular, and canon and context seem wide and unbridgeable; at other times, the distinctions seem to lose their relevance. Of course, Christianity began as a radical and struggling Jewish movement that became steadily more implicated in the world it sought to change. Initially, Christianity was a sect defined by its opposition to society, but it later became a massive church marked partly by its complicity with society. But once the sect became a church, this church itself spawned new oppositional and innovative sects that often became established churches in their own right. They sparked yet another round of protesting offshoots that ultimately found organizational stability through compromise and complacency. And so the process continues.

The chronological high points of this history begin with Jesus' birth in roughly 4 B.C.E. Other critical dates would include 313 C.E. when the Roman Emperor Constantine issued the Edict of Milan to legalize Christianity and anticipate his own conversion to the faith. This reminds us again of religion's dependence on and vulnerability to political power. In 1054 the pope excommunicated the patriarch of Constantinople and created the formal split between Western and Eastern churches, a division that would take on layers of political significance throughout the next millennium. In 1517 Martin Luther nailed his ninety-five "theses" to the Catholic church door in Wittenberg, Germany. The event sparked the "Protest-ant Reform-ation" and signaled the end of Catholic domi-nance over both sacred and secular spheres and opened the gates to changes affecting every aspect of life.

Two additional dates involve Christianity's migration to the west and subsequent change. In 1519 Cortés arrived in the "New World" and claimed Aztec Central America on behalf of Spain and Catholicism. In 1791 the United States adopted its Bill of Rights, including the First Amendment that proclaimed an uncoupling of church and state and marked a transition from established church hegemonies to increasing denominational variation and religious competition.

Of course, such a summary is gallingly inadequate from the stand-point of virtually any believer in any corner of the Christian world. But instead of pausing to consider its gaps, let us proceed on the premise that we shall learn much more about Christianity in the context of the five very different Christian societies described in this chapter and the next, not to mention the United States itself when it surfaces as the compara-tive focal point of part 2. Let us turn first to Brazil and then to Guate-mala as two countries that refract their similarities differently.

Brazil: Changing Bishops and Masses

The boy didn't look like a bodyguard. There was not even a gun in sight as he quietly observed my conversation with the local priest through the help of my sociologist guide and interpreter, Madeleine Cousineau Adriance.[1] But the boy was there to protect the priest, who was a leading advocate of land redistribution in this northern Brazilian state of Para. If one wanted to learn of the interpenetration of religion and politics in Brazil, it seemed appropriate to begin with this religious moth circling these political flames.

Less than a year before, shots had been fired at a window in the adja-cent bedroom. The priest had been almost killed by a hit-and-run driver several years before that. In fact, round-the-clock armed guards were in-sisted upon by Para state authorities concerned about death threats against the priest and the prospect of adding one more churchly martyr's assassina-tion to the seven that had already occurred in the area over the past decade. Nor did this include the Brazilian Catholic Pastoral Land Commission's estimate of some thousand peasants killed since 1985 by *pistoleiros* hired by landowners anxious to head off land reform at their expense.

Somehow guns and violence fit the scene. The town of Rio Maria is hot and dusty, with corrugated roofs and only one main street. It is a far cry from what was once part of the Amazon forest that had been stripped clear of rubber trees and "brazil nuts" to make way for more lucrative mining and ranching. This was not at all the Brazil I had envisioned. Rio de Janeiro, with its scalloped beaches and sensuous carnival, was more than a thousand miles to the southeast. By contrast, Rio Maria seemed like the sleepy setting of a stock Hollywood western, and with much the same primordial conflict between the few who had claimed the land and the many who sought it—in this case, with the priest's help.

Brazil as Cultural Multilith

Brazil is hardly the only Latin American nation to offer such contrasts. But it is exceptional on several other counts. It is the only country in Latin America claimed and settled by Portugal rather than by Spain, and this began in 1500 when Portuguese explorers were greeted by a relatively small population of coastal Indians—many of whom died from imported disease as others were driven into the Amazon interior, where they, like the jungles and the forests themselves, continue to disappear. Meanwhile, a third ethnic group began to arrive only shortly after the Portuguese and subject to their control, namely, African slaves. Today, they are the dominant ethnic group in northeast coastal Brazil, and the national population includes many *mamelucos* descended from the intermarriages of all three groups. Racism is generally held to be less extensive and pernicious than in the United States. Still, while the census estimates that 44 percent of the population is black, African-Brazilian rights groups argue that the figure would be at least 60 percent if more people were less constrained about admitting it.

Few North Americans appreciate the sheer size of Brazil. Occupying the continent's huge northeastern hump, it claims almost half of the entire landmass of South America. Its geographical area ranks fourth in the world behind only China, Canada, and the United States. Brazil's population size ranks fifth, though one wonders how many in the United States would answer "São Paulo" if asked to name the third most populous city in the world—or the single largest Catholic diocese.

Many other Latin American (especially Central American) countries revolve increasingly around the United States, both culturally and economically. But Brazil is now remarkably self-sufficient. If it tilts in any direction, it is toward Europe, and this is not just because of its Portuguese colonial past. Brazil declared its independence as early as 1822 and established itself as a republic in 1889. Portugal has long since ceased to be Brazil's primary reference point, though Portuguese continues as its national language.

Like most of Latin America, Brazil has three religious traditions that have grown increasingly competitive but not without some convergences. Of course, the Roman Catholic Church is the great institutional monolith. Until 1889, Brazil was officially a Catholic state, though in real political matters, the church was largely under the thumb of the Portuguese crown. The movie *The Mission* makes this clear as the seventeenth-century priests played by Robert De Niro and Jeremy Irons are finally forced to knuckle under rather than support the indigenous Indians near the spectacular Iguacu Falls at Brazil's southwestern border with Argentina and Paraguay. Following 1889, the Catholic Church was formally separated from the state, though it continued as part of the informal but effective ruling establishment.[2]

A second religious tradition involves various forms of pentecostal Protestantism that first appeared in 1908 through Swedish missionaries of the Assembly of God. This remains the largest but by no means the only such group. As elsewhere in Latin America, pentecostal and evangelical Protestantism are often described as "exploding" since the 1950s.[3] Including the Mormons, whose numbers are rapidly increasing, there are estimates that the broader movement will soon claim as many as a quarter of all Brazilians. While there are also reasons to be skeptical about such projections—given the typically high turnover rates and frequent multiple counting of members, who sometimes retain membership in two or more religious groups—there is no question that Protestantism is growing and makes good headline material. The most talked about church in Brazil today is the highly aggressive Universal Church of the Kingdom of God. Its leaders have been accused of fraudulent faith healings and fund raising, and in October 1995 one of its preachers created a furor by kicking a statue of Brazil's Catholic patron saint, Our Lady of Aparecida, during a televised sermon.

Finally, the country's third important religious tradition involves the Afro-Brazilian spiritist movement, variously known as *candomble* in the northeast and *umbanda* in the Rio de Janeiro area to the south. These cults bear some resemblance to what is often stereotyped as voodoo worship in Haiti. They combine strong emotionality with powerful folk arts. If the Catholics focus on institutional and societal scenarios and the pentecostals are more focused upon personal enhancement and salvation, these cults seek to influence the intervention of spirits.[4] Their rituals take the form of dramatic narrative structures. For example, here is my brief account of an evening in Salvadore, Bahia, on Brazil's northeast coast when four young girls were initiated into a cult with a fertility ritual comprising dance, drums, and singing:

> The temple is a cinder block structure with a dirt floor, roughly 40'
> by 60', in a working-class neighborhood where one could hear the

drums from a block away. There are some three hundred members of the "congregation" crowded inside, and men and women are segregated in both the audience and among the participants. As men drum, women dance. A dozen older women in white Bahian lace dresses with head kerchiefs and padding tied around their waists to represent pregnancy lead four young girls with shaved heads like babies around a central, perhaps phallic pole. The girls seem in a trance and grow increasingly dizzy, almost as if possessed by drinking "spirits" of a different kind. They need help to avoid falling or careening into the audience. Meanwhile, the drums grow more insistent, combining tribal rhythms with the cadences of a marching band. The singing involves more insistent chanting than lyrical melodies, and it too crescendos. Finally, each girl in turn is spun around three times before leaping into the air as a birth gesture that is greeted by much applause inside and firecrackers outside. In fact, there is a great deal of socializing outside the hall, as people coming home from work drop by to see friends. At least tonight, going inside requires a major commitment, since the humid temperature is well over one hundred, and at least two women have passed out, requiring assistance.

As different as this is from a conventional church service, there are also similarities. I attended a small-town Christian service in north-central Brazil that shared the same high level of emotional ritual participation, the emphasis on a spirit quest with eyes closed and hands raised high, and the same prominent roles given women. Surprisingly, this was not a pentecostal Protestant service but a Roman Catholic mass conducted by the priest in Rio Maria, who admitted that these were strategic accommodations. Catholics have begun to incorporate aspects of both pentecostal and Afro-Brazilian religious worship as a way of heading off further losses to these movements by fighting spiritual fire with fire. Another example is not far from the candomble temple in the same city of Salvadore where a large room in a Catholic church is filled with photos, carvings, and models of body parts that had been cured by spiritual healing—a leg here, an arm there, and heads of various descriptions. Syncretism has become part of Brazilian religious culture if not its formal ecclesiastical structures.

Introducing Liberation Theology

For more than four hundred years, the Catholic Church had fed off the fat of the Latin America land. But beginning in the 1960s—a turbulent decade throughout the West—church leaders began to bite the establishment hands that had been feeding them on behalf of those whose diets had been at best skimpy.[5] The Liberation Theology movement emerged from the convergent thinking of several radical Catholic leaders from various points in the hemisphere. These included the Colombian sociologist-priest Camilo Torres, whose assassination in 1966 marked only one of many moths caught up in the flames; the Peruvian theologian Gustavo Gutiérrez, who actually coined the phrase "Liberation Theology" in 1969 at a meeting of the World Council of Churches in Switzerland; and the popular Brazilian Bishop of Rio de Janeiro, Dom Helder Camera, who had begun the Latin American Episcopal Conference (CELAM) in 1955.[6] If there was any one galvanizing event, it was a meeting of that conference of Catholic bishops in Medellin, Colombia, in 1968.

The obvious challenge to which all of these were responses was the continuing poverty of the Latin American peasantry and urban underclass. But it was also a Catholic counteroffensive to the rapid rise of Protestantism and the continued presence of indigenous faiths and African spiritism. Catholicism was slipping and needed a boost.

From the beginning, Liberation Theology has had two fundamental objectives. The first and most controversial aspect entails a fundamental commitment to social justice. Ideologically, this involves a "preferential option for the poor"—the phrase coined at the 1968 Medellin conference. In practical terms, this requires attention to what Marxists call "praxis," or converting abstract theory (and theology) into concrete works by raising political consciousness and increasing solidarity. This was the radical message whose Marxist roots set teeth on edge in the fiercely anticommunist Vatican of Pope John Paul II.

A second aspect of Liberation Theology was equally alarming. This involved a massive effort to decentralize Latin American Catholicism by shifting initiatives and action away from the large, impersonal, patriarchal, and sometimes corrupt churches profiting from the status quo to a widespread network of small, intimate, and popularly controlled *communidades eclesiais de base*—CEBs, or base communities—working to change the status quo. CEBs now number some one hundred thousand in Brazil, each of which is larger than a family but smaller than a parish with an average of perhaps thirty members. These small communities represent a potentially profound change from the traditional top-down religious organization to one that is more bottom-up and grassroots oriented in both its means and its ends.

Such an objective is consistent with the 1965 Second Vatican Council, where Catholic bishops from all over the world resonated to the warm and open spirit of its convener, the late Pope John XXIII. But the objective poses a challenge to the current Vatican and Pope John Paul II. The vision underscores a major implication of Liberation Theology in giving voice and authority to the people themselves in countries throughout Latin America and indeed throughout the world. As a blow against the central and sacred power of Rome itself, this threatens a fundamental attribute of what is arguably the most successful continuous institution in world history. Power so carefully accrued and nurtured is not easily relinquished.

In the local Brazilian context, the change is also an adaptive response to a style that has proved so successful among Protestant pentecostals and the Afro-Brazilian spiritists. The Catholic priests and bishops with whom I talked all agreed with one who said, "We had to do something to reach out to the people and give them more of a voice in their religious life. Because the church has been so male dominated, this meant that we especially had to involve women in new ways." This was readily apparent in the Catholic worship described previously. Laywomen actually conducted most of the service, except for the priest's brief homily and administration of the Eucharist.

If Liberation Theology had been only a movement within the church, it would have attracted far less attention. But much of liberationism's national and international prominence stemmed from a sudden rupture in Brazilian politics and the Catholic Church's role within it. In the 1960s political discontent and upheaval were in the air not just in the United States but elsewhere around the world. The Latin American Catholic churches were by no means united in their response. In some cases such as Argentina, the episcopate remained allied with dictatorial forces in power; in others such as Chile, the bishops struck out in opposition.[7] As so often happened in the Third World, the military had become the real power behind the scenes, and one whose vested interest in stable traditions were challenged by radical developments, both sacred and secular. As one observer quipped, "It's better to have general discontent than a discontented general."

By the early 1960s Brazil had both. In 1964 a senator rose on the floor of the national Congress to say that the military had so overstepped its boundaries that no self-respecting Brazilian woman should sleep with any military man. As the story goes, that was a last straw—or at least a final pretext—for a dramatic change. The military suspended normal government functions and political activities in order to assume dictatorial powers that it would hold through three presidential marionettes until 1985. During these two decades, some 50,000 persons were politically detained, 10,000 exiled, almost 3,000 given long-term prison sentences, 2,000 tortured, 352 killed, and 152 "disappeared."

This was both a crisis and an opportunity for Brazilian Catholicism. On the one hand, it shredded the Church's traditional status as an establishment ally and beneficiary of the state. On the other, once the military had outlawed virtually all other public arenas such as political parties and trade unions, the Church became the only available venue for expressing discontent and opposition. In some settings, church officials—including pastoral agents, priests, bishops, and most especially Cardinal Arns of São Paulo—became forceful and prophetic opponents of the regime in their own right.

This gave new substance and a higher profile to the political dimension of Liberation Theology. The Catholic Church was suddenly identified with a populist social agenda on the left. Reforms within the Church went hand in fist with reforms outside the Church. A number of Brazilians whose Catholicism had lapsed began to find new meaning and new courage in the Church and many of its leaders. Yet even during the height of liberationist mobilization during the late 1970s, there were ecclesiastical officials who opposed its initiations and many others who took to the sidelines and abstained from involvement. At no point was there a real majority in support of the Church's new political agenda among the Catholic laity—even among the lower-class Catholics who stood to benefit the most from the social justice campaign.[8] As in many such episodes of institutional change, it is easy to confuse visions with realities and exaggerate change itself.

Liberation Theology Gone Normal

In 1985 the military relinquished control and the democratic republic resumed. But this posed a different combination of crisis and opportunity for the Catholic Church. The Church lost much of its broader political bully pulpit and was left with a more conventionally religious role. The Church had already lost some of its secular allies in 1982, when most of the trade unions and political movements left the Catholic umbrella in a conscious move to maintain their autonomy. But the return to democracy was by no means a return to a left-wing reform government. Both of the challenges that had led to Liberation Theology in the first place remained, that is, massive social injustice and the continuing loss of membership and dynamism to evangelical Protestants.

There are two basic issues on which assessments diverge concerning the CEBs. The first is to what extent they carry agendas for social action and ethical consciousness raising as opposed to serving as religious extension groups that allow like-minded people (mostly women) to experience religion closer to home, with their friends, and in conjunction with nonpolitical social activities.

Clearly both types of CEBs exist. Just as there are political communities within the *favelas*, or tin-roofed shantytowns, of urban areas such as Rio de Janeiro and São Paulo, so are there politicized base communities in violence-ridden frontier towns like Rio Maria in the north seeking land reform from wealthy landowners for dispossessed peasants. But even in towns like Rio Maria, some of the CEBs are more traditionally religious and non-political. Overall, the religious type has grown, while the political has subsided. This has disappointed some of the more prophetic liberation theologians themselves. But as one confided: "Of course, the progressive church has made mistakes—like expecting people to walk on their own two feet before giving them shoes. We have sometimes pushed the social at the expense of the personal, and we need to help people rediscover the internal mystery of liberation." In towns like Rio Maria, it is not uncommon to see married couples split in their Catholic-Protestant allegiances. I talked to one middle-aged couple, where the Catholic husband professed considerable respect for his wife's pentecostal activities—until she left the room. At that point, he whispered, "It's really an addiction, like cigarettes and liquor. And besides they're always asking for money, and I have enough expenses without giving them the ten per cent they want of what comes in."

Meanwhile, a second point of disagreement concerning the CEBs involves who determines whether a base community will be of one sort or another. In liberation theory, this should be a locally autonomous decision of the community members. In practice, the decision is sometimes made by priests, sisters, or pastoral agents with special skills and responsibilities. In theory, the members should seize the opportunity to develop and act upon a political agenda. In practice, members left to their own choices are more likely to opt for traditional religious rounds and nonpolitical activities.[9] After all, these are people who have long been politically dispossessed, and it is unreasonable to expect them to quickly toss aside their fatalism and their fears. As one might predict, many CEBs were torn by conflict between these options.

There is now evidence that CEBs once politicized with the help of leadership intervention rather quickly slide back into traditional religion once these leaders leave. There are some conservative bishops who welcomed the more radical CEBs despite the base communities' politics because it was one way to attract more young people. But it is in the more religious mode that the communities may offer Catholicism's most effective response to both Protestants and Afro-Brazilian spiritists—especially when the Catholics incorporate a more spiritualized ritual of their own and provide greater roles and voices for women within it.

Yet there is a growing religious conservatism overall in Catholic circles. In 1991 the National Conference of Bishops voted to approve the use of charismatic ritual—no doubt largely in response to pentecostalism. But the conservatism goes further. One priest in São Paulo remarked upon the struggle now going on between the CEBs and the arch-conservatives of the Catholicism's shadowy international lay movement, Opus

Dei: "In my novitiate class, all of them are from lower-class backgrounds but they are far more pious and far less political than before 1985. Out of fifteen, only two have any interest at all in learning about politics, much less doing anything about it. Five come from the Opus Dei, and seven are charismatics." The priest added that he has an increasing number of colleagues who are returning from secular garb to clerical collars and cassocks.

It has been about fifteen years since the republic was restored, and many members of Brazil's National Conference of Bishops are eager to return to their rightful place at the right hand of power. It is true that the new Brazilian Constitution of 1989 has religious clauses very similar to the U.S. Constitution's First Amendment's—and with the pentecostals' blessing in order to fend off Catholic state influence. However, many members of the National Conference of Bishops would like to negotiate a new concordat with the federal government that would somehow restore their de facto position at the establishment table, even if formal separation continues de jure. Far from insisting on a formal religious state, many would settle for an informal state religion. Here the moth's objective is more warmth than heat; here the risk is being co-opted as opposed to being consumed.

One development that has contributed to this mood involves the Vatican. Its recent appointments to positions of higher ecclesiastical authority have taken a clear conservative turn. In 1991, after years of Vatican censorship and harassment, Brazil's leading liberation theologian, Father Leonardo Boff, was finally saddled with a vow of total silence, which ultimately caused him to leave the priesthood but not the Church. In all of this, it is possible that Catholicism may win the institutional and ecclesiastical battle but lose the spiritual and cultural war.

It is true that there remain politically active priests and base communities in the Catholic community—recall the priest in Rio Maria. There is even some political mobilization among the Afro-Brazilian cults and the pentecostals. As one political veteran put it: "Only 35 of the nation's 576 Congressmen are pentecostal, but they're the only ones who list their religions in their bibliographies and the only religious group that votes as a bloc. They even support some conservative Catholic candidates for higher offices, but then they're not always as conservative as some people think."

One of the most swashbuckling political figures to emerge in recent years is known simply as "Lula." He is both a pentecostal and a leader of the Worker's Party (PT) on the political left. Another meteoric figure is Benedita da Silva, a woman who is also a PT member and was the first elected Afro-Brazilian senator.

But even in these cases, it is difficult to estimate the importance of religious factors themselves in politics. Many of my religious informants were understandably inclined to underscore religion's social and political importance even as they cited its problems. But when I consulted with the staff of a secular political think tank for an overall assessment of Brazilian politics, religion was never mentioned. When I asked a prominent ex-senator and current political journalist with no personal religious commitment to describe the most important trend concerning religion and politics, he responded, "That's easy. It's the march to religious irrelevancy." He may well be right, but then again . . .

Guatemala: Religion and Civil War in Central America

Although I had just arrived in Guatemala City, I was very much aware of a civil war that was almost forty years old with as many as two hundred thousand deaths and "disappearances." These victims were mostly Mayan *indigena* casualties of the military, but they included a number of priests, catechists, agricultural agents, and even anthropologists—some of whom were "gringos" from "the States" like me. My first interview in the country was with a human rights activist from California. After answering a number of my questions, he asked one of his own: "So are you going up to Santa Cruz del Quiche for the Memorial Service on Saturday? It's the first anniversary of the military's assassination of Julio Quevada. He was a very popular agricultural expert who did a lot to help the local women who have lost their husbands. Folks are coming from all over the country. Everyone will be there."

The town was only a few hours' drive from Guatemala City in the Quiche highlands to the northwest. But I had been warned to stay out of the area. Quiche is said to be the only diocese in the history of the Catholic Church to have formally closed and evacuated all religious personnel. This happened ten years earlier from 1981 to 1984, following the assassination of a priest.

> Isn't that area a little dangerous for someone who really doesn't know his way around?
> No problem. You can go with me. I'm driving up early Saturday morning. We'll just slip into town for the Mass and then slip out again before the local police or the military ever find out we're there.

My bluff was called; this was a command appearance I could hardly decline. The plan started out well enough. His car was a welcome relief from the acrid pollutants of the local buses; Guatemala seems to be one of many Third World countries where old U.S. school buses go to die. After a beautiful drive through rugged terrain, we arrived just in time to park outside the church and enter as the service was starting. Under

clouds of incense, the bishop was assisted by fifteen other priests of varying hues, though almost all were "Ladinos," that is, Guatemalans born
of mixed Spanish and indigenous backgrounds. The mass was said first
in Spanish and then translated into several of the twenty-one Mayan
languages. The music was led by a woman with an accordion accompanied by guitars and rolling gourd percussion.

The day's special congregation represented a cross section of the
Guatemalan class structure. But off to one side was a cluster of several
dozen small, dark indigena women with their braided black hair and
strikingly beautiful *huipiles*, or woven cotton blouses, that are the dis-
tinguishing daily attire of each village. The women sat just beneath a
commanding wall frieze of an alabaster Virgin Mary in a snow-white
wedding gown. The contrast seemed a stark image of the traditional power
of Euro-Catholicism looking down on a majority Mayan country.

Then I felt a tug at my sleeve and a whisper at my ear. "Damn. I just
realized I locked my keys in the car. Don't worry. Just stay here, and I'll
go out and jimmy it open." But he didn't return, and when the two-hour
mass ended, I walked out of the church to see the car surrounded by
circles of townspeople radiating outward from an inner core of police
and military. So much for getting in and out of town unnoticed. But
fortunately, all were intent on the common problem of unlocking the
door. Soon they succeeded, and despite our fears it was in fact "no problem." And yet problems have abounded for Guatemala.

A Civil War with Little Historical Relief

Tucked just south of Mexico to the northwest and just north of
Honduras and El Salvador to the southeast, Guatemala forms part of the
Central American isthmus. Conquered by Spain in the sixteenth century, Guatemala is one more example of the curse of an imposed culture
and exploitative political economy. In some ways, its civil war has been
going on for almost four hundred years as a sad struggle of class, ethnicity,
and religion.

Guatemala's early colonization was considerably abetted by the Spanish Catholic Church. For more than two hundred years, the Church was
a unifying force, but Guatemalan independence from Spain in 1821
brought about a quasi-separation of old church and new state, and this
was given more concrete status by the Liberal Reform of 1870. Still, in
the century to follow, Catholicism continued to define the unofficial
but universally acknowledged establishment even though it was more a
kept institution than the keeper of the kingdom's keys—more an appendage of the elite than a controlling force.

Guatemala began to change following World War II. The rise of a
new electoral democracy was heralded as a period of "springtime,"

marked by the presidency of Juan José Arévalo in 1944 and then the popular election of Jacabo Arbenz in 1951. But by this time, the United States had replaced Spain as a controlling force in the Central American economy and in Guatemalan politics. Largely at the behest of U.S. companies such as the powerful United Fruit Company concerned about local "Communists" nationalizing outside holdings, the Eisenhower administration approved—and later proudly proclaimed—the Central Intelligence Agency's (CIA) role in overthrowing Arbenz and aiding the strong Guatemalan military to fill the power vacuum. CIA files opened in June 1997, however, reveal a far more violent complicity than had been previously acknowledged.

Because Guatemalan politics is such a crucial context for its religious developments, it is worth recounting the nation's recent political history in some detail. [10] By 1960 civil strife had intensified into civil war. [11] On one side stood the shadow colonialists from the United States, the mostly Ladino or Spanish-descended old upper class, and the new middle class—all concerned to protect their vastly disproportionate stakes in the local economy, and using politics, the military, and the implied legitimation of the Church to that end. [12] On the other side was the great majority of Guatemalans, including many mestizos and the 60 percent of the population who were indigenous Indians. As these indigenas saw their own economic interests and cultural traditions being trampled, small but aggressive minorities in the northern highlands formed several insurgent movements that later coalesced under the umbrella of the Guatemalan National Revolutionary Unity (UNRG) in 1982 to coordinate their guerilla actions. [13]

Although it would be inaccurate to characterize this conflict as predominantly religious, religion was certainly implicated within it. Through much of this period, Catholic officialdom stood to one side, occasionally wringing its relatively powerless but by no means spotless hands. At the same time, there continued the rumbling long-standing conflict between imported and imposed Catholicism and the indigenous Mayan religion. Many Indians saw themselves as both, participating publicly in Catholicism while privately keeping alive the embers of their ancient Mayan tradition. Most higher-status mestizos or Ladinos were exclusively Catholic.

In the meantime, a third religious phalanx began to bring in its troops in the 1950s and 1960s. As Protestantism began to arrive from the United States, it flourished. Just as in Brazil, this was primarily evangelical and pentecostal rather than mainline Protestantism, but here the pipeline from the United States was even more direct. [14] Once again, the number of *evangelicos* began to explode, and by 1982 Guatemala had Latin America's first acknowledged Protestant chief of state.

President Efrain Rios Montt had converted from Catholicism to a

Protestant group called *El Verbo* (The Word) in 1977, after he had been denied election to the presidency in 1974 by the elite Catholic Christian Democratic Party.[15] This time he simply seized the office as the civilian face of a military regime supported by the country's business elite and a right-wing Catholic cardinal, some of whose liberal bishops and priests had become military targets in the highlands. Until leaving office in 1983, Rios Montt pursued order through terror and violence. His regime is often described as an unprecedented "scorched earth" campaign that obliterated more than four hundred villages and left an estimated hundred thousand dead or missing.

The military put an entire infrastructure into place that involved forced recruitment into Civilian Auto-Defense Patrols (PACs) to monitor and spy on their peers. Using a "beans and bullets" tactic by which peasants could only get the former by using the latter, at their peak these patrols involved more than a million indigenas, or almost half of the male peasant population.[16] At the same time, rebel groups also terrorized the countryside and committed atrocities in the villages against those suspected of betraying them to the government. However, the rebels' violence paled in comparison to the military's in both intensity and scale.

The country and the Pan-American community finally gagged. In 1985 the military bowed to the need for international legitimacy in order to avoid economic paralysis. It restored at least the form of democratic elections and enacted a new constitution. The constitution's opening phrase was "Invoking the name of God . . . ," and while Article 36 stipulates that the "exercise of all religions shall be totally free and by any means within the limits of public order and respect for others," Article 37 "recognizes the legal structure of the Catholic Church" and promises similar status to other churches, cults, and sects once their own legal statutes conform to public order. The government also promises to "give to the Catholic Church at no cost the titles of any properties they now own as part of their patrimony."

The 1985 elections resulted in a civilian government led by a Catholic president, Marco Vinicio Cerezo Arévalo, who was succeeded in 1991 by the first elected Protestant chief of state in Latin America, Jorge Serrano—a longtime compatriot of Rios Montt who was elected in part because Rios Montt's own candidacy was ruled unconstitutional. While Serrano was not a member of Rios Montt's church, he was a kindred, if less swashbuckling, political figure. Human rights abuses began to mount again, and by 1993 Serrano sought to suspend ordinary government to assume extraordinary powers. The effort failed, and politics resumed its bumpy course as the unacknowledged but unrelenting civil war continued.

Three Changing Religious Cultures

It would be unwarranted to infer any predeterminative religious causes or to assume that any one religious bloc had a corner on either civic virtue or political nefariousness. Still, religion is a key aspect of some broader cultural differences that continue to inflame the country. Recent developments among Protestants, Mayans, and Catholics each deserve accounts of their own, even though all three need to be understood partially in relation to each other.

As we have already seen, the growth of Protestantism is certainly the most politically conspicuous aspect of recent religion in Guatemala—more so than in perhaps any other Latin American country. But there are almost as many explanations for Protestant growth in Guatemala as there are Protestant groups in Guatemala—at last estimate more than three hundred, many from the United States, but with manifold variations among them. Consider the following two congregations as I described them in my field journal:

> "Mount Bason Iglesia" occupies a 20' by 35' lean-to with a concrete platform loosely connected to the rear wall of an electric power station in a hillside barrio on the outskirts of Guatemala City. The rain drums on its corrugated roof are supported by strategic 2 x 4's, but the water leaks in from its side walls of underlapping plastic sheeting and cardboard. Four bare bulbs attract mosquitoes and provide the light, while much of the heat comes from the fervent singing and almost competitively emotional prayers from individual adherents. Women conduct the service, except for the sermon. In fact, of the dozen-and-a-half persons scattered along the eight wooden benches on this regular weekday evening, there are only two males present: the young pastor, in a blue suit and tie, and our more informally dressed male host—an airline maintenance mechanic who remains a Catholic but made an exception to attend with his Protestant wife and daughters as a gesture of hospitality to me. Surprisingly, the pastor's sermon was more scholarly than perfervid: a careful exegesis of a Biblical text on suffering with no humor and few stories but using rolled r's and dynamic variations for dramatic effect. Just as every block along the barrio has a similar iglesia, the pastor himself has several others that he began and continues to serve.

One service in one church hardly constitutes a thick description. Still, there are some elements that resonate within wider evangelical Protestantism. What outsiders may see as a struggle for numbers, insiders experience as a welcome intimacy. They are bonded by strong emotionality and shared cultural consensus as opposed to rigid structure.

Then, too, the prominence of women in the congregation and the service is a striking characteristic of the new Protestantism in contrast with the old Catholicism. The paucity of men is partly because they are often demonized by preachers who promise there will be more money on the kitchen table each week and then sometimes manage the miracle by persuading husbands to curb their expenditures on the curse of alcohol. Of course, the theme of suffering and the emphasis on Christ and the biblical word are distinctive qualities of sectarian Protestantism everywhere.

The entrepreneurial character of many young Protestant pastors stands in contrast to the corporate bureaucracy of the Catholic priesthood. The Protestants start small congregations like small businesses. They hope either to grow with them or perhaps be drafted out of the religious minor leagues by a more established major league congregation such as the following:

"Fraternidad Cristiana de Guatemala" is in the upper middle-class "Roosevelt" district of Guatemala City—many of whose expensive homes are rumored to be owned by military officers linked to the drug trade. The church offers expansive parking for the late-model cars of the more than 1500 adherents (with a slight preponderance of women) who pack the Sunday morning service in a fan-shaped auditorium trimmed in the national colors of blue and white with marble floors. The two-hour service begins with thirty minutes of joyous singing, led by an engaging young man with hand-held microphone backed by an eight-person choir and a band of drums, bass, rhythm guitar and electric piano. The last hymn segues into personal testimony as a woman's voice soars over the congregation in a mixture of Spanish, Mayan, and glossolalia. The pastor is introduced and makes his first appearance wearing an all-white suit. A man in his 60's, he was one of Guatemala's early neo-pentecostals in the 1970s and has both boosted the tide and risen with it. He asks congregants not to chew gum and for the young men to leave their girlfriends outside. He then presides over a restrained healing session, as his assistants practice a sacramental laying-on-of-hands with no dramatic results. Following a guest keyboard and vocal artist, the pastor is reintroduced for a low-key, lengthy, but masterful sermon on the power of fear, with compelling anecdotes and engaging wit. He concludes by asserting that the country will remain mired in violence until all convert to Jesus. Next, some twenty-five come forward in response to a call to be saved. Then the pastor caresses the collection in soft and soothing tones, after which the congregation exits to a concluding song.

Much of this would not seem out of place in a mainstream Protestant service—or for that matter, many Catholic settings. However, it illustrates another strand of evangelical Protestantism in Guatemala—one that ministers more to the upwardly mobile middle class than to the working and lower classes. Here the church and the service are far more male dominated, and religious authority is accompanied by a more obtrusive church hierarchy. Both this and the preceding church emphasize individual betterment in this world and the world beyond. In neither church is there much of a political critique or agenda for society itself. If Mount Bason comforted society's losers, the Fraternidad Cristiana celebrates and certifies its winners. In the jobs wanted section of the local classifieds, personal ads often specify a Protestant affiliation but almost never a Catholic one.

Thirty percent of Guatemalans are now thought to be Protestants, though some estimates range as high as 40 percent, and hard numbers are elusive. Conversion and commitment scenarios vary widely. In some areas, fear itself is held to be a motive, that is, fear of the consequences from the military if one does not convert. There is no question that Protestantism has replaced Catholicism as a colonizing tool in some parts of the highlands where Protestants are given badges of identity unavailable to Catholics to assure safe passage from village to village. Although the military is not formally aligned with any religion, Protestant services are much more common than Catholic masses on its bases—in part because Protestant pastors are much more eager to cooperate than are Catholic priests.

Surely one can find evidence that suggests a major religious battle to establish hegemonic control. On the same day that a hundred thousand Guatemalans participated in a Catholic "Pastoral Synod," the military broadcast an anti-Catholic diatribe by a Californian leader of President Serrano's church. On the one hand, the Catholic archbishop gave an interview to a Panamanian newspaper alleging that the U.S. government is purposely subverting Guatemalan Catholicism by sending in and funding the Protestants. On the other hand, just prior to the pope's visit in 1996, evangelical truth squads toured the countryside with bullhorns to warn of the coming of the "Anti-Christ."

Yet Protestantism's politicization and the society's religious split can also be overstated. There is no overarching Protestant political force that applies a unified institutional shoulder to the political wheel. Many of the new pentecostal churches deliberately refrain from outright political involvement as a posture of otherworldly transcendence. Even those Protestants who are politically involved are not always on the same side. While most high-status Protestants support the military, some are opposed, including a few genuine martyrs to the indigenous cause. Rios

Montt was a Protestant pastor who actively proselytized for his church from the presidency. But his later Protestant successor, Serrano, was only a local church member, and his cabinet members and advisers included a good many Catholics whose political visibility confers important legitimacy on any regime. As the mother of one particularly prominent Catholic appointee put it: "He wouldn't dare not appoint my son."

Clearly Catholicism remains a major institution in Guatemala, though one undergoing significant changes and internal variations. While there is no single Protestant leader or spokesperson, at the top of the Catholic Church is a nervous archbishop who cut his ecclesiastical teeth under a reactionary cardinal but is now being pulled in the opposite direction by a young and predominantly liberal Council of Bishops. Perhaps as a compromise, the diocesan headquarters in Guatemala City hosted a human rights office but refused to pay a salary to the attorney in charge. There is far less talk of Liberation Theology as such in Guatemala than in Brazil, perhaps because Guatemala's civil strife affords less space for theological and theoretical discourse of any sort.

The archbishop was often described as a competent manager but by no means prophetic in his unsteady drift to the left. After ten years in office, he still had not won the "red hat" of cardinal rank. This is largely because following the death of his cardinal predecessor, the Vatican moved the ecclesiastical see to Nicaragua and has refused to moved it back, presumably because of the archbishop's liberalism and possible black-balls hurled by the Guatemalan chapter of Opus Dei.

Certainly it is little wonder that the archbishop was reluctant to meet me, a strange researcher from outside the country. It was almost comical to catch fleeting glimpses of him ducking furtively around court-yard corners to avoid meeting me. But, of course, his job was anything but easy. His office sits catercorner across the main Guatemalan City square from the sprawling, drab green buildings of the federal capital, and his role seems to have shifted from power player to tentative power broker. As one of my respondents put it in reflecting on the archbishop's burdens: "You can't have a clean church in a messy world." This is certainly true unless cleanliness is next to irrelevance, and canons are preserved without regard for context.

If this is Catholicism at the top, the scene is often far different at the parish level. It is here that one finds signs of Liberation Theology because it is here that religion and politics become embroiled in the struggles of everyday life. I asked one priest in a highlands parish how he differed from the padres of thirty years ago. "Well, they would have been Spanish and would have had very little interest in or knowledge of the local Indian languages and very little sympathy with the indigenous religion." This padre was different on all three counts, not least because he was actually from a U.S. diocese to which he was jointly answerable along with a local bishop.

But he was also jointly answerable in another sense as one who had taken pains to welcome different religious traditions into his parish. His office wall featured an organization chart that included not only the traditional elements of Catholic parish structure but several that reached beyond. Catholic Action groups pursue a social agenda in the community on behalf of the Church. Ladino groups are more middle-class social organizations, often separated by gender. *Cofradias* are small, mostly male, indigenous religious and fraternal cells that predate even the sixteenth-century Catholic Church and have been unevenly accommodated and sometimes co-opted. Despite their place under the church umbrella here, some are more Mayan than Catholic in substance and ritual. In fact, they provide one early model for the CEBs of Liberation Theology on the last line of the chart, where they function more as religious extension groups than political cells. The cofradias also offer some competition and resistance to the catechists seeking to extend the church's sacred and secular curricula into the surrounding community.

Catholic relations with local Protestants in this area are somewhat atypical because both Catholics and Protestants were recently victimized when local military panicked in response to a street disturbance and killed eleven Catholics and two Protestants while wounding forty Catholics and ten Protestants. For a time the two religious wings cooperated and cohosted town meetings to restore a sense of community, though the priest took affront at being referred to as *el sacerdote* rather than the more accessible padre. However, this ecumenism later ebbed, and Catholic-Protestant relations are once again distant and uneasy. While the majority of the townsfolk are Catholic, most of the city's leading citizens are Protestant—some of whom have also retained their Catholic standing for ceremonial purposes. Although the individual-centered Protestants have no political or social program, the Catholics are increasingly marginalized economically and politically despite their agenda.

Meanwhile, the two religious cultures have begun to change. Of course, both Catholics and Protestants have long-standing traditions of seeking zero-sum conversions. But recently Catholic catechists have even begun to adopt some successful Protestant techniques, such as stressing the figure of Christ, focusing on the Bible, accommodating the charismatic spirit, and emphasizing the voice and the lot of women.

There are also growing numbers of Catholic leaders—and some Protestants—who have marked an even greater departure from past practices by exchanging aggressive conversionism for a more tolerant syncretism. Many Catholic parishes and a few evangelical Protestant churches have made allowance for local mountain spirits and healing practices. Especially in the villages of the highlands, one finds a number of Mayan elements incorporated into Christian services—and vice versa.[17]

Mayan cultural identity hangs in the balance of religion, language, ethnicity, economics, and politics. And it is being refashioned nationally as well as in the villages. No person has been more symbolic of the indigenous struggle than Rigoberta Menchú—the young highlands woman whose father and brothers were killed by the military and whose best-selling book about her travails and determination ultimately led to her 1992 Nobel Peace Prize.[18] But as compelling an icon as Menchú has become in the villages and in the world outside of Guatemala, she remains predictably controversial among many Spanish and Ladinos who see her as a political puppet cleverly manipulated for ideological purposes. Recently a well-known anthropologist has provided a careful and not uncritical analysis of both her story and her stardom.[19]

Much of the future of Guatemala's Mayan majority depends upon the implementation of the recently signed peace accords between the government and the UNRG. The agreement signed on December 29, 1996, ended more than forty years of a civil conflict that overall claimed as many as two hundred thousand dead and fifty thousand missing from a population of some ten million. The United States became a more forceful outside party to negotiations following new revelations of government atrocities and cover-ups in both Guatemala City and Washington, D.C. But the most important brokering assistance came from the United Nations, which is also overseeing the difficult process of disarming and demobilizing approximately five thousand UNRG guerrillas and sixteen thousand Guatemalan military.

Coming after five hundred years of suppression, some of the accord's provisions are truly revolutionary. A new federal government Council of Elders includes twenty-one Mayan priests or shamans. There are numerous measures designed to protect and promote indigenous languages and customs, ranging from religion to the practice of community land-ownership. It remains to be seen how a predominantly Ladino Congress will put such matters into effect. However, the military has already been scaled back, and there is now a Historical Memory Project to uncover the grotesque abuses of the past in a manner similar to South Africa's Truth and Reconciliation Commission, which forgoes prosecuting suspects in order to extract their confessions. There is even a new national political party of indigenous people that has already elected the mayor of the country's second largest city, Quezaltenango.

But, of course, peace treaties are one thing and lasting peace another. Suspicions of mutual ulterior motives and hidden arms caches exist on both sides. And the class and cultural abrasions that provoked the struggle in the first place continue to throb.

An especially ominous sign was the April 1998 murder of the prominent Catholic bishop Juan Gerardi Conadera, who was bludgeoned to death late one night in his garage two days after he released a fourteen hundred-page report on human rights violations that was based on six thousand interviews with witnesses who placed the blame for 80 percent of the casualties on the army and its allied civilian patrols. Ironically, the report was titled *Nunca Mas*, or "Never Again." It is further ironic that Bishop Gerardi was the authority who closed down and evacuated the Catholic diocese of Quiche fifteen years earlier. While his murder remains formally unsolved, suspicions center on current and ex-military personnel. In the meantime, some PACs or civilian patrols are returning to action, and the dark form of Rios Montt continues to surface periodically and ominously in Guatemalan politics.

Guatemala is a country infamous for its earthquakes. Some have even argued that many Protestant groups gained their strongest foothold by providing crucial relief services following the devastating quake of 1976. But in addition to its natural fissures and seismic shocks, I am hardly the first to note their social equivalents. In neither case is the center holding reliably; there are continuing dangers on both levels, and it is almost as hard to predict one inevitably recurring disaster as the other.

As I was leaving the country, one of my very knowledgeable respondents said, "You are leaving just in time. You have learned a lot, and after three weeks everything is clear. After that, it just gets more and more confusing." The comment was intended seriously and sympathetically. It is good counsel for travelographers everywhere.

Conclusion

Brazil and Guatemala both illustrate the way in which religion shapes and is shaped by its changing social settings. Religion has been a source and a victim of upheaval. Although religion in Guatemala is not as directly implicated in politics and the state as in Brazil, religion burns with a smoldering intensity in both nations precisely because it has been touched by political flames. But the reverse is also true. Politics without religion in either country is scarcely imaginable. Religion is an important part of the cultural struggles that exacerbate political and economic class conflicts everywhere.

Moreover, Brazil and Guatemala both illustrate the paradox that religions out of power may have more power than religions in power. For almost four hundred years until the latter half of the nineteenth century, Latin America's colonial Catholicism was formally in power as the state church in virtually every nation. Even for another century following official separation of church and state, Catholicism remained a pillar of the popularly acknowledged establishment. Certainly elite standing carried important advantages for the church, culturally as well as economically. But it also led to characteristics of what has been called a "lazy monopoly," and there is no question that the church was hobbled politically.

During the last half century Brazil and Guatemala illustrate what can happen when religious moths leave the fetid chambers of the state and begin to fly closer to the flame of politics itself. Once religions become autonomous players, they are likely to exercise more influence rather than less. Certainly that is the lesson of the Catholicism's movement for Liberation Theology, although it was never a universal cause, and at least the Brazilian Church has shown signs of heading back into the state's embrace. Meanwhile, more indigenous religions and imported evangelical Protestantism have made independent headway of their own in each country. This has given new strength to the voices of religion and raised the stakes considerably for their mutual relationships, which range from imitative syncretism to intense competition.

2

Troubles and

Changes in

European

Christendom

*Poland, Northern
Ireland, and Sweden*

From the perspective of the New World, Europe has long represented the arch religious establishment. This was the early and enduring center of the great empire of Roman Catholicism, where politics and religion were mutually entrusted and encrusted. Even after the fragmenting Protestant Reformation of the sixteenth century, different religions enjoyed pride of political place in different countries. Catholicism retained its power in southern and eastern Europe; Lutheranism gained a strong foothold in Germany and became a controlling force in Scandinavia; Anglicanism flourished in England.

With historical hindsight, we Americans are often led to celebrate our own religious freedom in contrast to Europe's religious hegemony. But then hindsight is often self-congratulatory. Not long after the birth of European Protestantism, the United States was settled by religious Puritans and pilgrims who were anything but devotees of freedom. Nor were they denied all religious freedom in England—save for that somewhat arrogant freedom to mount a controlling political establishment there. This was precisely their objective in America, and for the first century and a half of the colonial experience the colonies were religious fiefdoms.

But what most Americans contrast with European religious establishments is our postindependence constitutional legacy and its heralded "separation of church and state." However, just as our separation is far from absolute, their establishments are far from dominant. Although the majority of European states remain religious enterprises in a formal sense, most have become increasingly thin veneers that no longer hide the tensions, conflicts, and in many cases, perceived irrelevance of religion.

Of course, it is equally presumptuous to describe Europe on the basis of three countries as it is to describe Latin America with only two. Once again, however, the cases are compelling in their own right, and they offer a triangulation of the European religious scene. Each provides different glimpses of moths aflutter, not to mention the interlarding of sacred and secular and the dependency of religious canons upon social context.

During the 1980s Poland became an inspiration in Eastern Europe and throughout the West because of its successful struggle to overthrow its longtime Communist government. The Polish Catholic Church played a major role, in cooperation with the Solidarity labor movement. But while the story leading up to and culminating in 1989 is often told, I shall focus more on what has occurred since. What has happened to Poland's once potent union of sacred and secular institutions? Where does the Catholic Church now stand—or stand to fall—in Poland today?

Certainly Northern Ireland is no stranger to the front pages of U.S. newspapers. Its "Troubles"—after 1969, Catholics began to refer simply but eloquently to the "Troubles"—continue to provoke headlines despite the peace that sometimes seems so tantalizingly close. A struggle often described as between Protestants and Catholics, this would appear a clear case of primordial religious conflict with high political stakes. Yet religion's involvement is not quite what this suggests, and there are other dimensions to the standoff that require attention.

Finally, shifting from Northern Ireland to Sweden is like moving from rapids to a backwater. Until very recently, Sweden was officially Lutheran; but it is not a country in which religious chords resonate deeply. What lies behind Sweden's decision to undergo religious disestablishment in the year 2000? What role can religion play in a country that seems to deny its standing so assiduously?

Poland: Catholicism as Both Solution and Problem

There are even Polish jokes in Poland. Question: How many Poles does it take to change the world? Answer: one. Of course, part of the humor is a matter of pride in playing off of the Polish jokes whose answers involve so many Poles. But another part of the humor suffers in translation across both cultures and time. So does the punch line. In the 1970s the solitary referent might well have been the new Polish Pope John Paul II, the former Cardinal Wojtyla of Kraków. But by the late 1980s another figure fit so perfectly that the joke needed no explanation in Poland or in much of the West generally. This was Lech Walesa, the former shipyard worker in Gdansk who won a Nobel Peace Prize for leading the Solidarity workers' movement that ultimately brought down the Communist government put in place by the Soviets just after World War II.

But it was really more than a one-man job. Walesa and Solidarity needed help, and they got a great deal of it from the Polish Catholic Church. Whereas Catholicism was systematically suppressed in other Eastern European countries behind the Iron Curtain, the Polish Church had been allowed to continue functioning as a kind of safety valve to relieve pressure on the unpopular Communist regime. It was virtually the only institution in Polish society that retained some independent public stature. As a result, when John Paul II began to broker a cooperative relationship between the Church and Solidarity in 1979, some saw it as a heaven-sent collaboration. It also sparked widespread discussion of a new concept, "civil society," which referred to those autonomous organizations that operated between the family and the state and gave new hope for freedom around the globe—though some of that hope has gradually given way to reconsideration and debate in Poland and elsewhere, as I shall elaborate in the second part of the book.[1]

Poland's struggle to overthrow Communism from 1979 to 1989 has been well and often chronicled.[2] Solidarity provided the driving force behind the surging political movement. The Catholic Church supplied a crucial legitimacy that extended the cause far beyond the reach of a labor union and allowed it to mobilize support from every segment of the populace. In 1989 the communists vacated the government and left it in the hands of Solidarity itself. In the first national elections in half a century, Lech Walesa was elected president.

But Walesa's victory was not the near unanimous anointment it was often assumed to be outside of Poland. No sooner did the Communists fall and Solidarity win than old conflicts began to resurface among the Polish citizenry at large. To many, Walesa quickly lost his charisma and reverted to working-class form as an unkempt rube with few of the skills necessary to lead a nation, as opposed to a movement. Heading down the electoral stretch, the outcome was decidedly unclear. At this point, Walesa again sought support from his prior ally in the struggle, the Catholic Church. Somewhat reluctantly, it delivered. With Catholic endorsement, Walesa won by a narrow margin; without Catholic support, he might have lost by a wide one.

At that point, Polish Catholicism was highly respected and very popular. Once its support of Solidarity through the 1980s was added to its role as an alternative institution over almost two centuries of foreign rule, the Church was perceived as not just a religious agency but the one continuous keeper of the national flame during a half-century of deep travail at the hands of outsiders.

World War II cost six million Polish lives. As a grotesque capstone to the Nazi occupation during World War II, Hitler's parting gesture in 1944 was to completely raze the central city of Warsaw in a spasm of spite and rage that involved a month of full-time destruction and some forty thousand deaths. When Allied troops arrived shortly thereafter, it was said that the only sounds were those of rats scurrying in the rubble.

Following the war, the city was hastily rebuilt, and some say with equal irrationality by an architecturally challenged Communist regime that confused sheer size with style. My visitor's home base—Warsaw University's Institute of Sociology—now occupies a building quickly constructed over the uncleared ruins of the old secret police headquarters, most likely with bodies still buried in the inaccessible basement. But building reconstruction was among the least of the Communist sins from the standpoint of most Poles. The country had exchanged one occupying force for another. Life continued to be drab, scant, and rigid in its constraints. Solidarity's victory in 1989 was akin to a spring sunrise following a winter night of fifty years. During my visit only a few years later, I took a streetcar across Warsaw with a young academic who suddenly pointed to a neighborhood market and said, "It is hard to believe how much life has changed for the better. I spent my entire youth standing in line—often at that very store—hoping to get the bare necessities for my family. Now there are no lines and no shortages of at least the essentials."

The current economic situation is not as upbeat as this may suggest, as salaries generally trail price increases. Still, Poland's quick shift to capitalism has been an inspiration to Eastern Europe, not to mention Russia and other countries of the former Soviet Union. There is now a Western glitz to shopping along Warsaw's equivalent of New York's Fifth Avenue, though the shelves of neighborhood grocers were conspicuously understocked. Meanwhile, the tilt away from Communism and in the direction of the West is seen in other ways. Imagine a national curriculum in the social sciences that turned virtually overnight from Marxist to non-Marxist. The shift in textbooks, let alone interpretive frameworks, was a wrench for teachers and students alike.

There was also another sort of revisionism afoot, this one concerning religion. It was not just that Catholicism had given legitimacy to Solidarity, but Solidarity had given legitimacy to Catholicism. Because of the Solidarity-enhanced stature of the Catholic Church, Catholicism became a criterion of national identity. To be Polish was to be Catholic; supporting the new Poland involved attending the old services. But there was now a tendency to forget that Catholicism was not the only Polish religion, and certainly not the only religion that had played a major role in Polish history.[3] It is true that Polish history is elusive, since the country's borders have shifted with virtually every war over some two hundred years. There have been times, however, when Poland was 40 percent non-Catholic and included large Lutheran and Jewish communities.

On the eve of World War II, Poland's 3.5 million Jews formed the largest Jewish community in Europe. This community bore the major brunt of the Holocaust that killed millions of Jews—along with substantial numbers of Romanies (known pejoratively as Gypsies) and many Christians who seemed threats or nuisances to the Nazi occupation.[4] Today it is hard to know how many Jews remain in Poland. Estimates range from five thousand to thirty thousand, but in a country where Catholicism is so dominant, many Jews conceal their identities; others have had their Jewishness concealed from them, only to discover it accidentally. Now there are stirrings of a new Jewish consciousness, aided by Jewish organizations from outside the country that have sparked some internal resentment. Not long ago a telephone hotline was set up to allow people to seek anonymous counsel concerning their identity. Calls have greatly exceeded anyone's expectations.

In the meantime, anti-Semitism remains virulent among roughly a quarter of the Polish population according to recent surveys. In April 1997, following an act of Parliament to restore Jewish properties confiscated during World War II, Warsaw's last remaining synagogue was set on fire two days after a bomb threat against offices of a Jewish foundation next door. Following parliamentary elections later that fall, a prominent Catholic priest used a sermon to argue that the newly appointed foreign minister should be excluded from office as a Jew.

Catholicism and Politics in the Revolutionary Aftermath

We have already seen how Brazilian Catholicism returned to a more traditional religious role with the restoration of democracy in the mid-1980s. In some ways, Polish Catholicism has experienced a similar process. But this did not occur overnight. Initially, the Church's successful collaboration in bringing down Communism left Catholicism not only riding high but aiming higher. Subsequently, it seems to have aimed too high and converted widespread adulation into considerable alienation. This resumes a long tradition of anticlericalism on the part of a laity that was fearful of the Church and a brand of impersonal, hierarchical, and authoritarian power that was often ecclesiastically self-serving if not outright corrupt.[5]

On a rainy day in Kraków, I was waiting at a neighborhood bus stop with a Polish professor who pointed at the adjacent lot containing an old frame hall and a brand new brick building: "That's our parish church. Just after 1989, the priests announced that it was now time to raise money for a new building. The economy was still in shambles and everyone was pretty destitute. Nevertheless we all scrimped and struggled to raise enough for the new building. But it was only then that the priests announced that the new building was for their quarters; the church is still the same drafty, dilapidated structure." Such incidents don't help the Church's image. Nor does the cynical Polish adage that if you want your son to live the good life and drive a Mercedes don't send him into law or medicine, but get him into the priesthood. Perhaps this accounts for Poland's surfeit of priests, in contrast to the shortages that plague the Church elsewhere in the West.

But there is another, more political reason for the rising disenchantment. Almost immediately after the new government was formed in 1989, the Catholic ecclesiastical leadership began to demand religion instruction in the public schools and government action that would effectively ban both elective abortion and divorce. After calling in its markers with President Walesa whom it helped elect, the Church won two out of three. Catechistic instruction in the schools continues to be widely accepted, even though it was implemented against the better judgment of the minister of education. However, the new limits on abortion were never popular to begin with and gradually became less so. As another observer has noted: "In Poland before 1989, one frequently heard the phrase 'the Church and us against them'; now one is as likely to hear the phrase 'the Church and them against us.' "[6]

In fact, a liberalization of abortion was among the first actions of Poland's new President Kwasniewski in 1996—just a few months after this Western-tilting former Communist had defeated Walesa himself. The liberal statute was subsequently overturned in the courts, but the issue remains on the public agenda, especially for women, many of whom are forced into the role of "abortion tourists" elsewhere. Yet Catholic officials were far less active in Walesa's campaign in 1996 than they had been in 1989. This was more a tactical decision to ward off growing disaffection than the result of any affection for Kwasniewski. His relations with the Church have been decidedly chilly. He conspicuously omitted the phrase "So help me God" from his oath of office; the Church denied him a burial plot for his mother. Kwasniewski's party suffered heavy losses in the 1997 parliamentary elections to a reborn and reconfigured Solidarity—ironically a case of an ex-Communist and probusiness coalition losing to an ex–labor union faction. But the Church gained little in the bargain. Surveys show that—while some three-quarters of the population agree that Catholicism is a major pillar of society and have no objection to religion in the schools—a majority believe that the Church ought to stay out of politics, a sentiment even shared by two-thirds of those who regularly attend church. Kwasniewski was easily reelected in 2000.

All of this comes at a time when the Church remains very much involved in politics as a way of protecting itself from sliding down the slippery slope to secularity that has characterized Western European religion. Italy offers an especially foreboding example, where the Catholic Church has lost much of its once commanding influence. As early as 1981, two-thirds of the population explicitly disobeyed its injunctions in voting to legalize divorce and abortion, and by 1984 the state and the Vatican had negotiated a new concordat that greatly diminished the latter's formal standing. Aware of such trends, the Polish Church has renegotiated a Polish concordat with the Vatican. But ratification by the Polish Parliament was delayed by a wariness of the document's stress on Catholicism as the dominant Polish religion with attendant political and property rights.

Although Parliament did pass a law requiring the media to respect "Christian values," action on a new Polish constitution was postponed until April 1997 in large part because of religion. Despite considerable opposition, "the Church" (in the person of Cardinal Jószef Glemp and his various bishops) finally secured inclusion of the old language from the 1921 Constitution: "The Roman Catholic faith, being the religion of the vast majority of the nation, has a leading position in the state among denominations with equal rights."

To critics, this sounds a bit reminiscent of George Orwell's fable *Animal Farm*, where some animals are more equal than others. Meanwhile, there may be a self-defeating boomerang effect in the Catholic leadership's efforts to have the nation as a whole invoke God as its highest loyalty, to pressure the state into its own concordat with the Vatican, to restrict if not illegalize abortion and divorce, and to secure economic privileges to the Church and its priesthood that are denied other faiths.[7] This is important background to the decline in the Church's overall approval ratings from close to 90 percent in 1989 to 57 percent in 1995.[8] As one of my interviewees put it, "They want too much, and they are making their business things that are not. By pushing too far into the private sphere, they are jeopardizing the public sense of community they once helped to build."

What then does it mean that more than 90 percent of Poles are Catholics? According to one observer-respondent, "There really are two types: the 'religious Catholics' and the 'family Catholics.'" But even the former vary. As another put it, "Being religious in Poland means one and only one thing—attending church on Sunday." The proportion claiming regular church attendance is well over 60 percent—an astonishingly high figure compared to countries in Western Europe or even the United States. While some experts expect the percentage to begin to decline, it has remained stubbornly resistant. At the same time, there are also religious Catholics who are more than just weekly attendees. Poland hosts a fervent Catholic renewal movement that is Bible-reading and pietistic, even if small and somewhat marginal within the population at large.

Meanwhile, what is a "family Catholic"? According to my respondent, these are not just people who think of the Trinity as Jesus, Mary, and Joseph—though many do. Family Catholics see the Church as an ethical ally in raising children at a time when youth are seen as anarchical, anomic, or perhaps worst of all postmodern. Youth are often depicted as lurching between meaningless self-indulgence and an intense enthrallment to the spirit of the moment. As one interviewee put it, "Many parents believe—or at least believe they believe—because they need the Church as an ally." They approve of religious instruction in the public schools not so much because it is religious as such but because any moral port will suffice in a relativistic storm. These are adherents who lean upon the Church even as they are suspicious of it, followers who seek out its communality even as they are recoil from its hierarchical verticality.

But perhaps there is a third form of Catholicism as well. While teaching a class at Warsaw University, I asked the students to talk a bit about their own religiosity. They all said they were Catholics but beyond that seemed puzzled, reticent, and not a little embarrassed. I wondered if the distinction between religious Jews and cultural Jews might be applicable? At that suggestion, they visibly brightened and clamored to speak. That was precisely it; they were cultural Catholics. They weren't really believers, and while they attended church at least sporadically, they had a good deal of contempt for some of the Church officials and policies. Still, Catholicism was part of their national and family cultural heritage, and they were proud of what the Church had done to help free Poland from the Communist regime.[9]

Today the phrase "cultural Catholicism" resonates throughout Western Europe. As Poland moves deeper into the Western economic and political orbit, this may be a religious concomitant. Certainly it is a far different way of reducing the possibility of religious hegemony than was recently demonstrated by nearby Russia to the east. Whereas Poland's response involves a voluntary cultural shift, Russia's answer as of 1997 took the form of draconian legislation that would essentially outlaw all but a few accepted religions, such as the Russian Orthodox Church, which claims the allegiance of half the population but will itself be placed under state controls. Aimed ostensibly at foreign sects and cults and their proselytizing, the action places all religions on guard in violation of the religious rights guaranteed under Russia's 1993 Constitution. Despite the efforts of some members of Poland's Catholic hierarchy, Polish politics seem to be working in a more modern—perhaps even postmodern—direction.

Northern Ireland: A Political Future Held Hostage to a Religious Past

The concussive thud quickly gave way to tinkling glass. It was shortly after 2 A.M. on my second night in Belfast, and I was suddenly awake thinking, "Welcome to the North of Ireland"—as the minority Catholics prefer to call it—or to "Ulster" in the parlance of the Protestant majority. Bombs are hardly unexpected in a country where violence is sometimes a round-the-clock phenomenon. Although I learned the next morning that the bomb had exploded six blocks away as a warning expertly designed to avoid actual injuries, it added a shiver of reality to the accounts I had been reading.[10]

Happily, much has changed in Northern Ireland since my visit. Although it took more than five years, a Catholic-initiated cease-fire finally led to a negotiated settlement, followed in turn by elections for a new Northern Irish political assembly. I will come back to this peace process later. Meanwhile, I want to describe the Northern Ireland that I encountered and the reasons why such peacemaking was so slow in coming. Whereas my account of Poland tended to focus on events since its political transformation in 1989, here I want to reverse the emphasis and stress factors that preceded the precarious Irish peace agreement of 1998. This involves a long-standing culture war between the long-dominant Protestant community—especially its militant Unionist factions—so loyal to England, on the one hand, and the nationalistic yearnings of a growing Catholic community—especially its militant "Republican" wing—eager to be reunited with the overwhelmingly Catholic Irish Republic to the south and hostile to England and its occupying military forces. The conflict has been both protracted and pervasive.

Violence in the Past and Present Tenseness

For many, violence has become a way of life in this society of 1.5 million residents. From 1969 to 1994 the civil strife cost some thirty-five hundred deaths in Northern Ireland and such "overspill" areas as England, the Irish Republic, and mainland Europe, where terrorism has been exported partly for political display.[11] Nor do these figures include the thousands who have been physically and psychologically injured. It is true that the violence crescendoed early in the 1970s, after which it grew mercifully more sporadic—if strategic. It is also true that the early predominance of Catholic Republican violence against Protestant Unionist victims has been reversed of late. But there is a bit of cynical irony that, in this war of sometimes amateurish terrorists, each side may have inflicted more casualties on its own ranks by accident than on the opposition by design.

But violence in Northern Ireland is apparent in other ways, too. Violence has long been a leading industry in this small corner of the United Kingdom. It is not just that the country has served as a site for British and U.S. military bases or that its capital, Belfast, was once a major shipbuilding center that produced a significant portion of the British fleet during World Wars I and II. Today its heavy industries are in decline, and they employ altogether a workforce smaller than that of Heathrow airport in London. Now civil violence itself has become a major occupation in Northern Ireland, as more than thirty thousand workers owe their livelihood to making, distributing, or deploying arms.

When I was there, the signs of a garrison state were not hard to find. One could not walk far in Belfast without coming across an armored tank-truck of either the local police—the mostly Protestant Royal Ulster Constabulary—or the British army. Troops in battle dress with submachine guns not only sit in the tank turrets but dash up and down the sidewalks for quick reconnaissance. But this, too, was routine, as I learned when one young man in full regalia looked up on passing, grinned, and said cheerfully, "Good Morning, Suh."

Such "security" forces can be comforting, if sometimes in retrospect. Because I enjoy walking, I spent part of a chilly, gray afternoon walking home from an interview along a route that I later learned few natives would follow. Having begun on the very Catholic Falls Road, where I stopped briefly in a Gaelic coffeehouse, I then took what I later learned was a naive and potentially dangerous turn on to the Protestant Donegal Road. The difference was abundantly clear in the brilliant political graffiti on the gables at the ends of the row houses on each block. One doesn't cross these boundary lines lightly in either direction, though I was relatively safe as a stranger. Despite my joint Catholic-Protestant heritage and a physical resemblance to many middle-aged Northern Irish males, my clothes, gait, and general demeanor marked me as a foreigner. I was out of the warring loop to the children who paused to stare at me with wide eyes and open mouths.

There are suspicions within the ranks as well as between them. At one point, a small-town respondent and her husband generously invited me to dinner along with several local couples—all old friends and all Catholic. The talk was socially convivial but politically superficial until one couple left late in the evening. At that point the conversation suddenly intensified and the war stories began. When I asked later about the change in mood I was told, "We've known and enjoyed that couple for twenty years, but where the 'Troubles' are concerned, we've never quite trusted them. And around here, you can never be too sure of who you're talking to." Many have had the experience of being shocked when close friends assumed to be mild-mannered bystanders to the "war" were arrested and convicted on ample evidence of arms smuggling or worse.

But why the warring at all? What are the issues that produced the cancer that has metastasized within this society? What is the conflict's past, and what seems its likely future?

As one might suppose in this part of the world, the conflict has deep historical roots. There have been Catholics in Ireland since Saint Patrick in 432 c.e. In 1170 Catholics came in force as Norman oppressors of the indigenous peasantry. But beginning in the seventeenth century, following the Protestant Reformation, the tables turned. Now the Catholics became the indigenous oppressed at the hands of a group of Calvinist Presbyterians sent from Scotland to look after England's interests. The culminating event of this early colonization occurred in 1689 when Protestants in Londonderry (or simply Derry to the anti-London Catholics) gathered in a fort to stave off a Catholic siege in a display of epochal heroism akin to that at the Texas Alamo in the United States.

For the next two hundred years and more, the English and the Protestants consolidated their economic and political power, as Catholics grew increasingly resentful. The Irish Republican movement began in the late eighteenth century after the example of the American and French revolutions. Sinn Fein (We Ourselves, often mistranslated as Ourselves Alone) was founded as a Catholic political movement in 1905 to fight for an independent Ireland. Gradually its underground guerilla wing, the Irish Republican Army (IRA), began to take shape. In 1916 Catholic alienation gave way to insurrection in what has been known ever since as the Easter Uprising.

The underground struggle grew increasingly savage until 1921, when England finally stepped in to broker a Solomonic solution that bitterly divided the ranks of the Irish Republicans themselves. Ireland's thirty-two counties were partitioned into two countries. The Irish Free State comprised twenty-six dominantly Catholic counties in an independent state to the south; the remaining six—majority Protestant—counties constituted what John Fulton refers to as the "statelet of Northern Ireland" and an extension of England itself.[12] By 1949 what had become the Irish Republic had seceded from the British Commonwealth after producing something England has never had, namely, a constitution—and one that declared unification with Northern Ireland a basic national objective.

Just as the U.S. African American civil rights struggle began a heralded surge of activism in the 1960s, so did the civil rights struggle of Catholic Republicans who, though of another country and color, saw their own experience in many ways similar to that of African Americans. The "Troubles" came to another head in Derry, where on Bloody Sunday in 1972, thirteen Catholic protesters were killed by British army troops. Shortly thereafter and following a loyalist strike, the power-sharing Northern Irish Parliament at Stormont collapsed, and the British imposed direct rule from London, though with Northern Irish representatives to the Westminster Parliament in London. However, violence continued—and continues—between the Catholic IRA and its two chief opponents—the occupying British presence, on the one hand, and the Protestant Ulster loyalists with their own extreme political and paramilitary groups, on the other.

As the Northern Irish economy turned decidedly cool, its local political climate grew progressively hot. The British tried on several occasions to arrange for a compromise withdrawal. Most notably in 1985, London and Dublin proposed an "Anglo-Irish" accord by which the British would share external governance with the Irish Republic. However, Protestant protests finally won out, and the initiative collapsed.

During my visit in 1993, John Hume, the leader of the country's largest nonviolent Nationalist Catholic party, the Social Democratic and Labour Party, joined with Gerry Adams, the leader of Sinn Fein and an ex-IRA member, to propose talks with Ireland and Britain. The proposal met predictable opposition from Unionist Protestants concerned that any possibility of reunification with the Irish Republic would jeopardize their religious birthright and their political standing. But there was also a dragging of heels in London. The Conservative government of Prime Minister John Major was unyielding in its condition that the IRA must first promise an unconditional cease-fire and a turning over of all weapons. In the words of one English acquaintance—a very prestigious and sophisticated academic—"Oh, well. You can't negotiate with terrorists, and besides those people are absolutely unreliable and not to be trusted, especially by each other."

A Religious Conflict?

If there is a true religious conflict anywhere in the world, this would appear to be it. But surprisingly, I found many there who dispute this diagnosis. Certainly this is not a battle of churches. The relatively small groups of extremists on both sides are mostly—but by no means exclusively—nonreligious. The majority of Catholic clergy have been consistently critical of the nominally Catholic IRA for its use of violence. The same is true of the mostly Anglican and Presbyterian clerics on the Protestant side. Even the best-known leader of the Ulster Unionists, the fulminating evangelical Rev. Ian Paisley, has sometimes faulted the violence on both sides.

There is a long history of dialogue between liberal Protestant and Catholic clergy, even involving those high on their respective ecclesiastical ladders, and many leading religious officials have backed away from the conflict altogether. Ironically, some of the most potent Catholic anticlericalism comes from lower-ranking Catholic clerics who are sympathetic with republicanism and see their leaders as pusillanimous. After noting that recent appointments to bishop are "Vatican civil servants" rather than real leaders, one of the rare Catholic priests with well-known Sinn Fein allegiances put it this way: "Just as politics is dominated by those with little religious interest, so is religion dominated by those with little political interest. I remember back in the 1970s a few of us entered into talks with the Red Hand Commandos and the Ulster Defence Association [both Protestant paramilitary squads] but it was frustrating because the Church hierarchy really didn't care—though, of course, they would have all come to our funeral if we'd gotten our heads blown off."

Meanwhile, another Catholic clergyman admitted that "the Church uses the State, and the State uses the Church." There is a good deal of rank-and-file suspicion that the Church has benefited financially from its cooperation with—and some say co-optation by—the British government. The state pays teacher salaries and gives student stipends even in parochial schools; there are handsome allowances for some social services run through the churches. But there is a fine line between state-church cooperation for the best of reasons and for the worst. When the British government put money into new housing in several working-class Catholic neighborhoods, many republicans scoffed at it as mere propaganda.

Overall religious participation is considerably higher in Northern Ireland than in the Irish Republic, the rest of Britain, or Europe in general even though the ranks of the nonreligious have grown from 1 percent to 12 percent over the past twenty-five years. Still, churchgoers are not the problem. There are other ways for religion to be implicated in conflict besides the formal actions of its clergy or its active parishioners.

Earlier I noted that cultural Catholics in Poland are analogous to cultural Jews. The phenomenon is also common here. Indeed, perhaps the most fundamental distinction in Northern Ireland is between cultural Catholics and cultural Protestants—neither are much involved in their churches, but both are caught up in the religious legacies handed down from family to family, neighborhood to neighborhood, and community to community. As one respondent put it, "When you meet a stranger here at a party or some other gathering, the first thing to be established is not your occupation but your religious identity." And as another noted, "Even if you are an atheist, you are either a Catholic or a Protestant atheist."

It is hard to escape these labels. Children quickly learn to distinguish Protestants from Catholics by their vocabulary, their pronunciation, and their dress. Sometimes safety depends upon it. But then, like most European societies—indeed like most societies in the world in contrast to our own—personal identity in Northern Ireland is more "retrospective" than "prospective." That is, you are judged more by what happened in your past than by what you are accomplishing now or are likely to in the future. Your parents' and grandparents' religion, ethnic origins, occupation, and educational attainment are all essential parts of your own identity, as are your own educational achievements—not just how much but from what schools and with what honors. Once this identity package is established by young adulthood, it is very difficult to shuck off. While some of this applies in the United States, at least the country's white middle-class culture orients more to the present and the future; it is more forgiving of the past but more demanding in the here and now.

It is not just in matters of personal identity that the present is haunted by the past. In Northern Ireland, one feels history hovering over every institution, and it is far more common to address what has occurred rather than what might or could. In the words of Maurice Goldring, "Ireland's evolution always wears the mask of tradition, and the country advances backwards into the future with its eyes firmly fixed on the past."[13]

A priestly informant was especially pointed in remarking that "the Catholic Church needs to address the future rather than the past." But the sentiment applies equally to Protestants. There is an almost audible sense of a clock ticking in the most infamous center of loyalist religion: Ian Paisley's evangelical "Martyrs' Memorial" Free Presbyterian Church in East Belfast. The church is something of a renegade since it is self-labeled Presbyterian and not a member of the official Presbyterian Church of Ireland. In a congregation so deeply enveloped in a past now fading, one must wonder how the parishioners interpret the motto chiseled above the entrance: "Time is Short."

If Northern Ireland is divided by different cultural religions at the individual level, it is also afflicted with competing civil religions at the societal level. "Civil religion" refers to a politically distilled religious common denominator that serves to unite a society or community despite its differences. The civil religion of the United States is a Christian-dominated amalgam that is celebrated on Memorial Day, the Fourth of July, and Thanksgiving, not to mention the nondenominational prayers offered during presidential inaugurations and at the beginning of each day in Congress or the motto "In God We Trust" on the nation's coins.

Ideally, a nation has only one consolidating civil religion. Having two involves not so much an embarrassment of riches as a nullifying conflict of competing principles. That is exactly the situation in Northern Ireland. Both religious communities have their own sacred events and symbols, their own fraternal orders, and their own versions of both the past and the future. Rather than unite the nation, civil religion has become an enduring source of division.

Clearly religion in Northern Ireland is important—though perhaps more negatively than positively, more politically than theologically. But there are compounding factors. One of these is ethnicity. After all, the tensions between the Irish and the English are long-standing. The (Catholic) nationalist—or in more extreme form, republican—agenda is defined by its eagerness for reunification with the Irish Republic, whereas the Protestant loyalists are more loyal to England where many trace their roots. Because the Anglican Church of Ireland was disestablished in 1869 and most Ulster Protestants are now Presbyterians, the tie would appear to be more ethnic than religious. At the same time, the basic ethnic split is certainly reinforced by the fundamental religious difference between Catholic and Protestant. Over the years, ethnic and religious differences have coalesced, but because the religious distinction carries greater institutional thrust with a higher public profile, it tends to dominate.

Another exacerbating factor involves the economy and considerations of social class.[14] If a rising economic tide lifts all boats, a receding tide may leave them all stranded. In recent years, the Northern Irish economy has been more bust than boom. Not surprisingly, the image of a class struggle is especially common among younger militants and Marxists on the Catholic left. Historically, there is no question that Protestants represented Ulster's bourgeoisie, with Catholics constituting the Northern Irish proletariat. But in recent years these labels have become less relevant. There are now more Protestants unemployed than Catholics, though the Catholic rate is higher. Catholic university enrollments and civil service employment are up, and Catholics have moved into the middle –class in increasing numbers. Many higher-status suburban Catholics now refer to the low-status Catholics of West Belfast as "a problem."

At the same time, there has been a leveling of Protestant status. Almost a fifth of Belfast's residents have emigrated out of the city since the "Troubles" began in 1970, and many of these are affluent Protestants who have left for England or the United States themselves or sent their children there for higher education. Meanwhile, although upwardly mobile Catholics are eager to move into Protestant suburbs, the Protestants are not anxious to have them. The aspirations of the upwardly mobile are often resisted by those who find their own status threatened. Indeed, a good deal of recent loyalist violence against Catholics is aimed at precisely those who have moved into previously all-Protestant areas— what some observers refer to as neighborhood "ethnic cleansing." The few Protestant members of Sinn Fein are clearly motivated by continuing class grievances rather than any affinity for Catholicism itself. Because the world of Northern Irish class differences is also retrospective, old relationships are culturally perpetuated even after they become structurally passé.

Approaching the Endgame
Optimists were rare in Northern Ireland in 1993; skepticism had become a matter of course. After all, if rain today can seem a predictor of rain tomorrow, the country has every reason to carry umbrellas at the ready. The Hume-Adams initiative mentioned earlier was by no means the first attempt to negotiate an end to the country's "Troubles"—though it was the first to be supported publicly by Sinn Fein. Anyone expressing more than the most guarded hope is apt to be regarded as either deluded or uninformed.

Surely there were reasons for continued pessimism. Other than a few benighted mavericks, there had been no groundswell of Protestant enthusiasm for negotiations of any sort—though by the time of the May 1998 referendum on the peace agreement, half of the Unionists voted for it. A Protestant businessman assured me, "This is a great place to live. Most Protestants and Catholics get along splendidly. After all, only 5 percent are involved in violence." Still, mutual suspicions remain rampant especially among the working classes, though Protestant prejudice toward Catholics is commonly acknowledged to be greater than Catholic antipathy to Protestants as such. In recent years Protestant violence directed toward Catholics has been more common than vice versa.[15] The larger target of the antistate Catholic IRA has been the British, and this involves not only attacks on the British occupying forces but major bombings in England itself—some of which are claimed to warn rather than injure.

It is true that the extremists on both sides constitute very small minorities, and it is also the case that the IRA is reputed to be more tightly regimented. However, one sympathetic Catholic remarked, "They also have their share of gangsters and murderers." As a liberal Protestant churchman put it, "Each side needs to be protected from its own flanks and to protect the other from its worst fears." Thus, among Catholics, "nationalists" are understood as favoring reunification with Ireland but without the use of violence, whereas "republicans" approve violence as a means to such an end—whether justified politically by Sinn Fein, conducted professionally by the long-standing IRA, or involving the less controlled and more volatile actions of the Irish National Liberation Army. Similarly among Protestants, "unionists" are those who favor continuing ties to England, while "loyalists" are those willing to use violence in its behalf—whether the more disciplined Ulster Volunteer Force or the less disciplined Ulster Freedom Fighters.

But protecting the centers from the periphery has not been easy. It is a measure of the stalemate's perversity that it may be partially understood by standing two common explanatory frameworks on their heads. First, instead of regarding violence solely as a consequence, it has become a cause in its own right. Second, solutions to the conflict have become part of the problem.

Over the years, violence has begotten violence in a tit-for-tat spiral that soon loses touch with first blame and first causes. As both a way of life and a means of livelihood for its perpetrators, it has also become a point of orientation for its victims and bystanders. Northern Ireland's routinization of violence resembles the family that so adjusts to an alcoholic in its midst that it comes to depend upon the pathology as the node of all interactions. Moreover, requiring a total cease-fire and surrender of arms as preconditions for negotiations simply puts more power in the hands of the violent few—including those idiosyncratic misanthropes on each side who are beyond even the control of the IRA and its Ulster equivalent.

As for solutions becoming problems, each possible denouement has been so tainted by past disappointments and continuing fears that it becomes another reason to maintain the status quo. Of course, Protestants seek to maintain their ties with Protestant Britain—and the Catholics see them as both obdurate and manipulative to that end. Catholics seek a reunification with the Irish Republic to the south, and many Protestants view this as an apocalyptic scenario. To the extent that each side holds to its own "solution," there is no solution at all.

All of this underlies what Padraig O'Malley calls a "too manageable conflict." [16] That is, the "Troubles" were sufficiently constrained and confined that they failed either to threaten other nations sufficiently to force their involvement or penetrate to the heart of the matter and compel an internally generated settlement. In O'Malley's terms, the "conflict is about the conflict." While it reflects what one interviewee called a "balance of fear," it also provides its participants an important sense of public purpose and private identity.

Such were among the various grounds for the mood of pessimism and fatalism that had seeped to the core of the culture on both sides. Nonetheless, when I returned from Northern Ireland, I was strangely buoyant. I had the palpable feeling of change occurring, and much more in the offing. While I realized the danger of being seduced as a naive foreign observer, I also knew that resident veterans of the conflict could be seduced by cynicism.

If there was a single word that accounted for my mood, it was "demography." At the time of partition in 1921, Catholics constituted roughly a quarter of the Northern Irish population; they now comprise more than 40 percent and are closing fast on the voting majority necessary to control the country's political fate. The change is only partly (and decliningly) a matter of differential fertility. Some one in sixteen marriages are now Protestant-Catholic unions, with the great majority of these landing in the Catholic fold. As noted earlier, many Protestants see the political writing on the graffiti-emblazoned walls and are emigrating out of Northern Ireland. According to a recent survey, some 80 percent of Belfast's churchgoing Protestants foresee a Catholic majority in their lifetime.

In fact, some of the Protestants without the resources to leave Belfast or the country at large are increasingly desperate and paranoid. They see themselves as involved in the same sort of heroic siege that occupied their Londonderry ancestors in 1689. But in the unkind phrase of one Catholic republican: "As some rats jump ship, it leaves others cornered." Under these circumstances, one perverse portent of change is the last paroxysm of violence that often stems from the extremist fringes of the once powerful who are now threatened with powerlessness. The syndrome is a global recurrence, and we have already seen it among the military death squads of Guatemala as well as the Nazis who destroyed Warsaw. Quite apart from the moral issues here, the sociological dynamic is in the time-honored tradition of losers everywhere for whom violence is a final option.

Some of my respondents referred to Londonderry as a harbinger of the sort of devolved joint sovereignty that could someday characterize Northern Ireland as a whole—if only as a stage en route to reunification with the republic. Here the Catholics have already achieved a majority, and they have developed a power-sharing relationship with the Protestants that involves alternating mayors. The arrangement has not been totally idyllic—and many Protestants have simply bailed out of city government and city affairs altogether, including attendance at the games of its popular professional football (soccer) team. Still, it is a model and a microcosm that offers hope. It also offers another dose of irony, since this is a town that has been a frequent center of religious conflict throughout its history.

A Settlement at Hand and at Last

On April 9, 1998, a peace agreement was finally concluded between Unionists and Nationalists in Northern Ireland. The agreement was brokered by outside figures such as the new prime ministers of both Britain and the Irish Republic and former senator George Mitchell of the United States acting as both mediator and liaison from the White House. Over the next several months, the agreement received 71 percent approval from a referendum vote, and a new political assembly was elected. Both suggest that this time the peace may endure in the long run despite predictable short-run vicissitudes.

As we shall see in many other countries, the leaders of conflicting communities who agree to negotiate tend to expose their flanks in turning to the middle. In this case, both Protestant and Catholic leaders of the peace process have been seen as betraying their causes and have been subject to as much scorn and suspicion from within their own ranks as from their opponents. This is a common political scenario, but it is exacerbated when the intense feelings of religion are added to the mix. Violence will continue to erupt sporadically, especially around holy days and holy sites that have special meaning for either Catholics or Protestants but require tolerance on each side amid close quarters. As the United States learned from its own civil rights struggle, the only way to reduce cultural hostility is to constrain the behavior associated with it. Once the offending behavior is ended, the associated cultural and psychological dispositions tend to wither for lack of enactment and reinforcement. But the process is neither quick nor easy, and there must be sufficient political resolve to stay the course.

Northern Ireland is a peculiarly compelling story of civil warfare. Here is another case in which religion and politics seem to play moth to each other's flames. It is a cautionary tale for many other countries around the world, and Northern Ireland has been at the center of a number of comparative analyses by outside observers. Various studies have compared it to countries such as Israel, Hungary, the former Yugoslavia, South Africa, and, of course, the United States.[17] It is hardly flattering to be selected for such inclusion, but it does illustrate the potential of using comparisons to probe beneath encrusted surfaces and reach beyond the contaminated perspectives of the insider.

Sweden: The Twilight of a Religious Establishment

When I began my cross-cultural odyssey, I was eager to find countries as unlike the United States as possible. In particular, I looked for countries that had an officially established national church—as opposed to our church-state separation—and societies where traditional religion was an acknowledged dying ember—as opposed to the licking flames of our own religious firebox. Little did I realize that I would find both attributes in a single case. But then Sweden is a country whose religious paradox has been a mirror image of our own. Here the dominant religion is both official and an anachronism—although as we shall see, the first of these characteristics was shortly to change.

Lutheranism was the first product of the sixteenth century Protestant Reformation, but much of the Catholic decorum remained within the Protestant church, and Protestantism soon began to follow some of the Catholic patterns against which it rebelled. In 1523 the Lutheran Evangelical Church of Sweden became the country's de facto state religion, when Gustavus Vasa took charge of both the state and the church; in 1593 the establishment was proclaimed as de jure.[18] After almost two hundred years of hegemony, the arrangement began to be modified. Sweden enacted a law of "tolerance" in 1781, adopted a constitutional guarantee of religious freedom in 1809, repealed compulsory church attendance in 1858, and in 1860 allowed the citizenry to leave the Lutheran Church—but only for another state-recognized Christian faith.

By the turn of the twentieth century rural communities in the throes of winter's darkness near the Arctic Circle continued to huddle around church congregations, but this was much less true of Stockholm and other growing urban areas to the south. Ingmar Bergman's great film *Fanny and Alexander* captures the growing rift between secular and sacred by contrasting the colorful delights of an irreverent Christmas celebration in a wealthy home with the stark and gloomy pessimism of an evangelical Lutheran parish with all of its patriarchal authoritarianism intact. The latter was even then fighting a losing war.

Sweden was constitutionally Lutheran until the very last day of the twentieth century. But the initial public consideration of disestablishing the church and separating it from the state occurred in the first decade of the century, though it was not until 1951 that citizens were allowed legally to sever all ties to religion. By the mid-twentieth century the church's official status was increasingly belied by religion's declining participation and ebbing cultural salience. Today Swedish religiosity falls at the bottom of virtually every ranking of the world's industrialized nations—whether the measure involves church attendance, belief in God, or any other test of religiosity. Nor is this simply a matter of public lassitude and indifference to churches on the part of the privately pious. Only 44 percent of Swedes agreed that "the world would be better if people followed the Christian ideals," and only 37 percent say, "I myself try to live like a Christian."[19]

Unlike countries where religion is on the tip of both the popular and demagogic tongue, here it elicits more yawns than passion. Lennart Ejerfelt has summarized the pertinent changes over the past forty years: "After the Second World War the Swedish state church system underwent a thorough change. The organizational structures, the parishes' status as public bodies with the right to levy taxes from the citizens, the population register, the cemeteries, and the "burial administration" remained, but the content of this polity has been largely lost. In most countries state-church problems refer to education and to family legislation. In those areas the Swedish church has lost all institutional influence whatsoever."[20]

In many respects, Sweden's state religion is more a nostalgic vestige than a vital institution. The great majority of its active parishioners are over the age of sixty. The church is respected more in death than in life, for church burials are the one ritual that continues to be compelling for more than 90 percent of the population. Even nonchurch members continue to pay 40 percent of the annual church tax to be eligible for such burials—an amount that may exceed $100 each year. This is not just a burial fee but also a way of paying for other civil services that the church renders. It is true that some 65 percent of marriages involve church weddings (5 percent of which are in Catholic or other nonstate denominations). But apart from such rites of passage, ritual observance is very low indeed. Less than 60 percent of the Church of Sweden's members are formally baptized, and the proportion of church membership in the population has declined further since a 1996 law required actual baptism for church membership and held that membership was no longer inherited and automatic if one's parents had belonged. All of this has produced a widening gulf between what some have called "folk" versus "personal" religion.[21] The former is similar to what I have identified earlier as cultural religion in both Poland and Northern Ireland.

However, there is still at least an impish sense in which Lutheranism continues to be a matter of life and death in Sweden. The most important state function rendered by the Church is compiling national census figures. In each of the nation's twenty-five hundred parishes, the clergy serve as vastly overtrained census takers, for which the church receives government remuneration. While some of the "free churches" have complained about possible biases in this system, the system passes formal demographic muster quite well.

But as we shall see repeatedly in other settings, it is one thing for the church to serve the state and quite another to wield influence over it. When asked for recent instances of the latter, most respondents were hard-pressed to respond with anything at all. The last concerted effort occurred in the 1960s and involved increasing the hours devoted to religion in the public school curriculum. The church won the battle but lost the war when the curriculum itself was greatly changed shortly thereafter. In the 1970s the church sought to produce a major governmental reconsideration of family law and abortion, but the effort was to little avail and ultimately abandoned.

Note, however, that church policies themselves reflected input from the broader political scene, since political parties ran their own representatives for parish council positions and bishops are selected by the government from among candidates generated by the church. Of course, individual church leaders have taken prophetic positions (for example, the Bishop of Stockholm's upbraiding of those who shift their legal residence elsewhere to avoid paying state taxes). But these tend to be both rare and ineffectual.

Even the church's national symbolic stature is limited. Perhaps the clearest test here involves religion's role in a societal crisis. Consider, for example, the still unsolved 1986 assassination of the country's prime minister—the social scientist Olaf Palme—as he emerged from a Stockholm movie theater.[22] As in the deaths of many other Swedish national figures, there was no state funeral. While church attendance in the week following the assassination was high, it was not easy to disentangle the religious, political, and national sentiments involved. Responses of appreciation to a widely circulated prayer composed by the Bishop of Stockholm may be especially revealing. They tended to refer not to the bishop's prayer as such but rather to his "poem." Some might interpret this as evidence that Swedish religion has become so deeply privatized as to be inexpressible; an alternative explanation is that religion may be disappearing altogether.

Sweden may be one of the few societies in the world whose civil religion bears little relation to its conventional religion.[23] Instead the nation's most sacred sense of itself is organized far more around its commitment to democratic welfare liberalism. Reinhold Brakenheilm remarks on "the increasing secularization of Sweden which, in light of the widening gap between Christian beliefs and contemporary culture, is characterized by the polarity between an ecological-oriented egalitarian value-system and an individualistic value-system."[24] A number of respondents commented on this devotion to the Swedish welfare state, and I was puzzled when many expressed an eagerness to come to the United States. I asked why they should want to leave a society where problems have been minimized for one where they continue to fester?

"Ah," said one, as if speaking for many, "it is so boring here and so exciting there."

The larger pattern of secularization applies across Scandinavia, where Sweden, Denmark, and Norway vie for standing. Official religion is increasingly taken for granted as a historical legacy.[25] Nowadays the Lutheran Church even has religious competition that is still slight but growing. The country's nearly nine million people remain almost 90 percent Lutheran by heritage if not conviction. However, the growing numbers of immigrant "guest workers" who have decided to remain in the country continue to add to the numbers of Catholics, "free" Protestants, Muslims, and Jews.

When new religious competition is set alongside the old religious lethargy, one might ask how the state remained officially Lutheran for so long. Yet there was little urgency about changing a pattern that had become an innocuous anachronism on its own. Less than half of the polled citizenry (48 percent) opposed such a change as early as 1968, and the figure had dropped to 31 percent by 1987. The breach very nearly occurred in 1978 when the government shrugged and withdrew its proposal at the eleventh hour in response to minority opposition from a national organization of parish officials largely concerned about losing government stipends for services rendered. Opposition to disestablishment continued to decline even among church leaders themselves. Many hoped that an independent church would be revitalized without the real and symbolic constraints of being a state institution; many would prefer to work with small but committed remnants than a large but desultory mass adherence. Opposition remained among clergy and laity associated with declining rural parishes and among those concerned about the loss of extensive and valuable church properties. But these problems were more organizational than theological.

Finally, in 1995 Parliament acted to sever the cord in the millennial year 2000 following a series of gradual stages and commission studies concerned with taxes, burial, property, and the like. The rewritten constitution of 2000 reflects this "change of relationship" as a compromise between full church-state separation and continued state-church subvention for secular services rendered and as a historical legacy. Lutheran doctrine and procedures are described in the law but as a historical legacy and current option, not as part of an officially established linkage. The Church will be allowed to select its bishops without state involvement. Concerning church finances—a major sticking point that continues to loom as a problem for the future—only actual church members will be obliged to pay church dues, though the government has pledged assistance in collecting them for the first ten years.

Sweden is not the only Western European country where the question of disestablishment has emerged. Nor is the issue restricted to Scandinavia. As we saw earlier, Italy has renegotiated and greatly minimized its concordat with the Vatican. There is also loose talk about a severing of British ties with the Anglican Church.[26] Indeed, I recall raising the matter in Britain during a small conference on religion and democracy held in a country estate outside of Oxford. The conference soon devolved into a dulcet shouting match between elite British Anglicans from Parliament, Oxford and Cambridge universities, and the media establishment on the one side, and a number of prominent leaders of the growing British Muslim community on the other. As an American visitor, I wondered aloud if Parliament had given any serious consideration to disestablishment. One particularly prominent Conservative Party member chuckled and then congratulated me for being so "wry": "My dear fellow, that is a very amusing question. Everyone knows that the Anglican Church is only a matter of historical style not substance. Because it has become merely charming and has no influence whatsoever, there would be no point in ending its official status."

One could fairly hear the Muslim teeth grind around the table, and one could easily imagine the response of Northern Irish Catholics. Just as Sweden will retain its Lutheran traces for some time to come, much of British politics, personal law, and criminal law remain stamped by their Anglican origins. However, a recent report from the British Home Office has raised the first official doubts about the country's Anglican standing and the first official consideration of disestablishment.

Conclusion

At first blush, it is hard to see what Poland, Northern Ireland, and Sweden share in the midst of a major religious renegotiation, a putative religious war, and an anticlimactic religious disestablishment, respectively. However, one syndrome that is common to all three societies involves what I have called cultural religion—or an identification with a religious heritage without any religious participation or sense of personal involvement per se. In many societies around the world—and perhaps especially in Europe—cultural religion may represent the most common form of religious orientation.[27] But Europe also reminds us that, even in this form, religion can be an important force.

At the same time, one might ask whether the culturally religious need deeper commitments with more compelling participation, and if so, where they might find them. Students of religion spend far more time debating the secularization of older faiths than examining the sacralization of possible "religious" equivalents such as ethnic, class, and national identities. Certainly we have seen an abundance of sacred causes, ranging from Ulster loyalism to England, Irish republican opposition to England, Polish allegiance to the Solidarity labor movement and its antipathy to Communism, and Sweden's commitment to a welfare state. At the same time, while European Christendom is clearly not what it once was, it is far from exiting the stage either quietly or altogether, and it is difficult to know what it will ultimately become.

3

Four Islamic Societies and

Four Political Scenarios

Egypt, Turkey, Pakistan, and Indonesia

For most Westerners, leaving the Judeo-Christian world represents a step into a dark void of ignorance and uncertainty. It is not that we haven't heard of other religions. But in addition to hearing too little, we have sometimes heard too much. This applies especially to the religion of Islam.

Not long ago Islam and its Muslim, or Moslem, adherents—once commonly called "Muhammadans" for reasons to become clear momentarily—were so distant as to have little bearing on Western lives. But that has changed. Islam is now the world's second largest faith tradition, with its 1.3 billion adherents second only to Christianity's 1.9 billion. Islam is also among the fastest growing faiths in the United States, and by some estimates Muslims outnumber each of the great liberal Protestant denominations that have shaped so much of America's cultural heritage: Episcopalians, Presbyterians, and Congregationalists (United Church of Christ). In addition, the politics of predominantly Islamic countries around the world are increasingly relevant to Americans. The U.S. hostages held captive in Iran from 1979 to 1981 were martyrs to a chilling new form of Muslim fundamentalism under the presumed leadership of the Ayatollah Khomeini. Although the Persian Gulf War of 1990/91 was more a conflict over oil than religion, it was sometimes portrayed as a religious conflict by Middle Eastern leaders concerned about the massive presence of Western military forces. It is by now a commonplace for our newspapers to carry stories of the latest terrorist attacks of Muslim extremists from North Africa to the Pacific.

Under such circumstances, it is little wonder that stereotypes of Muslims abound and that the problem of too little knowledge has been replaced by the problem of distorted and incomplete knowledge. Consider, for example, the recent Disney hit *Aladdin*, which begins with the sinister line, "On a dark night, where a dark man waits with a dark purpose" and goes on to portray the dark Muslim Arab as a diabolical figure. In addition to Hollywood's efforts, journalists and political officials have cooperated in demonizing Muslims. Of course, no society or culture can be responsibly described by focusing on its aberrants and extremists alone. Identifying all of Islam with fundamentalism is an atrocity in its own right.

But Egypt, Turkey, Pakistan, and Indonesia all face internal challenges in their uneasy relationships between Islam, politics, and the state. As yet another illustration that social context is at least as important as religious canon, each country has met the challenge in different ways within different historical scenarios. But before turning to these national contexts, it is important to become acquainted with the canon at issue.

Introducing Islam

Great founding figures are important to great religions, and Islam's founder was Muhammad the Prophet, born around 570 c.e. in the city of Mecca in what is now Saudi Arabia. It was not until he was forty that Muhammad had his first divine revelation. Virtually alone among major religious figures, he actually wrote down what was revealed with the help of angel scribes. As part of God's work, he denounced the idolatry of Mecca so aggressively that he was forced to leave town for the city of Medina—also in Saudi Arabia. He spent eight years in exile, during which he built a powerful military and political movement and continued to record God's message in Islam's holy book, the Koran—like all Islamic terms, an Arabic word, and one that is sometimes transliterated into English as Qur'an.

Muhammad returned to take over Mecca in 630. He died in 632, but within another twenty years, most of the Arab world had been converted to Islam and the religion was virtually at its political zenith.[1] While Muhammad's initial revelations in Mecca had been highly personal and emotional, his Medina phase involved a heavy emphasis on social justice and the injunction to spread the message by political and even military means if necessary. Relative to its time and place in a remote area of the Middle East not yet fully penetrated by either Judaism or Christianity, early Islam was a liberal and liberating force. Its legal system (the Sharia) included reform measures on everything from the status of women and obligations to the poor to bans on slavery, alcohol, and charging interest on loans.

Islam is part of the same prophetic tradition that had earlier spawned Judaism and then Christianity. Muslims are enjoined to defend Christian churches and Jewish temples while regarding the Bible's Old Testament as a sacred work, though not on the same level as the Koran, with its accompanying interpretive narrative, the *hadith*. Moses and Jesus are both venerated as important prophetic figures, though neither is the son of God in the same singular sense as Muhammad.

Like Judaism and Christianity, Islam is strongly monotheistic. Its most basic belief, prayer, or mantra for the ritual of conversion is known as the *shahaada*: "There is no God but Allah, and Muhammad is his prophet." The phrase is the first of "five pillars" of the faith, the four others involving *salaat*, or prayers facing Mecca five times daily; hajj, or the pilgrimage to Mecca at least once during one's life for those who are able; *siyam*, or fasting through the daylight hours on the Friday sabbatt and especially during the month-long observance of Ramadan with no food or water from dawn to sunset; and finally *zakaat*, or giving alms to the poor, often through a state tax.

Several other Islamic practices are often stereotyped far out of proportion. Thus, the notion of jihad (just war) conjures up visions of marauding bands shrieking "Allahu akbar" (God is great) and using whatever means necessary to conquer and convert. In actuality, jihad is highly circumscribed by various social preconditions, and religious tolerance is the more common norm. Then, too, there is Islam's version of what Christians refer to as Old Testament punitive justice—an eye for an eye or, more to the point, a knuckle for a first property offense and a finger for the second, with a stoning death in store for the most serious crimes against the person. As with jihad, these sanctions are honored far more in the breach than the observance. This is partly because of the development of secular law and partly because, even within the Sharia, they can only be applied under conditions that offer no mitigating circumstances or motivations.

Islam's strong opposition to idolatry is readily apparent in its *masjids*, or mosques, as centers of worship. In contrast to many Christian churches and Jewish synagogues, mosque interiors are strikingly unadorned. There are no images of God, Muhammad, or other religious beings or events. While the walls may be beautifully covered by geometric tiles and there may be elaborate stained glass windows, there are no displays of representational religious art. In humbler mosques, the only source of color is the oriental carpets so common on the floors. In lieu of pews or benches, the carpets are intended for the Islamic prayer ritual. After washing one's feet before entering, the adherent moves through various postures, from kneeling to prone to erect and back again.

A common external characteristic of the mosque is the minaret from which the muezzin issue their five daily calls to prayer—now often through recordings. The voices float piercingly and hauntingly, but they are more cajoling than commanding. Prayers can be given anywhere by dropping to one's knees and facing Mecca. Moreover, mosque attendance is not obligatory for men and even less expected of women. Women who do attend are generally set off to one side for more seemly privacy in exercising their prayers—a practice intended not as discrimination against females but as a way of protecting males from sexual distractions.

The rationale is similar for purdah, or the tradition in which women use ritual coverings for their heads, faces, or sometimes their entire bodies, leaving only slits for their eyes. Although veiling was an Arab practice even before Islam, its adoption as religious tradition reflects a concern over carnality that characterizes most religions—but not all, as we shall see in Hinduism.

Like every other world religion and any other culture of long standing, Islam has known considerable internal discord. This is partly because it lacks the kind of organizational mechanisms that help to maintain control. Islam has little of the ecclesiastical structure that characterizes Christianity, especially Catholicism's pyramid of worldwide power that radiates from the Vatican. It is at least arguable that this is one reason why Islam has spawned so many political movements that play this role informally.[2] This also helps account for Islam's frequent close relationship to the state as an allied polity that can exercise authority in the name of the faith. In contrast to the Protestant Christian tradition, it is conventionally argued that there is no Muslim distinction between mosque and state or between sacred and secular governance—though this has long been debated.[3]

As with virtually all religions, Islamic history is a record of increasing differentiation. Following the great days of the caliphs in Baghdad in the eighth century, locally powerful sultans and emirs gained more autonomy. While the guardians of orthodoxy—the priestly ulema—exercised control by dominating education, even they had difficulty with local clerics, or mullahs. There were also challenging splinter movements such as the highly lyrical and emotional Sufis whose "whirling dervishes" sought ecstasy and religious release through dance.

Islam's deepest division between the Sunni and Shia factions occurred only twenty-four years after Muhammad's death in a dispute over the rightful heir to power following the murder of the Third Caliph in

656. Since then, both have produced offshoots of their own: the spiritu-alistic Sufis were a tenth-century development out of Sunni Islam, and the Bahai faith began as a nineteenth-century Shia reform movement. Today the Sunnis now claim 90 percent of Muslims around the world. However, the minority Shia are more highly structured and closely dis-ciplined under their system of ayatollahs. Partly for this reason, they account for many more instances of political Islam, and it is no accident that the one dominantly Shia country is generally regarded as the most politically militant, namely, Iran.

Meanwhile, more recent internal disputes involve Islam's response to change itself. Not long ago at a conference-ending dinner, I was seated beside a very able Muslim educator, who suddenly turned to me and asked, "Why don't people like us?" His plaintive candor was moving, and no amount of polite protest on my part could shake his concern. As we explored the topic together, a recurrent theme was Islam's perceived resistance to change. Lisa Anderson puts the perceptions this way in an account of Islamic politics in North Africa: "The popular Western view of Islam today is remarkably unchanged from that of twelve century European Christendom: as both a civilization and a religion, Islam ap-pears menacing, recalcitrant, corrupt. . . . This apparent continuity in Western views of Islam conveys the impression that Islam is fundamen-tally wicked but also that it has an essential, primordial, unchanging character."[4]

Although Islam's actual historical record is replete with change, there remains a quality of changelessness that is both a curse and a blessing. The Koran itself shares this double valence. On the one hand, it provides a unique record of the faith's founding vision—one that is long enough to provide a wide variety of theological and moral guidelines but also one that is short enough to be memorized in its entirety not just by holy men but by ambitious schoolchildren eager for prizes. In some places, the Koran is printed on eatable paper and consumed as a ritual act. On the other hand, this very document for the ages tends to bind Islam to its past. Literal readings can be a heavy constraint against adapting to chang-ing circumstances. What was once a reformist view of women, polygyny, and criminal law may now seem reactionary.

Consider the Iranian fatwa (religious edict) placing a death sentence on Salman Rushdie, the Muslim novelist who left India for England where he wrote simultaneously trenchant and satirical accounts of Islam that were deemed "blasphemous." Satirizing the old is a major source of the new, and at the end of the day, expunging blasphemy is as futile as ban-ning slang.

In both the distant and recent past, there is little doubt that Islam's greatest challenge has come from the West—a challenge that began in the twelfth century when Islamic civilization reached its zenith only to fall victim to the Christian crusades from Europe. Today the quandary involves possible reactions to modernity.[5] Of course, modernity has many dimensions—cultural, economic, and political —and Islam has demonstrated at least four different responses. One is the aggressive and often nationalist tack of actively combating modernity—sometimes using "modern," high-tech weapons in a struggle that is frequently stereotyped as fundamentalism. This is illustrated by Egypt. A second option is to minimize Islam as anything more than a cultural legacy and join the ranks of the purposely secularized, as exemplified by Turkey. A third response involves turning away from modernizing developments and withdrawing into a religious cocoon, a tendency found in Pakistan. Finally, a fourth response is to modernize Islam in a fashion somewhat akin to liberal Protestantism or Reform Judaism.[6] This characterizes very recent developments in Indonesia.

Different countries have indeed reacted in different ways. At the same time, all four of these responses can be found in all four of these countries, to which I turn to next. In each case, it is partly the conflict and competition among these responses that provides much of the religion's political dynamic. As we saw with Christianity, it would be a mistake to try and isolate a single authentic, canonical Islam that is invariant across time and space. This religion, like all others, is lived locally with important variations between genders and generations.

Egypt: Fundamentalism Rears Its Head

On my first morning in the crowded center of Cairo, I was awakened half an hour before dawn by no less than four calls to prayer from four different mosques in the immediate neighborhood. The result was an unintended polyphony—at some points caressing and at others discordant. But it was not always thus in Cairo and Egypt. In fact, few countries have known a greater gap between their past and their present.[7] Egypt has long been a must stop on the Western tourist circuit, but it is visited far more for the splendor of its antiquities than the complexities of its contemporary life.

The fabled world of the pharaohs, the pyramids, and the Sphinx, with the fabulous tombs of the great Tutankhamen and the Ramses occurred some four thousand years ago. Located in the northeast corner of Africa, on the western flank of the Middle East, and just across the Mediterranean from Europe, Egypt has always been a natural node of the world's commerce in material goods, political force, and culture. It has been subjugated by Macedonia, Greece, Christianity, Islam, France, Turkey, and finally the British from 1882 to 1954, when General Gamal

Abdel Nasser finally secured the country's independence. Of all these influences, Islam is now the most pervasive. About 90 percent of Egypt's sixty-five million people are now classified as Muslims, though another 6 percent constitute a declining and increasingly beleaguered minority of Coptic Christians. Now the largest Christian community in the Middle East, the "Copts" date from the efforts of Saint Mark the evangelist in 60 C.E. and retain the name given by Arabs several centuries later. They are mostly Eastern Orthodox but include some Roman Catholics and Anglican Protestants.

Neither Egypt's Muslims nor its Christians have any roots in the country's pharaonic past. As the great Sphinx looks out to the east from its post just outside of the sprawling city of Cairo, it seems oblivious to the new culture that has grown up around it. Most tourists treat Cairo as just a point of entry and exit, pausing only long enough to visit the Sphinx and its surrounding pyramids before heading south up the Nile River to the pharaonic majesties of Luxor and Abu Simbel. Cairo intimidates the unknowing. It is easily seen as a teeming, dusty center of raucous urban life.

But Cairo is also one of the world's great cultural centers, straddling the razor's edge between past and present just as it straddles the Nile itself. A fount of the arts and intellectual life, it is home to great universities, newspapers, and literature. Like Egypt overall, Cairo represents both high and low points in the trajectory of Islam. Its tradition of highly sophisticated Muslim theology and ideology reflects the early influence of the Turkish Ottoman Empire, while it has more recently become a battleground for the struggle between mosque and state and between various versions of contemporary Islam.

When Egypt secured its independence from the British in the 1950s under the towering leadership of General Nasser, the model for the future was socialism rather than the Sharia. A truly charismatic but personally secular figure, Nasser varied his political response to religion. He was not averse to waving the green color of Islam during times of social crisis. At the same time, he had little patience for Islamic activists, and he imprisoned almost the entire senior leadership cadre of the Muslim Brotherhood (MB)—one of Islam's first radical political movements of the twentieth century. Originally formed in 1928, the MB had been a major underground presence, while exporting its ideology and techniques across the Islamic world. The MB was held responsible for the assassination of two Egyptian prime ministers under colonial rule, and it was far more of a retrogressive threat than a forward-looking ally to Nasser's efforts to mobilize the country and propel it into a new economic era.

When Nasser died in 1970, he was succeeded by Anwar Sadat. Sadat and his wife, Jehan, cut an elegant swath through the West with their impeccable manners and command of English. He shared a Nobel Peace Prize with Israel's Prime Minister Menachem Begin for cooperating with U.S. President Jimmy Carter in the breakthrough Camp David Accords of 1979. But Sadat's successes at home were more limited and more contested. While he was able to arrange for the Israeli army to vacate Egyptian land gained during the humiliating Six-Day War in 1967, many economically disadvantaged Egyptians saw this as a hollow victory. Civic temperatures rose as the economy sagged.

In a major play for support and an effort to bridge the gaps between Egypt's secular politics and its religious community, Sadat sought an alliance with Islamic activists by releasing many from prison. But as so often happens when politicians court militant groups, he was not able to carry through all of his envisioned programs, and some saw him as betraying the faith he had promised to keep. The political moth was ultimately consumed by the religious flame. In 1981 a small band of Muslim terrorists assassinated Sadat, making him the fourth Egyptian head of state to be assassinated in the twentieth century.[8]

His successor was and continues to be Hosni Mubarak, an air force general who rose through the ranks and learned how to secure power in the process. Lacking Nasser's magnetism and Sadat's polish, Mubarak has built a political machine that has turned elections into anointments. In a system in which winning "only" 70 percent of the vote seems tantamount to defeat, he pushed hard for a near unanimous endorsement through a series of electoral laws that severely hobble opposition groups while censoring their ideas. In his most recent election victory in 1998, Mubarak claimed 94 percent of the vote, although this was really a simple "yes or no" referendum on his administration, and the tally was "down" from his 96 percent in 1993, not to mention Sadat's 99.9 percent in 1981.

Mubarak is especially wary of religious groups that threaten to dissolve the semblance of democracy altogether. Like every other national political leader across the Koran Belt from Nigeria to Indonesia, Mubarak is only too aware of the Islamic theocracy that characterized the Iranian Republic under the Ayatollah Khomeini from 1979 to 1989 and the current Taliban of Afghanistan. From a politician's perspective, these represent cautionary tales from hell.

Yet like his predecessors in office, Mubarak also plays the mainstream Muslim religious card in his search for legitimacy. For example, in recent outbreaks of violence, Muslims have been widely suspected of killing Coptic Christians. But the Egyptian police and military have not only failed to pursue and prosecute the suspects, they have actually blamed the offenses on other Christians.

It is quite a different matter when Islamic extremists move against the state. Mubarak's struggle against Islamic extremists has taken that conflict to new highs—and new lows. By all measures of civil disruption—such as strikes, riots, arrests, assassinations, and public violence—there has been a crescendoing rise in Islamic insurrection and state oppression during Mubarak's rule.[9] The violent conflict between the movement and the state has become so entrenched and routinized as to form part of the "normal" way of Egyptian life.[10]

As one newspaper editorial suggested, the country is under "double siege"—both from the Muslim terrorists and from the government and its state security apparatus. During the first eleven years of the Mubarak regime, there were more than fifteen hundred government-inflicted casualties and some twenty-five thousand arrests, including twenty-seven death sentences. If Iranian Muslims placed a death sentence on the head of the writer Salman Rushdie, the Mubarak regime gave a quick trial and quicker hanging to the Muslim intellectual Sayid Qutb for writings deemed subversive of the state.

As in many other countries, one has the distinct sense of the cultural core dissolving. There is polarization along almost every conceivable continuum. In matters of social class, it is not simply that the tiny and mostly secular upper class continues to gain while the sprawling and much more religious lower class continues to suffer. But many who once occupied the ground between them are being emiserated and proletarianized; hence, there is little sense of a politically stabilizing middle class. A similar scenario applies to age and generation. As young people see their future prospects dim, significant minorities are drawn into webs of passive alienation and active protest that sometimes take religious forms and sets them apart from the more religiously and politically moderate older generations. Again, there is little common ground for a centrist majority.

Or consider the public-private distinction between the government and the citizenry. In most stable societies, this depends on a civil society layer of civic nongovernmental organizations and professional associations that provide the cartilage in the social joints. But in Egypt this is also threatened—and from both sides. The state has chosen a strategy of insulation rather than inclusion, and several recent laws not only curtail freedom of assembly by banning nongovernmental organizations from politics but strike at freedom of speech by providing for government censorship. Significantly, when Egypt was hit hard by an earthquake in October 1992 and the various Islamic organizations responded far more quickly than the government in providing aid, thereby gaining legitimacy, Parliament passed a law making it illegal for nongovernmental groups to assist in earthquake relief.

Meanwhile, like most growing movements, the Muslim Brotherhood has reached a wider audience by mellowing its tactics since its early days. It is no longer on the left flank of Egyptian or Middle Eastern Islamic activism, and it has increasingly pursued its objectives through politics rather than violence. Banned from conventional elections, it has concentrated on gaining control of aspects of the civil society infrastructure, including professional associations representing Egypt's doctors, lawyers, pharmacists, engineers, and university professors. This is not quite as earth shaking as it sounds, because these groups are politically constrained in their own right, and they had such small minorities voting on the MB alliance that is was possible to claim landslide results by moving only a few grains of electoral sand. Still, this is another respect in which the very center of Egyptian society is now politically and religiously contested.

But Egypt's Islamic movement is not monolithic.[11] In the struggle against a secular state perceived as corrupt and oppressive and on behalf of a new Islamic hegemony, the torch of terrorism has now passed from the MB to several more extreme groups. Their targets have included the New York World Trade Center under Sheikh Omar Abdul-Rahman now serving a lengthy sentence in a federal prison in Missouri;[12] Western tourists in Egypt as a way of crippling this principal component of the Egyptian economy; Egypt's small minority of Coptic Christians, who remain a stone in the shoe of an otherwise dominantly Muslim culture; political officials and cabinet ministers, who are seen as too secular and too corrupt; women who are unveiled in public; and leading Islamic intellectuals, who are seen as betraying the faith by questioning some of its more traditional tenets and practices.[13]

Terrorists even stabbed and critically wounded Egypt's leading novelist and winner of the 1988 Nobel Prize for Literature, Naguib Mahfouz. Many of Mahfouz's works are deeply etched accounts of the Egyptian underclass. They contain not only implicit criticisms of state policy but also potentially blasphemous images of Islam that are similar to those that led Iranians to put a price on the head of the more infamous Salman Rushdie. The question is not so much why Mahfouz was finally attacked but why it took so long to do so. The answer may be that, unlike Rushdie, who publicly left both India and Islam behind for the West, Mahfouz remained in Egypt as a loyal citizen who continued to experience the burdens of the society he commented upon in his widely read novels and newspaper column.

One of the most prominent extremist groups is the sophisticated Al Jihad, which draws many of its members from the ranks of recent college graduates who are increasingly bitter about their persistent underemployment. During a day at Cairo University—where I narrowly avoided a herd of camels being driven along the campus's edge to a nearby slaughterhouse—I was walking in the company of a journalist who had been a student there in the 1970s. He pointed to the throngs of undergraduates around us and remarked, "You know, I used to be like those people. When I graduated, there weren't any jobs, and I was bitter and joined the ranks of the local Marxist protesters on the left. When these people graduate, they'll face the same situation, and the only difference is that they will find their protest group among the so-called fundamentalists."

It may seem surprising that these extremists are often drawn from the educated middle class rather than the desperate poor. It may seem paradoxical that the basic motives behind such religious extremism are not necessarily religious. But a related pattern emerges from a second extremist group—the more rural, lower-status *Gama'a Islamiya* (Islamic Group), whose members are sometimes not religious at all. This group has many of the characteristics of the classic proletarian movement in a class war rather than a religious war. Saad Ibrahim makes the broader point this way: "[T]hroughout Arab-Islamic history in the last thirteen centuries . . . politicized Islam (is) an idiom for expressing profound worldly grievances. Staying close to the Egyptian case, it seems clear . . . that swift rise and spread of Islamic activism, with all its violent and non-violent strands, is [sic] associated with real or perceived crises— social, economic, political, cultural, regional, international."[14]

Regardless of the mix of sacred and secular motives pushing Egypt's Islamic extremists, there is no question that they have cast a long shadow across the country.[15] But there is considerable question as to their provocation. There is truth in both sides' depiction of the other. Just as the Islamicists have evidence of a state gone sour, so does the government have credibility in claiming its repressive actions are necessary for protecting democracy and stability from willful disruption. But then this is another instance in which violence feeds upon itself. It is almost inevitable that sooner or later those who challenge the status quo will receive their day in power. Every thing that goes wrong seems to symbolically underscore the deficiencies of the incumbents while commending the virtues of their opponents. The grass often seems greener on the other side of a political fence.

The theme of imperiled democracy resonates widely across Northern Africa and the Middle East following the convulsion that seized neighboring Algeria in early 1992. Regardless of the facts, Algeria is perceived as a case in which the national elite allowed the local Islamic movement to participate in national elections only until it appeared that the Islamic faction was on the threshold of a sweeping victory that would carry it to national control. When new elections were scheduled for five years hence, the Islamic party was banned from participating, and the incumbents won by a large majority amid echoing charges of fraud.

To many liberals, this seemed a betrayal of the democratic faith; after all, the justification of elections cannot be contingent on their results. But what if democracy is interpreted more broadly to refer to constitutional governance generally and a willingness to abide by elections that would end a period of power rather than begin one? Again, those with a wary eye on Iran wonder whether it is not democratically justified to suspend any election whose victors promise to end all elections and replace the constituted government with an imposed theocracy— even if it is true that the constituted government is itself corrupt and controlled by the same elites who have the coercive power to suspend democracy in the first place. Such questions are as important as their answers are elusive. Egypt is not the only country where they hang heavy in the air.[16]

Turkey: A Secular State, Cultural Islam, and Fundamentalism Lite

Few national identities are so conflicted by their history and geography as is Turkey's. It is a country that has shifted from a capital of Christianity to a world center of Islam, and then to a symbol of modernist secularity in the Middle East. As a nation whose people are longtime intellectual admirers of France, a founding member of the Western military alliance, the North Atlantic Treaty Organization (NATO), and Europe's only Muslim nation, Turkey had high hopes when its prime minister, Turgut Ozol, went to Brussels in 1989 to apply formally for full standing in the European Union. Ozol was prominently seated up front for the European Union's opening ceremonies. The French chairperson began by reporting the results of his recent search for the real essence of what it means to be European. When he triumphantly proclaimed the answer to be nothing less than the Christian religion, it was like flicking a velvet glove across the face of Ozol individually and Turkey collectively.

Turkey's relation to the West is not only a key to its future but to the world's. Unless Turkey is granted full standing in European circles, there is a very good prospect that it will turn eastward to join Islamic countries such as Syria, Iraq, Iran, Turkmenistan, Afghanistan, and Pakistan in an invigorated economic, military, and religious coalition. This could lead to a polarized regional struggle with global impact and a possible religious struggle reminiscent of the ancient Christian crusades against Muslims in the eleventh through thirteenth centuries. All of this would confirm Samuel Huntington's prediction of a mounting "clash of civilizations."[17]

Yet the issue of West versus East has never been fully resolved within

Turkey itself. Even its location suggests a geographical ambivalence. Sharing a western border with Greece and Bulgaria, it is bordered to the east by Syria, Iraq, Iran, and the new nations of the former Soviet Union, Armenia and Georgia. Even its largest city, Istanbul, is divided between west and east. Straddling the Bosporus Straits that connect the Black Sea to the northeast with the Aegean Sea to the southwest, commuting ferries connect the metropolis's European and Asian sides. But then the fairies of history make similar connections. Once the center of Orthodox Christendom, the city was originally named Constantinople, for the Roman Emperor Constantine, who gave Christianity its first stable legitimacy. Constantinople thrived for a millennium and a half as the capital of the great Byzantine Empire. However, by the mid-sixteenth century the city had succumbed to conquering Muslims and become the capital of the no less great Ottoman Empire. As with many empires, this one had overextended itself with triumphant advances in two westerly directions—through the Balkans and to the very gates of Vienna in the north and through Egypt and to Algeria in the south. The Ottomans needed a point of consolidation, so Constantinople's Christianity gave way to Islam. Many of its churches were restyled into mosques, and the great cathedral of Saint Sophia acquired an imposing new neighbor only several hundred yards away in the famed Blue Mosque with its blue-tiled interior and six minarets.

The Ottoman sultans ruled Turkey until the beginning of the twentieth century with an iron hand but an increasingly inquisitive mind. They took special interest in the rise of French positivism, with its double postulate that rational humans could scientifically understand and systematically perfect rational society. However, as the again overextended Ottomans grew more in touch with France, they grew less in touch with Turkey itself. The 1908 constitutional regime of the so-called Young Turks sought major changes without cutting the Ottoman cord. But fifteen years later—following a genocidal campaign to forcibly evict some 1.7 million Armenian Christians with an estimated six hundred thousand deaths, the turbulence of World War I and the humiliation of an allied occupation—a single young Turk stepped forward to remake Turkey almost overnight.

Judged by the magnitude and endurance of his changes, Mustafa Kemal Ataturk is arguably the world's most effective statesman of the twentieth century. Ataturk was born near the country's far west border with Greece and not far from Mount Olympus. The son of a small-town Muslim merchant, young Mustafa chose an army education and career rather than his father's trade or his mother's deep-seated faith. After rising through the military ranks, he wrested order out of confusion by proclaiming the current Turkish Republic on October 29, 1923. But as he well knew, political changes come and go unless accompanied by cultural changes.

The next dozen years saw a series of seismic transformations that converted the Ottoman fascination with the West into full-blown emulation. In establishing the Turkish Republic with one-eye cocked on the French Revolution and the French Republic, Ataturk moved the capital to Ankara, a small town in the center of the country and its Anatolian Plateau, leaving Constantinople stranded and renamed as Istanbul. Working through his democratically elected Grand National Assembly, he severed the two heads of Ottoman power: its political sultanate and its religious caliphate—describing the latter act as "cutting out this tumor of the Middle Ages."[18]

In his determined pursuit of a thoroughly secular state, Ataturk substituted new civil laws for the old sharia law, abolished public religious schools, and ordered the government to exchange the Muslim's traditional Friday day off for the conventional Western weekend. He abandoned traditional Muslim dress and made himself something of a role model dandy in Western clothes. As part of a major drive to enhance and equalize the status of women, he forbade them to wear the veils of purdah in public. But then he also outlawed the Muslim fez as male headgear. He banned the several dervish groups as being too superstitious, ecstatic, and nonrational in their mystical religious practices. He changed the country's very alphabet from Arabic to Latin. Finally, he set the style of adopting Western surnames and devised his own. Like most Turks he had only one given name, in his case "Mustafa." "Kemal" (meaning roughly a perfectionist) had been fixed upon him in military school, and he himself chose the name "Ataturk," meaning Father Turk. He had filled the description admirably by the time of his death in 1938 at age fifty-seven.

Turkey has hardly been immune to internal discord. Ataturk himself was involved in the country's heinous massacre and displacement of Armenian Christians prior to World War I, though Ataturk later secured the treaty that created an Armenian state within the Soviet Union. Meanwhile, the ethnically distinct Kurds have become the country's leading "minority problem."[19] Located primarily in the country's southeast corner at its borders with Iran and Iraq, the Kurds remain a distinct ethnic group that poses distinct difficulties for all three countries. Because the Kurds are physically indistinguishable from the Turks and share their Muslim faith, many have moved to Ankara and Istanbul to join the economic mainstream. However, those remaining in their native environs are subject to predations from all three of the contiguous nations, and this has produced several movements whose aggressive actions on behalf of a Kurdish nation have increased the stakes and the violence.

Like many parents, Ataturk left an ironic legacy. Despite his Western bent, Ataturk was also a strong Turkish nationalist. And despite his public secularism, he saw Islam as part of the Turkish heritage and never recanted his Muslim identity—though he was a private agnostic who sought to make religion as rational as possible. Ataturk's seeming ambivalence on these matters is reflected in Turkey's own inconsistencies over the years.[20] In fact, one can plausibly describe two Turkeys with a tension between them that has erupted into outright conflict at ever more frequent intervals.

There is no question that Ataturk's reforms found a receptive audience among the urban middle and upper classes who had already tilted westward. They rallied around his call to "unity and progress" and basked in the relaxation of religious authority. There was widespread approval of the laicization of public religion—meaning laypersons exercising control from within the state as opposed to Muslim clerics arrogating all power unto themselves. For many, secularism became a credo in its own right, especially when coupled with the quasi-cult of "kemalism" to fill what might otherwise be a cultural void. As one of my sources put it while we drove near her old residential area: "Turkey became a nation of forgetters. Many in my parents' generation were eager to renounce the past in favor of a new westward-looking way of life. My family even got rid of our heirloom Turkish rugs in favor of chic, wall-to-wall carpeting. I recently learned that some of those rugs are now in museum shows in the United States."

Just as the Turkish state sometimes seemed to vacillate between being antireligious and religiously neutral, so the quality of Muslim adherence eludes easy labeling for many Turkish individuals. Many in the middle class are not sure themselves whether they are best described as nonreligious, cultural Muslims, or what now passes in Turkey for conventional Muslims.[21] As one remarked, "Most Turks can't even conceive of a 'Muslim intellectual.' It is an oxymoron, like being a 'liberal Muslim.' " As this suggests, a sizeable portion of the Turkish population remained rooted in tradition even as it was enthralled by Ataturk himself. According to another observer, "There is a sense in which changes at the center never fully penetrated the periphery." As one moves from urban to rural and from western Turkey eastward, one has the sense of leaving Europe for the Middle East and Asia and of leaving the First World for the Third.

Meanwhile, some Turkish Muslims have also resisted Ataturk's vision of the state and its politics. Although it is not clear whether the secular dam is holding back a religious trickle or a flood, there have been a number of instances suggesting sacred water in store. In 1961, 1971, and 1980 the Turkish military stepped in to take over the government and maintain its laicized secularity against a mounting religious tide. In each case, democratic governance was restored once the crisis dissipated, and in general the intellectual elite is surprisingly uncritical of its military counterpart owing to their shared secular leanings. But lest one suppose that the military functioned purely through rational persuasion instead of time-honored coercion, one of my contacts reported that both of her grandparents had been imprisoned for political activities. While her grandmother died there, her grandfather was released because of an illness that suggested death was near—only to live almost two decades longer, perhaps partly out of spite.

During its last takeover, however, the military made some unexpected concessions to religion as a strategy to recruit right-wing Muslim allies against a perceived left-wing Communist movement. Today the government has a Directorate of Religious Affairs with headquarters in the largest mosque in Ankara and responsibilities for funding and overseeing new religious curricula in the public schools, new mosque construction, and trips to Mecca on the part of pilgrims undertaking hajj. While there may be some question whether the government is promoting religion or controlling it, this is a far cry from the strict state secularism so important to the republic's founding.

Another controversial indication of increasing Islamic sentiment involves women and the veil. Of course, it is not surprising to see women fully veiled in rural, peasant circumstances or in countries such as Egypt where veiling is often enforced by extremist factions. But it seems incongruous to see only the eyes of even a small minority of Turkish middle-class women—especially university students—who don the veils voluntarily. The veils are technically illegal for students as well as civil servants, lawyers, judges and others in public offices. But policing the law is lax, and in most universities it has been bucked down from the government to the campus and from higher administrators to lower.

Since Turkey has given considerable impetus to the movement to liberalize Islam and liberate women, donning the veil would appear to be a step backward. The full head-to-toe, face-covering black dress of *burka* is much more rare in Turkey than in other Islamic societies, but *hajab*, or the use of head scarves, is readily apparent—now more than in the past. What is its appeal and significance in these circles?

Some of the people I talked with were downright cynical. One indicated that funds provided by orthodox Saudi Arabia paid some women students to wear the veil with a monthly stipend that actually exceeded their government scholarship. A male university administrator said: "Just yesterday there were four women in veils in my office who wanted me to set aside a room for Muslim prayers. I said that education is my number one priority and the quality of student facilities number two. I told them that I couldn't do it, and that I didn't care if they wore veils or bikinis. Actually you see them in veils one day and necking openly the next. I had a student who went from a beauty contest candidate in a bikini one year to wearing veils the next. She was an insecure kid who was seeking attention."

Because veiling was once associated with the wives of the prophet, it still carries a high status connotation within the faith, not to mention the status implications of the expensive high-fashion veils now available in boutiques across the Muslim world. Turkey is virtually unmatched among Muslim societies in the inroads women have made into previously male enclaves such as business, the professions, academia, and government—witness its recent prime minister, Tansu Ciller. When I was there, people were buzzing about a television show in which a young woman suddenly bared her breasts to signal her rebellion against her mother's antediluvianism.

Still, a significant proportion of young middle-class Muslim women find it hard to establish a secure identity in a fully secularized context where new gender differences have replaced traditional distinctions. Under these circumstances, a return to the veil is a return to a more stable and protected way of life in which women are set apart rather than thrown in among the hunters and the hunted.[22] Hijab can also be a powerful form of self-assertion in some contexts. Recently, a woman newly elected to the national parliament created an uproar by appearing for her first day in session wearing the scarf of hijab. The woman is actually a computer engineer and an Islamic moderate. But her point was directed against a political system whose secularism had reached authoritarian lengths. While public opinion polls show overwhelming opposition to an Islamic state, they also show that a strong majority favors the right to wear scarves among public employees and students.

There are also other, more political evidences of a persistent Islamic traditionalism.[23] Muslim leaders have always enjoyed more leadership positions at the local rather than the national level. But astonishingly enough, Turkey has recently had a public advocate of Islam in the prime ministership for the first time in seventy-three years.

Prime Minister Necmettin Erbakan is not a Muslim cleric swept into office on an Islamic tidal wave. He is an establishment politician who was part of the loyal opposition for forty-five years, and he even served a stint as deputy prime minister under a previous administration. Actually a forthright religious party would be illegal in Turkey, but "everyone knows" that Erbakan's party serves the role in all but name. Once called the Refah Party (generally translated as the Welfare Party, though some prefer Prosperity to avoid any mistaken Marxian connotations), it is now known as the Virtue Party.

Among the dozen parties that contested the 1995 national elections, Virtue won only 21.3 percent of the vote, but this was more than any other party achieved. When the political dust settled, Virtue entered into a power-sharing arrangement with a more conventionally secular party. The two party leaders agreed to rotate the prime minister's office between them for the balance of the term. During his brief time at the helm, Erbakan agreed to uphold the Ataturk model of state secularism, and he ultimately bowed to pressure from the military elite in closing some Islamic schools, constraining the Islamic media, and setting new limits on Islamic dress. More recently, the Virtue Party has been frozen out of power by a coalition of parties whose shared commitments to secularism overrides differences that otherwise extend from the left to the right of the political spectrum.

This hardly sounds like the stuff of a revolutionary religious regime. It certainly bears little similarity to what occurred almost twenty years earlier in Iran—Turkey's neighbor and longtime competitor. Compared to Iran, some secular Turks describe their recent Muslim push somewhat smugly as "fundamentalism lite." Some even argue that the move of religion into politics actually strengthens Turkey's democracy while underscoring the country's general secularization and the reasonableness of the religious groups themselves. For others, recent developments suggest the beginnings of a dual society amicably divided between two pillars, one secular and the other Islamic.

Clearly, there are a variety of possibilities in store. However, there is now a sense that religion is on the offensive and secularism on the defensive in Turkey. Even though religion's field position is poor and the military will insure that the playing field is anything but level, here is another case in which mounting national problems of whatever sort redound to the detriment of the political incumbents while making the challenger's grass appear ever greener.

In the meantime, the European Union has declared Turkey an official candidate for inclusion. A final decision is still years away, and during this period Turkey will be on a short probationary leash, especially concerning its record on human rights for both Kurdish and Muslim activists. Turkey remains in suspension and suspense.

Pakistan: The Specter of Islamization

When I began my travels in 1986 in search of countries different from the United States, Pakistan was my first stop. I was to attend an August conference in bordering India, so it made sense to leave early and spend several weeks in Pakistan. This would be my first trip outside the

West, my first trip to a Third World nation, and my first visit to a Muslim society.

Since planes from the Europe to South Asia tend to arrive after midnight, my arrival in Karachi spared me the daytime heat but at the cost of an almost surreal introduction to the country in early morning darkness. When I emerged from the airport, I was quickly surrounded by taxi drivers shouting for my attention and my business. After somehow settling on one and agreeing on a price in advance, I stuffed myself into the backseat of a small and seemingly ancient car that inspired little confidence. Even at 2 A.M., the highways were busy, and I had my first taste of Pakistani traffic. Headlights were turned on only when there was a sense of something worth seeing—including the rear ends of huge trucks that suddenly loomed out of the darkness with no warning, since their taillights were often masked by the tin ornamentation that has become an elaborate folk art.

When I awoke the next morning, my first order of business was to canvas the local English-language newspapers. I was especially taken by a story about a young lawyer's concerns over Pakistan's possible shift from Western secular law to Islamic sharia law. Wonder of wonders, his name was in the phone book, he happened to be free at the time, and he came to the hotel within the hour for a valuable session that was my first interview on the project. I said to myself, "This is going to be easy." So much for misleading first experiences.

I shall return to the lawyer later. Meanwhile, a bit of background is in order. From a Western perspective, Pakistan may seem almost as much a prototype of the Islamic society as its more extreme neighbor, Iran. Founded half a century ago through the Muslim-Hindu partitioning that marked India's own independence in 1947, both West Pakistan in the northwest and East Pakistan (now Bangladesh) in the northeast were set aside as a combined national homeland for Muslims on the subcontinent. I shall describe those hopeful yet tragic days in more detail while describing India in the next chapter. Suffice it to say here that the partition caused a frantic migration of Muslims from India to Pakistan and Hindus from Pakistan to India, with massive killing on both sides. When the exchange was finished, Pakistan was more than 95 percent Muslim, though there continued to be a greater number of Muslims in India, where they constituted 12 percent of a population many times larger.

Demographics aside, Pakistan raises again the question of what constitutes an "Islamic state" in traditional theory or contemporary practice. Egypt and Turkey both struggle with the issue in their own very different ways. Pakistan represents a third scenario.

Of course, there is no question that Pakistan's dominant culture is

Islamic, and it has produced one of the great Islamic philosophers of the twentieth century: Sayyid Abu'l-A'la Mawdudi has had a singular influence on Islamic revivalism from Africa to Asia.[24] Yet it would be simplistic to describe Pakistan as an Islamic state in the fullest sense of that phrase. Even its history is ambiguous on the point. Its founder, Muhammad Ali Jinnah, was a British-educated secularist for whom religious freedom and pluralism were more important than an official Islamic state. Moreover, many of its current Islamic laws were enacted by another Western-influenced secularist, the charismatic yet enigmatic Zulfikar Ali Bhutto.

Bhutto was elected to office following a civil war between two parts of a country that were two thousand miles apart—a war that led to East Pakistan's secession to become Bangladesh in 1971. Toward the end of Bhutto's troubled regime from 1972 to 1977, he sought legitimacy from any and every quarter, including religion. Personal disinclinations aside, Bhutto made national the Muslim ban on charging interest in financial transactions, its observance of Friday as the national sabbatt, and its prohibition of alcoholic beverages. Finally, Bhutto was undermined by his authoritarian rule and widely rumored corruption. A series of internal crises culminated in an army takeover. Following a quick trial, Bhutto was executed in 1979 as an enemy of the state under its new military leader, General Zia-ul-Haq.

President Zia also sought legitimacy through religion, but in his case the campaign was not as patently cynical. After all, Zia was known to be a practicing member of the Wahabis, a branch of Sunni Islam that is especially strong in Saudi Arabia. At the same time that his military regime was ironhanded, his public rhetoric was laced with injunctions for Pakistan to become a Koranic state by adopting the Sharia and its courts as the ultimate law of the land, especially in matters of criminal justice. As part of this "Islamization" campaign, there was much talk of a pending Sharia Bill that would set up a council of Muslim mullahs as supreme arbiters of the nation's laws and state decisions to insure that they are in keeping with the Koran.

Nonetheless, there were widespread doubts over both the sincerity and merits of Islamization.[25] Some referred to it cynically as "Saudization," since Saudi Arabia supplied much of the money for its most conspicuous projects such the enormous new mosque and the Islamic National University in the country's capital city of Islamabad. Zia's close ties to Saudi Arabia were also a factor in Pakistan's substitution of Arabic for English as the second language taught in the public schools, in addition to the indigenous Urdu.

There were powerful opponents of Islamization, though many preferred not to express their position publicly, and some covered their options by affiliating with different positions in different contexts. I interviewed one prominent political journalist who was very much a Western-leaning secularist with me but—as I later learned—was also a member of Pakistani's largest and most active religious party, the Jamat'e'Islami. This is just another confirmation that where we stand depends in part on with whom we are standing.

Many Pakistani business leaders were concerned that stricter Islamic financial constraints would cripple their dealings in the international political economy; this certainly included Islam's ban on *riba*—the charging or paying of interest. Another issue concerned the status of women. Some middle-class women who had experienced considerable emancipation under the constitutional revisions of the 1960s and early 1970s were among the most vocal opponents of the regression in rights that occurred under the Zia regime. They were especially incensed about an instance in which a woman who had brought charges against two men for rape was herself convicted of unlawful sexual intercourse and making unsubstantiated charges under an ancient law giving women virtually no independent standing in the courts.

While the nation's lawyers were prepared to work within (and around) any law, many shared the bitter despair of the young lawyer whom I met on my first day in Karachi: "At the moment my library consists of fifteen thousand books. Am I to replace them all with one sheet of paper, which is what the Sharia Bill consists of?" Even many in the villages saw Islamization as too ideological and impractical. Islamization also raised hackles among some of the devoutly religious, who were reluctant to place such power in the hands of mullahs of uneven quality.

A side issue that threatened to move front and center concerned relations between Pakistan's majority Sunni and minority Shia communities. For most of the nation's history, little has been made of the distinction, although other Islamic sects have been subject to discrimination. But problems have begun to escalate. For example, when the state took over the administration of the zakaat tax for social welfare to the disadvantaged, the proportion of the population claiming to be Shia suddenly jumped from 15 percent to 35 percent—quite possibly because Shia don't believe in such state administration and are therefore exempt from the requirement. More ominously, the rivalry between Sunnis and Shia has recently taken a more violent turn. Once real Islamic power became a possibility, the obvious questions were who will exercise that power and on which terms? Several Shia informants told me that they were prepared to die rather than see the Sunnis dominate such an arrangement—and some have. Such comments are now frequent newspaper fare, and sectarianism appears to be an increasing obstacle to any sort of pan-Islamic state.

Finally, many members of the government opposed Islamization, albeit in different ways and at different levels, all of them discrete. Several agency heads actually described the campaign to me as a "hoax." Informants drew a sharp distinction between religion in politics and religion in government. A number of highly placed sources indicated that President Zia himself realized the disadvantages of state religion and in 1985 began a subtle process of de-Islamization.[26]

It is hardly surprising that Zia—like many politicians in Pakistan and elsewhere—sought to use religion as a source of political support without having it built into the government as a source of traditional constraints. Islamization may be initially appealing as a source of political legitimacy, but it is also a potential threat when it becomes an open-ended arrangement whose details are to be filled in by religious leaders over whom the government has little control.

All of this provides a background to the political events that began to dominate the country in 1986. Pressure had mounted on Zia to fulfill his vague pledge to allow the country to resume democracy with full national elections. My visit coincided with the return from exile of former Prime Minister Bhutto's daughter, Benazir Bhutto, to take over his old political party and lead it to victory. A Harvard and Oxford graduate, Benazir Bhutto and her mother had been placed under house arrest for a time before being allowed to leave the country for temporary residence in the West. She was now returning to the triumphal strains of a martyr's welcome—adored in the villages of Pakistan as well as in the corridors of power in Washington and London. Often defying government regulations, her political rallies overspilled with both numbers and emotions. My one chance to attend such a gathering was in Lahore, but a stomach bug rendered me unable to move from my bed, let alone my room. As it happened, violence erupted at the rally and left five dead and many wounded.

Just as Benazir Bhutto's campaign was intensifying, Zia and several of his closest aides were killed in a plane crash that remains shrouded in mystery. An election was now critical, and Bhutto's November victory as prime minister was widely acclaimed as a final corner turned in Pakistan's march into the international arena. In fact, it was the beginning of more problems than solutions. Part of Zia's legacy was a law that gave the country's largely symbolic president one major power, the ability to relieve a prime minister of office and require new elections. This sword hung over Bhutto's tangled relations with her (and her father's) bitter parliamentary rivals. Nor were her family relationships any help. While her marriage was publicly arranged according to Islamic custom and linked her family with another landholding clan of enormous wealth, her husband was anything but popular as a perceived ne'er-do-well who came to be called "Mr. Thirty Percent" for the cut he required on economic deals approved by the government. Finally, the president acted, and prime minister Bhutto was forced out of office in 1990.

As if to confirm Marx's axiom that history is condemned to repeat itself, the first time as tragedy and the second as farce, the cycle recurred. Because Bhutto claimed that she had been victimized by foul play and because her successor as prime minister had problems of his own, she soon began a successful campaign to return to office in the 1993 elections. Once again, however, she found it much easier to gain the office than to fulfill it. Her administration wallowed indecisively, as she found herself falling between the several stools of sacred and secular, elite and mass, men and women. Charges of corruption mounted against her and her husband, and there were revelations of huge personal expenditures in England. Her estranged brother was killed in a shoot-out with the Karachi police—an episode that some blamed on her husband. In 1996 Bhutto was once again sacked by the president, and once again she and her now divided Pakistan Peoples' Party were badly beaten by the same old rivals. Parliamentary control and the prime ministership was returned to the hands of her longtime competitor, Nawaz Sharif—like Bhutto, a member of a feudal landowning family in which peremptory power and massive wealth form part of a lineage that has little room for democracy.

Old questions remain concerning Pakistan as an Islamic state. The linchpin of Islamization—the controversial Sharia Bill—finally passed in 1991 while Bhutto was out of office. Of course, a law passed is not necessarily a law fully implemented. Moreover, this one omitted a controversial clause rolling back women's rights, and its most traditional elements only really apply to family and criminal matters, where they are often disregarded. The bill does not cover more complicated issues of international law and corporate economics. Still, the reaction among many middle-class Pakistanis was similar to that of a character in *My Beautiful Laundrette*, a film about Pakistanis living in England: "The whole country is being sodomized by religion. It is beginning to interfere with making money." Pakistan's national dispute over sacred versus secular power continues to simmer both nationally and locally. Not long ago, a barely literate fourteen-year-old boy spent five months in jail for the alleged "blasphemy" of writing anti-Islamic graffiti on one of the mud walls in his village.

Meanwhile, Sharif used his Muslim credentials as a partial cover for buttressing his personal position as prime minister. He ousted the president and stripped the office of its power to force new elections and a new government; he also sacked the chief justice of the Supreme Court, the head of Parliament, the chief election commissioner, and the army chief of staff. But any move against the military in Pakistan can be fatal. In

1999 Sharif succumbed to pressures from the West and the United States and ordered a withdrawal of Pakistani forces from the overwhelmingly Muslim but Indian-occupied areas of the disputed border territory of Kashmir. This represented a loss of face for the nation generally and the military in particular. It ultimately led to a military coup led by the new army chief, General Pervez Musharraf, and a trial against Sharif that was reminiscent of the trial of Benazir Bhutto's father some twenty years earlier. In this case, Sharif was sentenced to life imprisonment rather than death, and later permitted exile in Saudi Arabia.

Pakistan has been under direct military control for almost half of its national history—twenty-four of its fifty-three years. Unlike Turkey's military so devoted to secularism, the Pakistani military has a record of supporting Islam—although experts disagree on the actual level of Muslim faith and practice among the senior officer corps, including some in the shadows thought more powerful than Musharraf himself. With democracy in indefinite abeyance, religion continues to be feverish in the continuing dispute with dominantly Hindu India over dominantly Muslim Kashmir. Most of Kashmir is formally an Indian state subject to Indian-Pakistani negotiations, which were agreed to in the indefinite future fifty years ago but have never materialized. Now that India and Pakistan both have nuclear weapons, the negotiations are both more important and more difficult.

In addition to Islamization's strictly religious appeal and political significance, other matters hang in its balance. In the eyes of many scholars, Islamization symbolizes a larger retreat from the myriad disjunctions and dislocations entailed in the country's stagger toward modern parity.[27] But then some also suggest that Islamization is actually encouraged by the old plutocracy who find the faith a convenient distraction from the misery and exploitation involved in these developments. Whatever Pakistan's future holds, it will contain important lessons for others.

Indonesia: Islamic Syncretism and Modernization

Mention Islam and Muslims to most Westerners, and the countries that come to mind are those of the Arab Middle East. However, these countries account for less than a fifth of the world's Muslims. According to government statistics, the largest single Islamic nation is Indonesia, the fourth most populous country in the world. With some 88 percent of its 210 million people commonly classified as Muslim, Indonesia greatly exceeds even Pakistan, Bangladesh, and India—the next three largest Muslim societies, in that order.

But government statistics are sometimes affected by government ideologies. Some unofficial estimates of the proportion of Indonesian

Muslims place the figure as low as 30 percent. The problem is that definitive religious identities are elusive in a society where multiple religious allegiances are common. When I asked Indonesians about their religion, a typical response was: "Muslim, but not like the Iranians or the Pakistanis, because we are also part Hindu, part Buddhist, part Christian, and even part *abangan* [animist] in keeping with our roots." Even more than with other Muslim countries, there is some question whether Indonesia has been "Islamicized" or Islam has been "Indonesianized."

Compared to Indonesia, with its religious and ethnic mega-pluralism, another vaunted pluralistic country on the opposite side of the globe—the United States—seems like a tightly cloistered community. Indonesia is a country of some three hundred ethnic and tribal groups, speaking four hundred languages and dialects, and scattered over six thousand of its almost fourteen thousand islands, though 70 percent live on the principal island of Java and use a dozen major languages. The anthropologist Clifford Geertz describes the country's somewhat inchoate history in a single, breathtaking sentence:

> Settled by Austronesians coming, in God knows how many waves, by God knows how many routes, out of what is now south China and north Vietnam a millennium or two before Christ; scene of elaborate Indic state building, Borobudur and all that, from about the fifth century to about the fifteenth; progressively honeycombed with rather single-minded Chinese settler-traders from the Han on; subject to intense Islamic missionization, some orthodox, some less, from the twelfth century; colonized inchmeal, region by region, by the Dutch from 1598 to 1942 (with an English interlude, bringing eminent domain and left side driving, around the time of the Napoleonic wars); occupied, and rather generally manhandled, by the Japanese Army from 1942 to 1945; and now variously intruded upon by American, East Asian, Australian, European, Soviet, and Middle Eastern political and economic interests—there is hardly a form of legal sensibility (African, perhaps, and Eskimo) to which it has not been exposed.[28]

Like its neighbor Malaysia to the north, east, and west, Indonesia's government has cultivated a moderate Islamic identification while warding off the threat of Islamic fundamentalism. The state itself is neither officially secular nor officially Islamic, and it has steered a middle course between them since its independence from the Dutch via the Japanese in 1945.

Indonesia's postindependence history has been dominated by two presidents, first the Western-oriented secularist Sukarno until the bloody coup of 1965, when the state was taken over by the more traditional

Javanese leader Suharto. The pretext for the coup was an incipient Communist takeover, against which the military used Islam itself as a mobilizing device in a politically manipulated Islamic jihad. Many believe the considerable threat was exaggerated, but the episode was nonetheless grotesque.[29] Estimates of five hundred thousand deaths are uncorroborated, but 1.4 million were arrested and subjected to long-term gulag-style imprisonments without formal charges. The military coerced accusations that were followed up by impatient "justice." One of my respondents described a neighbor who was forced at gun point to accuse an innocent lifelong friend of treason—a neighbor who is still haunted by the friend's look of betrayal just before she was executed.

President Suharto held power for more than thirty years until his forced resignation by mass demonstrations in 1998. He claimed a personal allegiance to Islam, but he was well known as more of a Javanese animist, and his government was frequently criticized for being anti-Islamic.[30] In 1984 on the docks of Jakarta, as many as three hundred Muslims were killed in protesting the defiling and defacing of a mosque by two military officers. Muslim "extremists" have also been involved in arson and vandalism against some of Indonesia's most revered historic monuments as well as against evangelical Christian churches and ethnic Chinese banks and stores, groups that are perceived as outsiders. The evangelicals are seen as religious boat-rockers, while the Chinese constitute a small but powerful merchant class long characterized as avaricious. Whatever the overall tally of victims in 1965 and again in 1998, the Chinese were disproportionate among them.

In the midst of all of this, President Suharto, his government, and even his corrupt entrepreneurial offspring were doubly insulated, structurally and culturally. Structurally, the Suharto regime developed a political apparatus, Golkar, which was part party machine, part civil service, and part Big Brother.[31] The organization's tentacles reached down to the village level where it monitored the political activities of local officials who have been the traditional source of authority in Javanese society. Virtually every voluntary association in the country was pressured to formally affiliate with Golkar, hence its network was continually expanding.

Meanwhile, the government's cultural insulation comes from *Pancasila*, a pledge of national allegiance that functions as a kind of religious common denominator.[32] It was originally conceived by Sukarno in 1945 as a unifying umbrella for a heterogeneous new nation. It includes five simple principles with very little elaboration: belief in one God, national unity, guided democracy, social justice, and humanitarianism. Pancasila's roots are variously traced to Indonesia's major religious traditions, Javanese culture, and the competing political factions requiring mollification. The generic monotheism was designed to accommodate all five of Indonesia's world religions, including Islam, Buddhism, Hinduism, and the separate strands of Protestantism and Catholicism—though, as we shall see, the fit was somewhat procrustean in the case of Hinduism, and the credo was revised at the last minute to delete specific injunctions for Muslims to obey the Koran and for the national presidency to be reserved for a Muslim. More recent discussions have considered adding a sixth acceptable religious component, namely, Javanese animism, which is the culture's oldest but least codified religious tradition. Meanwhile, organizations and associations all across Indonesia are asked to sign pledges of loyalty to its principles, not unlike oaths of fealty to a feudal patriarchy. Some intellectual observers scoff at Pancasila as something of a charade whose form is more important than its content and a tabula rasa on which only the government can write to fill in the specifics convenient at the moment.

If both Golkar and Pancasila are walls of insulation, they have also been platforms for assertiveness. The Suharto government was increasingly involved in managing religious affairs—often funding them in order to control them. This included supervising religion in the schools (where the government has aroused opposition by not allowing Muslim girls to wear veils or long-sleeves and long trousers for gym), dictating to Islamic organizations the terms (and the candidates) for their elections, and arranging for hajj to Mecca—including President Suharto's own well-publicized trips.

In all of this, Suharto operated within the tradition of an Indonesian culture that often eludes Western sensibilities. For example, Indonesia's traditional status system was once so refined that a seemingly oxymoronic language was reserved exclusively for the king—a language that only he could understand. Or consider the sometimes blurred parallels between the real world and the world of the shadow puppets in the great Indonesian art form. David Moberg has elaborated the observation that Indonesia is an "as if" society:

> It looks as if political parties, elections, labor unions, a free press, and other foundations of democracy exist. But they don't. After more than three decades, an authoritarian regime rooted in the military still calls the shots as a restive population is denied a voice for its discontents. . . . Indonesia's "as if" politics often seem like a performance of Java's famed shadow puppets, which render epic battles between good and evil in fleeting, hazy images and keep the puppeteer hidden from view. The puppeteer behind the drama of

Indonesian public life is Suharto. . . . Meanwhile, in the political
shadows, many Indonesians are becoming absorbed in the question
of what happens when the puppeteer Suharto leaves the stage.[33]

It is understandable that prospects of insurgency and upheaval should
be unsettling in any society that so prizes status etiquette—especially
one still recovering from the horrors of 1965 and lesser intervening events.
While Suharto's authoritarian style was jarringly coarse in a culture so
subtly nuanced, he nonetheless played upon fears of a still greater rupture. Rumors of another wave of Communism were predictable during
periods of political uneasiness. Pancasila and Islam itself were often
rushed to the rhetorical fore to provide reassurance and shore up support
for the status quo. But religion can be a two-edged sword. Although Communist rallies and demonstrations could be outlawed, Muslim movements could not be suppressed without the possibility of creating martyrs
and jeopardizing the state's own legitimacy. Since fundamentalism was
more acceptable than Communism even in the post-Cold War climate,
this helped to explain many of the rallies under the green Muslim banner. Religious demonstrations were the only legal way to express secular
grievances, at least indirectly.

As Suharto prepared for yet another election in 1997, two figures
emerged from the wings as potential threats. One was Abdurrahman
Wahid, the director of the country's largest Muslim movement, Nahdlatul
Ulama (NU)—a phrase roughly translated as "Awakening of the Learned."
The other was Megawati Sukarnoputri, the daughter of former President
Sukarno and a quietly persistent early candidate of the left-wing Indonesian Democratic Party (PDI). A coalition between the two would have
posed a major problem for Suharto and Golkar. But Wahid and Sukarnoputri represented very different constituencies and agendas. Like most
Indonesians—even intellectuals—Wahid is a moderate who valued
Suharto's efforts on behalf of social and economic development and gave
the president an early and much-publicized handshake of benediction as
a fellow Muslim.[34] Megawati was less conciliatory, and government-
planted rumors begun to bloom concerning charges of Communist infil-
tration into her party. The party itself responded by removing her from
leadership, hence electoral candidacy.

In the end, Suharto received more than 70 percent of the vote and
steamrolled to yet another victory, despite charges of electoral irregu-
larities by opponents and foreign observers alike. But one of the paradoxes of democracy is that parties that win too overwhelmingly are
sometimes parties that are overcompensating for their own precarious-
ness. Suharto's future was finally doomed by a sham election that drained
his legitimacy and credibility. His international reputation had suffered

greatly within the human rights community because of his government's heavy-handed oppression in East Timor, where two of his local opponents shared the 1996 Nobel Peace Prize. Even Suharto's economic reviews were tattered by a sudden plummeting of the Indonesian economy as part of the widespread fiscal "Asian flu." His standing was further tainted by increasing evidence of corruption within his administration and his family.

The crescendoing and often violent demonstrations of the winter and spring of 1998 finally drove Suharto out of office in May of that year. The protest movement was largely fueled by a potent combination of student and Muslim groups. Suharto's designated successor, B. J. Habibie, was a longtime Suharto veteran and presidential stopgap who inspired little confidence but at least presided over two further votes crucial to the nation's history. One was a promised referendum in East Timor, where independence from Indonesia carried overwhelmingly. The other was a new all-Indonesian national election won somewhat surprisingly by the Muslim leader Wahid, who quickly built a new coalition government of those formerly out of power by including his old competitor, Sukarnoputri, as vice president.

Wahid offers compelling evidence that charisma is as much a property of circumstances as of the person. A man in his late fifties who is nearly blind and cursed by diabetes, Wahid had a long history of moderate—even liberal—Islamic leadership that followed his education in Cairo and took him all across the Koran Belt in meetings with other major figures of the faith while developing tastes in films, German classical music, and the Western literature of the sociology of religion. His election was a signal that extremism is not the only path to political power. Islam and democracy are indeed compatible.

However, subsequent events have belied Indonesia's stereotypic status as a "pacific" nation both socially and geographically. Amid the celebrations of Pancasila, liberal Islam, and the moderating effects of what I have called "internal religious pluralism," violence has once again spread. At this point, it is hard to weigh the causes or the future of the killings that have resulted. Muslim-Christian conflict is partly a result of competitive proselytizing on both sides, as hostilities have long surged from the bottom up. When I left Indonesia in 1987, my plane-mates included a Christian evangelical pastor and his family who had been effectively expelled from the country for their aggressive conversion efforts.

But somehow the current conflict has an added dimension and can be seen as instigated from the top down. The old regimes of Suharto and the Indonesian military did not go quietly, however. Both of these reactionary elements sought to discredit Wahid and his ability to control the nation by provoking riots and instability across the great stretch of Indonesia.[35] Violence spread from East Timor in the southeast to Aceh in the northwest and from South Sumatra in the southwest to the Moluccas (or Spice) Islands in the northeast. The terror involved more than a thousand deaths in 1999 alone—Muslims versus Muslims, Muslims versus Christians, and both against Chinese ethnics as the common out-group. As Wahid struggles against opposition charges of corruption and faces in impeachment, Indonesia remains another country whose fate depends upon a new relation between religion and politics. The nation is charting a new course in its vast waters.

Conclusion

How then to summarize Islam and its relation to the state? Once one leaves the pages of the canonical Koran, one is immediately sucked into a set of centrifugal forces that produce very different syndromes in different contexts.

Egypt is caught up in a continuing struggle between a secular elite and Islamic extremists who have directed violence against the state itself as well as noncomplying Muslims and Christians. Turkey has been simultaneously Muslim and secular since 1923, though its proud history of tilting toward the West is now being challenged by a minority Islamic movement that has become a portentous political movement.

Pakistan was born in 1947 as the Indian subcontinent's independence from Britain produced nationalist twins. Pakistan was smaller and almost exclusively Muslim; the Republic of India was much larger and dominantly Hindu. Pakistan's current politics reflect Western influences as well as recent pressure toward Islamization. This pressure has had sometimes turbulent consequences, as the faith has become a veil for both political corruption and military intervention. Finally, Indonesia is both officially Islamic and the most religiously pluralistic nation in the world, with Buddhist, Christian, Hindu, and indigenously animist elements added. The country's political leadership has sought to control Islam rather than be controlled by it. But the recent change at the top has produced a sea change in the rise of a precarious new leadership of moderate Muslims committed to democratic practices.

As centrifugal as these countries may seem, they share a basic centripetal quality in bringing their moths ever closer to their flames. Without suggesting that there are no religious movements that have chosen to avoid the political heat—or vice versa—it is clear that each of these Islamic societies has much at stake in the way religion and politics flutter around each other.

Yet these countries are not the only Muslim countries one might examine. They are neither exhaustive nor quintessential, and one could just as easily consider another four. I tried unsuccessfully to gain access to Iran, and neither Algeria nor Afghanistan had become open wounds of religion and politics at the time I was designing this project. However, Islam is certainly implicated in the two countries that follow in the next chapter. In both cases, I shall be examining the dynamics of Islam as a minority rather than a majority.

4

Two

Multireligious

"Mindfields"

Israel and India

Sacred turf can be shaky ground and is not easily shared. No countries offer more compelling testimony here than Israel and India. Both have been important sites for the early development of several of the great world religions. Both have been controlled by different religious groups during their long histories of multireligious coexistence. Both have also hosted some of the bloodiest religious carnage the world has ever known.

Jews, Muslims, and Christians have all played major roles in Israel's history, and all claim sacred areas not only within the country at large but within an area of less than a single square mile in East Jerusalem known as the Old City capped by what Jews call the "Temple Mount" and the Muslims refer to as the "Noble Sanctuary." While Christians no longer have hopes of hegemony there, the persisting visions of Jews and Muslims remain in conflict. If the land that is now Israel is the great spawning ground of Western religion beginning with the Judaism of Abraham some three thousand years ago, India is the East's religious womb, beginning with Hinduism's origins even earlier. Hinduism has in turn given birth to Buddhism, Jainism, and Sikhism. But the country has also played reluctant host to the power of both Islam and Christianity.

In sheer scale, Israel and India could not be farther apart. Israel occupies a small swatch of land the size of Massachusetts on the southeastern shore of the Mediterranean where it is dwarfed by its often hostile Arab neighbors. By contrast, India has a land mass roughly equal to a third of the United States but a population four times larger at nearly one billion (almost 170 times greater than Israel's six million). But size aside, Israel and India share the blessing and the curse of religious fecundity. Trying to understand either country without understanding the often violent mix of religion and politics in each is a bit like trying to understand procreation with no grasp of sex.

Israel: Religious Crucible and War Zone

Israeli psychologists know the syndrome well. It is called the "Jerusalem complex," and it describes those who are so affected by the city's sacred aura that they adopt a messiah's identity for themselves. One of my respondents has often seen them walking what he calls "the messianic mile"—an approach to the now closed Golden Gate of the Temple Mount, where they hope that crowds will gather to affirm their divinity and follow their prophecy. Alas, the only commotion on the path while I was there occurred when Israeli police shot and wounded a twelve-year-old Muslim boy for throwing stones at them.

Jerusalem as a Religious Fount

No city in the world can match Jerusalem's status as the sacred ground of three major religions. Jews staked their claim first, but Judaism's own beginnings defy conventional chronology. More an intense ethical pact than an elaborate vision of supernatural realms within a divine cosmology, its basic scriptures involve the Torah—revealed by God to Moses on Mount Sinai and which Christians know as the Pentateuch, or the first five books of the Bible's Old Testament—and the Talmud, which is a vast series of exquisite ethical deliberations on and learned arguments with the Torah.

The prophet Abraham is believed by many to have founded Judaism proper on the large rock table that crowns the Temple Mount—the same stone that the Muslims used in 691 C.E. as the base for their still-standing Dome of the Rock. A steep western approach to the mount includes the single holiest site of Judaism, the "western wall"—sometimes known more fatalistically and pejoratively as the Wailing Wall.

Judaism's claim to Jerusalem moved from storydom to history in 1000 B.C.E. when King David captured the city and made it the center of his empire. Not long after in 960 B.C.E., Solomon expanded the city and built the Jews' First Temple. The Second Temple followed some four hundred years later when Jews returned to the city after its destruction and their forced departure by the infamous King Nebuchadezzar of Babylon. Never lacking enemies, however, Judaism was next banned—and Jerusalem next razed—by the Romans, whose scourge continued until the early fourth century when Constantine acknowledged a new religious presence and converted his empire to Christianity. The destruction of the Second Temple marked a traumatic and enduring shift from a once highly centralized system of "temple Judaism" to a more local and autonomous form of "rabbinic Judaism."

Of course, the story of Jesus and the early Christians is familiar to even the most casual Christmas and Easter service attendees. The site of Jesus' crucifixion, burial, and, according to Christian doctrine, miraculous resurrection is within the Church of the Holy Sepulchre of the Old City. The Bethlehem of the stable and crèche is now a Jerusalem suburb in the West Bank, and most of Jesus' life transpired only a few hours' drive away on the northern shore of the inland Sea of Galilee. It is possible to take local public buses from Jerusalem through Jericho and Tiberias to the Tobgah site where Jesus is reported to have fed thousands with but a few "loaves and fishes." One can then amble two miles along a quiet country road to Jesus' synagogue in Capurnaum, passing en route the unmarked and unremarkable grassy hillside that is held to be the site of his Sermon on the Mount.

In walking this terrain, even I had a momentary glimpse of the miraculous. There is a small chapel on the lake shore commemorating Jesus' instructions to the frustrated fisherman, Peter, to take his boat back out again, and fish would then materialize in great abundance. It seemed to me that the five large stones extending out into the water from that point were all strangely heart-shaped, as if to represent the spirit that infused Jesus and the four disciples present. Surely I am not alone in the perception, and the authentic modern miracle may be that no healing cult or souvenir stand selling stone replicas has yet materialized on the spot.

Following Constantine's anointment of Christianity in the Roman Empire, one might think that the question of religion was settled once and for all. But in fact its religious battles were just beginning. As Rome waned, Islam waxed. Islamic forces captured Jerusalem in 637 C.E.—only five years after the prophet Muhammad's death. Indeed, the rock table is believed to be the spot from which Muhammad ascended to heaven; some Muslims point out his footsteps on the rock, and many regard the Temple Mount as Islam's third most sacred spot, behind only Mecca and Medina. By 1099 the Muslim presence had attracted the return of Christian crusaders who killed Jews and Muslims alike and captured Jerusalem. A century later the Muslims recaptured the city, only to lose it to the Mongols in 1244. Finally, a temporary stability followed the conquest by the Ottoman Turks in 1516. For the next four hundred years, Jerusalem and surrounding "Palestine" were largely under Muslim control, though communities of both Jews and Christians remained.

An Embattled Statehood

By the second half of the nineteenth century, the great majority of the world's Jews were scattered around the world throughout the diaspora in Russia, Europe, and increasingly the United States. In most areas, they were relegated to ghettos or shtetls that were in but not of the host countries. Understandably, Jews longed for both a common home and the original homeland. In the late nineteenth century Theodor Herzl gave prominence and persuasiveness to a Zionist movement on behalf of a new state of Israel in the old Palestinian territory.

In 1917 Britain weighed in with a declaration of support from Foreign Secretary Lord Balfour. In 1920—after the British captured the territory from the Ottomans during World War I—the League of Nations recognized a British mandate in the area on behalf of Jews everywhere with provision for a separate Arab territory as well. Over the next thirty years, conflicts and eruptions mounted between Jews, Arabs, and the controlling British administration. In the aftermath of World War II and while people around the world were still reeling from the horrors of the Nazi Holocaust, the new United Nations created separate Jewish and Arab states in the area in 1947. But in the 1948 War of Independence, Jews prevailed to establish the single State of Israel with both Jewish and Arab-Muslim residents.[1]

From the outset, Israel was opposed by its neighbors. Jordan had secured control of East Jerusalem in 1948, prohibiting Jewish access to the Temple Mount and the Wailing Wall. Syria had increasing influence in Lebanon to the immediate north and controlled the Golan Heights in the northeast overlooking the Galilee area, which became a target for shelling. To the south across the Gaza Strip and the Sinai peninsula, Egypt sought to deny Israel access to the Suez Canal between the Mediterranean and the Red Sea, despite the treaty forged in 1956 when Nasser's Egypt lost its battle with the British and French. Israel was growing rapidly from Jewish immigration, but it was also experiencing mounting tensions with non-Jewish opponents. It was developing a siege mentality as a garrison state.

The fabled Six-Day War of 1967 marked a dramatic change. Israel's powerful military launched strikes in several directions against its overmatched neighbors, and Israel quickly seized the Sinai and the Gaza areas, the Golan Heights, and the West Bank, including most particularly such hallowed sites as Bethlehem, Hebron, and East Jerusalem with its Temple Mount and the Wailing Wall. To the beleaguered Jewish people, God seemed to look upon them with favor again. A state that had begun in surprisingly secular terms was given a major sacred jolt. A nation that once depended on secular statecraft and military mobilization now seemed to have a messianic destiny.

Some Israeli leaders—including the country's founder David Ben-Gurion—urged a return of much of the territory won, claiming that it was unnecessary to Israel and that such an act would help placate the country's opponents. But power had shifted into the hands of those who saw the seized territory as part of the sacred land that was the Jewish birthright. Far from being returned, Israel had to fight again to protect it while repelling the invasions of Egypt and Syria in the brief but bloody Yom Kippur War of 1973.

By the late 1970s it was clear that such wars served no one's interest. Accordingly, Egypt's President Anwar Sadat and Israel's Prime Minister Menachem Begin—a former guerilla hero and hawkish leader of the conservative Likud Party—accepted U.S. President Jimmy Carter's invitation to come to his Camp David retreat in Maryland and negotiate a phased settlement that involved, among other things, a return of land in the Sinai in exchange for guaranteed Jewish access to its sacred sites. Sadat and Begin shared a Nobel Peace Prize for the 1979 Camp David Accords. But if this eased problems with Egypt (and Jordan) to the south and east, Israel continued to have border problems in the north with Syria and the imploding Lebanon. These problems were to continue through the 1980s and 1990s, with alternating bursts of military hostilities and wary negotiations. Meanwhile, external hostilities were being upstaged by internal conflicts.

Cracks in the Rock

A state is not necessarily a nation, let alone a fully bonded society. From the beginning, it was apparent that the very notion of an Israeli consensus was a futile fiction. We know the Jewish justification of an Israeli state that finally provided a safe haven and a return to religious home base. Later we shall examine important and sometimes bitterly contested differences among Jews themselves. In the meantime, it is crucial to understand that the new Israel was not exclusively Jewish. The largest segment of the host population were Arab-Muslim Palestinians, who comprised almost a fifth of the population and whose growth through high fertility held pace with Jewish growth through continued immigration.

From the Palestinian perspective, of course, the Israelis who poured in largely from Europe, the United States, and North Africa were an unwelcome incursion arranged through devious great power politics and conspiring elites. A land originally sacred to Muslims had been additionally sanctified by a millennium of continued residence. It was one thing to share the land but quite another to find themselves dealt losing hands as a relatively powerless underclass within a political and economic system that was stacked against them from the start. Ever since 1967, Palestinian communities in both the West Bank and the Gaza Strip were under Israeli military occupation to protect the Jewish settlements that had grown up illegally and despite the increasing disapproval of other Israeli Jews.

The results were hardly surprising. Under the leadership of young militants such as Yasser Arafat, the Palestine Liberation Organization (PLO) emerged as a guerilla movement and a major thorn in the side of the state. With the blurring of distance and hindsight, the last fifty years seem to represent a continuing reciprocity of state military and police brutality, on the one hand, and terrorist attacks, on the other.[2] Religion was by no means the only factor in producing conflict, since both ethnic and class differences were also at issue, and the three sources of tension built upon each other. But ultimate and even proximate causes are easily lost in violence's own self-provoking and self-perpetuating cycles.

Gradually the PLO followed the pattern of radical movements everywhere. As part of an aging process of both the organization and its leaders—and in response to the stick of continued armed suppression and the carrot of an increased political voice—the PLO began to mature from a military cadre to an administrative organization capable of negotiation. Yet all was not quiescent. In December 1987 a new pattern of resistance began in an *intifada* (uprising) that arose spontaneously following a Gaza Strip traffic collision in which an Israeli vehicle killed several Palestinian workers. From this point on, ordinary citizens—especially young people—launched a regular series of actions against the Israeli military presence in their areas. These included public demonstrations, work stoppages, and staged confrontations in which rock throwing provoked military responses. In 1988 a part of this civil insurrection took a religious turn with the emergence of a Muslim group known as Hamas (an Arabic acronym for Islamic Resistance Movement). Hamas was in turn an extension of the Islamic Jihad, a group formed in the early 1980s with assistance from Egypt's Muslim Brotherhood.

Hamas saw itself pursuing a jihad against the Israeli state.[3] Many other Israelis regarded it scornfully as fundamentalist terrorism. In any case, the cycle of violence was again spurred forward. Prepubescent youngsters comprised a high percentage of the Hamas recruits, and Hamas initiated them into a violently xenophobic world during the most critical phase of their life socialization. This was a new Palestinian offensive—

but one whose aggressive radicalism even put many Palestinians, including the PLO, on the defensive.

By the early 1990s new political arrangements were obviously necessary. The early democratic dream of a common Israeli citizenship under a single state authority had now turned into a nightmare. The 1993 Oslo Accords represented a widely applauded breakthrough. They partitioned the country in a way that allowed the Palestinians to control their own areas in the Gaza Strip and the West Bank. For this purpose, the PLO took another step away from its founding characteristics as a guerilla movement and segued into the Palestine National Authority (PNA)—again under the leadership of Arafat.

The solution was fraught with problems, even from the Palestinian perspective. The PNA areas suffered from inadequate political and economic infrastructures. Lacking the domestic resources (and foreign assistance) of the country's affluent Jewish majority, many Arab-Muslims had little to fall back upon and continued to blame Jews and the Israeli government for their poverty. Of course, the blame was reciprocated. In the words of one Jewish social scientist respondent, "They do nothing for themselves." However, another noted the asymmetry in the stand-off: "Jews moving into Muslim areas is okay, but not vice versa. Curtailing Jewish rights is an 'abridgement of freedom,' but curtailing Muslim rights is a matter of security.' "

The high levels of suspicion and resulting violence were readily apparent. On my second day in Jerusalem, one of its quotidian tragedies occurred in the shop-lined alleyways of the Muslim quarter of the Old City—the *suk*—where a Jewish extremist's grenade killed a Muslim blacksmith and injured twelve others. In this climate of reciprocal violence, the incident was less remarkable than its aftermath. After a few days, the blacksmith's family requested pension assistance from the government. They learned that the law provides for the survivors of Jewish victims of Muslim violence but not Muslim victims of Jewish violence. Although a number of Jewish politicians claimed that the matter was "really more complicated" and others sought to right the wrong, the imbroglio mirrored the larger problems faced by the Palestinian minority.

In the meantime, Arafat was caught in the middle and on a hot spot, desperately trying to put a lid on a pot that was boiling over. Still regarded suspiciously by most Jews, he was also making enemies as well as friends among the Palestinians themselves. Many viewed his governance as authoritarian and unsympathetic if not outright treasonous. Crime rates rose, and Hamas continued its campaign of sacred violence with a haughty disdain for anyone who would compromise with the hated Israeli state to achieve personal power. During an evening spent with the family of another Muslim shopkeeper in the suk, I asked the man and his twenty-year-old son their reactions to the situation. The son said, "I support the intifada and the need to keep applying pressure, though, of course, not Hamas." Perhaps because the Hamas demurral was merely for the benefit of his father and myself, the father visibly cringed and said, "I am too old to know about that. I just want police protection for my shop. They don't listen to me and never seem to be there when you need them."

Clearly the Palestinian community falls short of any communal ideal. But this is also true of Israel's Jewish community. Here, too, there are fissures of long standing that sometimes close in the face of a common enemy only to widen again once power is being allocated. So far I have concentrated largely on the Arab-Muslim fifth of the Israeli population. It is now time to turn to the discordant Jewish four-fifths and examine the collision of religion and politics from another series of vantage points.

Jews, Jewishness, and Zionism

Surprisingly, Israel's founding leaders had no aspirations of a "Torahcracy," or an exclusively Jewish religious nation. The principal architect of statehood was a secular Jew, David Ben-Gurion, for whom Judaism was a historical and cultural identity that transcended any religious observance or lack of it. In fact, Ben-Gurion wanted to keep religion "under his thumb." While he appreciated Israel's religious significance, he was eager to avoid having the country defined or controlled in narrowly religious terms. In this, he had much in common with a generation of early-twentieth-century secular statesmen, including Turkey's Ataturk, Egypt's Nasser, Pakistan's Jinnah, Indonesia's Sukarno and, as we shall see later, even India's Gandhi and China's Mao Zedong. Like another of Israel's early political leaders, Golda Meir, Ben-Gurion had spent time in the United States. Perhaps this is why he opposed introducing television into Israel. After all, the creation of a new nation was to be a precarious venture that would require the hard work and deep commitment of the traditional kibbutzim, or collective farms, rather than the narcotizing self-indulgence so characteristic of post-World War II America.

Religion itself has long been a source of irony in a country so widely depicted as a Jewish religious state.[4] Even among Jews themselves, religion has been almost as divisive as it has been unifying. Moreover, support of the Israeli state is by no means perfectly correlated with the degree of religious adherence. On this point, Israel's Jews include at least three discernible factions. First are the secular Zionists in the socialist—even antireligious—tradition of Ben-Gurion and Meir. These are citizens who are not personally religious but whose cultural Judaism pivots around

their steadfast commitment to Israel as a nation. Second are the Orthodox Jewish Zionists, including those within a messianic political movement known as the Gush Emunim (Bloc of the Faithful), an early Jewish
parallel to the Hamas. Finally, the third community is the Haredim on
the far religious right who are—again ironically—conspicuous for both
their ultra-Jewishness and their opposition to Zionism and the Israeli
state. Each of these clusters merits brief consideration.

Of the three, the secular Zionists are by far the largest. It is variously estimated that anywhere from 40 to 60 percent of Israelis (a term
often used inaccurately to refer to only Jews) are nonreligious, including
the overwhelming majority of the current political elite. Israel's nonreligious proportion is certainly far larger than is customarily cited for the
United States. According to a recent survey, 20 percent of the country's
Jews are totally nonobservant, while another 40 percent designate themselves as somewhat observant. By comparison, about 25 percent see themselves as observant to a great extent and only 14 percent as strictly
observant. Much of this is reflected in attitudes toward religion and the
state. A substantial majority favors a separation of religion and the state.
In interviewing Israelis about their religion and their country, the following response was typical: "Everyone thinks of this as such a religious
country, but it's really not. I'm not religious at all, really, and most of the
young people see themselves as Israelis rather than Jews."

Yet the question, "Who is a Jew?" remains a very pressing issue in
Israel. If it perplexes Jews, it can be even more confusing to those outside the faith and outside the country. For example, Friday nights are the
Jewish shabbat, and on this particular Friday my wife and I were dining
at the home of friends in Jerusalem. The husband was a rabbi, and before
supper he led the customary prayers and singing while lighting the sacred candles. Like virtually all religious rituals, it had a beauty and mystery that was enveloping even to the uninitiated. But suddenly the mood
was broken. The husband interrupted the ceremony and looked up at us
grinning: "You know, we don't believe in any of this. But then in Judaism, it doesn't matter what you believe. What's important is what you
do. Judaism is a religion of the act, whereas Christianity is a religion of
the word."

The self-description may have been stretched a bit for effect. However, it correctly implies that Orthodox Jews are perhaps better described
as "orthoprax" and that many Jews who are not believers are in some
measure "behavers." The Israeli citizenship of even the nonbelievers
and nonbehavers is prima facie evidence of their Jewishness. They have
at least a minimal loyalty to Israel as both a concept and a state, though
they often disagree with overtly religious policies. The notion of Israel
as a homeland remains, even when the homeland is defined in cultural

or ethnic terms instead of religion per se. All of this recalls the importance of cultural religion in Poland, Northern Ireland, and Turkey.

However, there are certainly those who see the state as very much a
religious project. As noted earlier, the 1967 Six-Day War tended to
sacralize a nation that was originally conceived in relative secular and
pluralistic terms—albeit with Jews in control. Following the near defeat
in 1973 and the Camp David Accords in 1977, religion took on greater
prominence in the political arena—this was less out of celebration than
of fear that Israel was in jeopardy through either war or diplomacy. In
the years since, it became a commonplace to refer to the "Judaization"
of Israel and to see the country as a religious mission. Some even refer to
a "Judaization industry" as a whole series of educational programs and
retreats devoted to stemming the tide of secularization and producing a
return to the faith.[5]

The most extreme movement here is that of the messianic "Kookists"
founded by Rabbi Abraham Isaac Kook and his son some seventy years
ago.[6] This was another group often depicted as fundamentalist. However, as with movements such as Hamas, the stereotype is only accurate
in suggesting high levels of religious intensity; it fails to capture the
innovative departures from the past as pathways to a much different
future. Kookists were eager to seize the day on behalf of a newly authen-
ticated and invigorated Judaism. Their religious prophecy led to a hard-
core political movement that sought to translate God's will into concrete
power relationships, namely, the Gush Emunim.

The Gush are Zionists whose zealousness has led to assaults on Arab
groups and even an infamous bombing attempt on the Muslim Noble
Sanctuary.[7] It is true that not all members of the Gush are religiously
fervent, and some use religion as a means to Zionism rather than a Zionist end in its own right. But for the most part, the Gush represented a
new form of Israeli underground activism—one in which sacred commitments overcame secular constraints. This was not at all the movement that had initially created Israel and spawned leaders ranging from
Ben-Gurion to recent figures such as Begin and Rabin.

A tight relation between Judaism and Zionism is also characteristic
of Israel's less messianic Orthodox Jews. But it is not easy to isolate, let
alone enumerate, just who is Orthodox. Israel contains some fifteen different Jewish sects, each with slightly different versions of orthodoxy.
Overall, it is estimated that no more than 40 percent of the Israeli population is even minimally Orthodox in its basic beliefs and ritual practices, including some combination of (almost) daily synagogue attendance;
head coverings for both men and women; not traveling, watching television, or using the telephone on the Sabbath; believing that the Torah has
divine origins; and believing that the Messiah will return to end the

tribulations of the Jews and proclaim them as the chosen people. Other aspects of Judaism associated with orthodoxy in the United States (for example, observing a strictly kosher diet and keeping a kosher kitchen that fully separates meat and dairy preparations) are more common in Israel as part of a broader cultural legacy. Nonetheless, not all Orthodox Jews have an activist commitment to religion as their primary political agenda.

A last component of Israel's Jewish mosaic involves the Haredim, or ultra-Orthodox, who are notable not only for their religious zeal but for their opposition to Zionism and any Israeli nation established before the Messiah returns. These Jewish opponents of the Jewish state are sometimes portrayed as typical Israeli citizens because the men seem so stereotypically Jewish with their full beards, single hair curls hanging from each temple, and wide-brimmed black hats.

The Haredim constitute yet another embattled minority, many of whom are Sephardim from North Africa. Although they have now moved into some smaller towns, they are particularly concentrated and conspicuous in large, self-defined neighborhoods within both Tel Aviv and Jerusalem.[8] The Jerusalem neighborhood—known as Mea Shearim—frequently erupts into minibattles with the state itself. The neighborhood's streets are periodically closed—even to the police—by barricades of burning automobile tires. Inside, life follows an ancient rhythm set largely by the schools—whether state-supported ultra-Orthodox schools for the children or community-supported Talmudic schools for the men who attend every evening (but the Sabbath) to engage in ritualized debates over the finer points of the Torah. For the most part, strangers remain just that, and to be caught on the nearby streets in a car after sundown on the Sabbath is to risk calumny or worse. After one visit to the area, as our car exited near dusk, I glanced out of the rear window to see a small boy spit contemptuously after us.

The Haredim account for about a fifth of the Israeli population, as do the Arab-Muslims. The numbers of both groups are increasing due to disproportionately high fertility, and in Jerusalem (East and West combined) the two populations are becoming even larger factions as other citizens leave the city to escape its mounting tensions.

But the Haredim and the Palestinians share more than a demographic pattern: both are scorned by many Israelis, albeit for different reasons. The Haredim are seen by many as parasitic, hypocritical gadflies. While they receive high levels of state financial support, especially for their special ultra-Orthodox schools and neighborhood projects, their men remain full-time students until they are beyond draft age and hence manage to avoid compulsory military service. Moreover, the Haredim community continues to bark at and sometimes bite the hand of the state that feeds it. As a result, the Haredim are bitterly derided by a substantial portion of Israeli Jews, and the tension is so great that it could well outlast the Palestinian stalemate. Once stability with the Muslims is attained, it is at least conceivable that the less religious Jews will turn on the hyperreligious. The Haredim could even become the next community to be a scapegoat target of violence, and it is perhaps portentous that the government has floated proposals to strip away some of the ultra-Orthodox privileges.

Synagogue and State

If any country in this collection qualifies as officially religious, one might think it would be Israel. But as most Israelis would be quick to point out, the formal reality is otherwise. We have already seen that the country's founding leaders were secular Jews who envisioned a secular state, albeit an ethnic Jewish homeland. In this respect, Israel is a deliberately constructed national enclave whose creation is similar to that of Pakistan a year earlier in 1947 or Northern Ireland in 1921.

Certainly Israel is not constitutionally Jewish, in large part because it still lacks a final constitution of any sort.[9] There is a perennially pending "Torah" Constitution whose first line specifies that "the State of Israel is a Torah-cratic Republic." However, it is too controversial to pass. In the meantime, the country's basic governance is covered by a Transition Law passed in 1949 plus half a dozen other basic laws passed since.

One manifestation of the country's original commitment to the free exercise of religion and state religious neutrality is that each major religious community—including Muslims and Christians—is allowed to apply its own traditions to such personal matters as marriage, divorce, and burial. Yet Orthodox rabbis are the only members of the rabbinical court that is the sole arbiter of such matters for Israel's Jewish citizens—Orthodox or not. As this suggests, Orthodox Judaism is a distinct minority but also a distinctly powerful one. A number of matters of state policy reflect Orthodox standards. State-funded religious—even ultra-Orthodox—schools are commonplace. To honor the Sabbath, many government services are closed, and no state buses operate from sundown Friday to sundown Saturday. Recent religious demands in Jerusalem have ranged from Sabbath road closings in Jewish areas and relocating a sports stadium so that it would not disturb a particular neighborhood's Sabbath to halting the sale of nonkosher food in Jewish sectors. The responses of what has been called "the overburdened polity" have been both reluctant and controversial, but they amount to providing oil for the squeakiest wheel.[10] In six of the eight cases that Ira Sharkansky analyzed, the religious petitioners won most of what they had sought.[11]

Another tradition currently being contested concerns Israel's Law of Return, a statute enacted in 1950 with quite liberal qualifications for immigrating to Israel and attaining state-recognized "Jewish religious identity." Despite the law, Orthodox rabbis have continually insisted on more rigorous standards for Jewish citizenship, and they have tended to prevail informally while lobbying for a bill that would cement their formal authority. As one prominent Jewish politician remarked to me, "Israel is very generous to its citizens, though the standards for citizenship are stricter than the Talmud." He was, of course, talking only of Jewish citizens. In any event, the question "Who is a Jew?" has become a matter of considerable debate. Orthodox criteria would extend automatic admission only to immigrants whose mothers are Jewish (and by strict standards, only Orthodox Jewish mothers at that); all others must be converted by an Orthodox rabbi into orthodoxy.

The consequences of such a policy are especially troublesome in the United States, where moderate Conservative and liberal Reform Jewish communities are far larger—and the Orthodox minority much smaller—than in Israel. Ordinarily, one would suppose that opposition from two wings of Judaism that are so small within Israel itself would be of little political consequence. However, a vast majority of the private funds raised for Israel in the diaspora comes from the United States, where the United Jewish Appeal digs deeply into Reform and Conservative pockets. Because these two communities also have massive lobbying leverage over the billions of dollars sent to Israel from the U.S. government, their concerns are not easily dismissed.

Neither of Israel's two major political parties—the more liberal Labor or the more conservative Likud—is religiously rooted. The two primary differences between them involve economic policy and the hardness of their attitudes toward Israel's Palestinians. In the latter case, the question has recently come down to how much of the Gaza and the West Bank will be turned over to the Palestinians, in particular the land that the government has allowed Jewish settlers to build on as a form of religious stake claiming that violates prior understandings. Although Orthodox Jewish factions in the Israeli Knesset, or parliament, fall far short of even a numerically significant minority, here again they have disproportionate power. Since the two major parties rarely attain clear majorities of their own, both must rely on fragile coalitions with the remaining dozen or so parties. Several small Orthodox parties have been particularly influential in various coalitions because the parties have just enough votes to tip the balance and are obdurate in charging a high policy price. These parties have not infrequently held the kingdom hostage while playing the roles of both kingmaker and kingbreaker.

Religion's influence in Israeli politics was tragically illustrated in

November 1995, when Labor Prime Minister Yitzhak Rabin was assassinated at the conclusion of a peace rally. The nation held its breath while awaiting word as to who was responsible; in such a charged atmosphere the religion of the assailant was critical to the response—whether a paroxysm of vengeance or an encirclement of mourning. As it turned out, the latter was more the case. The lone assassin was not a Muslim concerned that Rabin was giving up too little land to the Palestinians but an extremist Jew convinced that Rabin was willing to relinquish too much land that was too sacred.

A single bullet often changes history more than a protracted war. Rabin's death led to elections five months later in which his long-time comrade—first in the Zionist underground and then in Labor politics— Shimon Peres lost very narrowly to the Likud Party and its leader, the Philadelphia high school graduate Benjamin Netanyahu. Because Likud could not mount a majority by itself, coalition politics were again the order of the day, as it was once more with Netanyahu's successor, Labor's Ehud Barak, followed by Likud's Ariel Sharon.

Almost regardless of party, any Israeli leader of the moment is squeezed between majority pressure for negotiated peace and a critical religious minority's continued opposition to negotiations. Behind the rhetorical feints and jabs that characterize every cornered politician is deep pressure for Israel to avoid any accord with Syria that involves ceding the strategic ground of the Golan Heights, to refuse to withdraw military forces from southern Lebanon, to continue to approve construction of new Jewish settlements in Palestinian areas, to stall withdrawal from old settlements despite their low occupancy rates, and to keep off the table any possibility of giving up part of Jerusalem for a Palestinian capital of a prospective Palestinian state. Of course, there is no less pressure on the Palestinian leadership in just the opposite directions.

Zionism as a Quasi-Religion

Is Israel a Jewish country? Even if it is not officially a Jewish state, it is certainly a Jewish-dominated society. But many would argue that Judaism is the wrong word and Zionism the right word in discussing this troubled nation. It is not at all unusual for nonreligious Israelis to be Zionists—even militantly so. However, Zionism itself is subject to different interpretations.

From one perspective, Zionism is tantamount to racism—at least according to a 1975 United Nations resolution that passed despite U.S. objections but with considerable Third World support, especially from Muslim nations. Certainly one must understand this ideological declaration in political context, as Muslims and the Third World came to the defense of their Palestinian allies. However, the label of racism is too loose a term to cover such a multitude of disputes and conflicts. It tends to confuse causes with consequences. In a world of unintended effects that are often institutionally rooted and protracted, it is not easy to discern the motivations behind even widespread patterns of unequal and discriminatory outcomes. Moreover, the accusation sometimes haunts the accuser as much as the accused. Filing a charge of racism is sometimes like hurling a bomb at one's own feet.

As a cultural force within Judaism, Zionism has an ethnic nationalist connotation along with a sense of grievances to be redressed. Justifying a present and future homeland with reference to past victimization is a dominant refrain echoing throughout the Jewish community—both in Israel and across the diaspora. Of course, no single episode of victimization is so grotesquely compelling as the Holocaust. The unspeakable tragedy of six million deaths at the hands of the Nazis is spoken of often as an example of racism in all its pathological horror. The Holocaust has become iconic, and Holocaust museums have burgeoned to crystallize the collective memory.

It is now not uncommon to hear Jewish harshness against others defended in terms of Jewish suffering at the hands of others. Yet even some Jewish respondents expressed cautious reservations about an almost exclusive appropriation of the tragedy by Jews who little acknowledge the genocidal sufferings of the Gypsies, and the admittedly more political mass deaths of Christians and other non-Jewish Nazi enemies and "nuisances" throughout eastern Europe and Russia. As one Jerusalem Christian commented to me, "God knows, the Holocaust was one of humanity's lowest points. But Jews are not the only people to suffer millions of dead in orgies of violence. And I have to confess that I get a bit offended by the way the Holocaust is now symbolically manipulated. It seems to me that some people tend to use their martyrdom and our guilt to exonerate their current abuses of groups like the Palestinians."

Meanwhile, there are at least two respects in which the frequent phrase "secular Zionism" may be an oxymoron and Zionism itself may qualify as religious. First, insofar as Zionism draws upon the religious legacy of the Jewish historical experience, it is certainly redolent of religion. Events like the Holocaust and the Six-Day War have taken on distinct religious overlays. Even many nonreligious or cultural Jews continue to resonate to the religion of their forbears. One reason why Orthodox Judaism still wields powerful influence is that its spiritual themes and moral agendas invoke a sacred past that continues to hover even over those who dismiss the religion itself as irrational superstition. To reject or simply ignore this religious legacy is to diminish a part of oneself.

A second reason why Zionism qualifies as at least a quasi-religion is its importance in bonding Israeli Jews and consecrating the Israeli state.

In this sense, Zionism qualifies as a partial civil religion of the nation itself—though one that obviously does not apply to most of Israel's non-Jewish citizens.[12] As I have argued throughout, it is important to analyze religion in contextual action rather than canonical isolation. Just as the sacred may undergo secularization, so may the secular undergo sacralization. One way of defining religion is in terms of what it does rather than what it is. Any set of deeply held commitments that brings a society together may be defined as a sacred civil religion even if it lacks conventional religious doctrine or rituals. As in the cases of Sweden and Turkey and to a developing degree in Poland, not to mention China, Israel is not the only society with a civil religion that is widely galvanizing even among the nonreligious.

The struggle over this sacred land continues as various national templates float above it.[13] Recent Muslim-Christian violence over a holy site claimed by both faiths in the city of Nazareth indicates that Jews are not always involved. Still, from a political perspective, Israel has been dominantly Jewish turf. As pressure for a separate Palestinian state mounts and receives quiet and unofficial support from the United States, one can only wonder what the new millennium will bring. The question becomes especially chilling during periods such as the fall of 2000 when the latest intifada and its violent repercussions took more than three hundred lives.

India: Its Splendor and Its Violence

How long does it take to destroy an almost 450–year-old Muslim mosque? Only one day if you have the labor of more than two hundred thousand Hindu *kar sevaks* (holy volunteers). At least that was the case on December 6, 1992, in the north-central Indian city of Ayodhya, when followers of the Hindu nationalist Bharatiya Janata Party (BJP) broke ranks from a demonstration protesting the location of the Babri masjid on what many Hindus considered the exact birthplace of their revered god, Rama. The mob razed the structure stone by stone, leaving only a pile of rubble at day's end. The incident triggered another round in the communal religious violence that has become a tragic trademark of India. The resulting riots in cities like Bombay ultimately left some seventeen hundred dead and almost six thousand injured.

Why? How can one account for such civil strife in a country often described as the world's largest successful democracy since its independence from Britain in 1947? A resolute demographic determinist might argue that size and density alone are the problem. After all, India now claims roughly a sixth of the world's population and not long into the twenty-first century will overtake China as the globe's most populous country. However, China's own relatively low level of civil strife rebuts the population factor, as we shall see in the next chapter. Clearly there are other cancers gnawing at India's simultaneously new and ancient corpus.

There is a sense in India that all of its history leads to Ayodhya. In order to understand the orgies of destruction and violence that have occurred in Ayodhya and elsewhere, we need to appreciate the religious and political factors involved and how their trajectories converge. Like a social scientific detective, we need first to inspect the scene of such crimes before we go on to consider some of the most likely suspects.

India's visitors often find the country a bewildering conundrum—both a stimulant and a depressant, sensuously seductive in its sounds, tastes, and colors but gloweringly formidable in its poverty, pollution, and alien uniqueness of manners and custom. There is no denying its splendor, its violence, or its singularity. Indeed, these sometimes coalesce in a single image—for example, the bright vermilion sari worn by a woman picking through the trash on one of Calcutta's mountains of garbage with her naked children searching nearby. India is unique in so many ways, including its temporal status as the world's only major nation that is on the half-hour relative to the rest—for example, not just ten hours ahead of New York but ten and a half hours. Until just a few years ago, India was also the one remaining great civilization that had not yet been invaded by McDonald's. Alas, in India's transition from a closed socialism to a more open capitalism, McDonald's has arrived with its lamb-based Maharajah Macs designed to offend neither the cow-revering Hindus nor the pork-abstaining Muslims.

India has been more a culture quilt than a tightly bound nation for most of its history.[14] In one sense it was waiting to be conquered because it was already divided, and its political unity is the bittersweet legacy of two outside incursions—first, a dynasty of Muslim Mogul emperors who ruled in the north from the early sixteenth to the late eighteenth century, and second, the British East India Company and then the British government itself that ruled until 1947. Even independence combined the bitter with the sweet. Under the leadership of Mohandas Gandhi, achieving freedom from the British climaxed one of the greatest social movements in world history and the fulfillment of a democratic dream. But it also involved a nightmare of Hindu-Muslim violence. As I described in my earlier visit to Pakistan, the negotiations for independence had finally yielded not one but two new nations—the gigantic, polycultural but predominantly Hindu India, and the Muslim state of a combined West and East Pakistan (the latter becoming a third independent state, Bangladesh, in 1971). When independence was originally realized in August 1947, Hindus and Muslims alike were stranded away from their new homelands; violence ran amok during the desperate migra-tions across the borders. In the thirty years or so that followed, India's government shimmered as a political exemplar. But beginning in the 1980s the country's past began to catch up with its present, and its reli-gious conflict began to infect its politics. Ayodhya is not the only recent case of religious violence.

Introducing Hinduism(s) and India's Religious Profusion

Who is a Hindu? The answer is surprisingly varied. According to perhaps the oldest criterion, a Hindu is anyone who resides in or is descended from the great Indus River valley that now—ironically enough—runs down the center of Muslim Pakistan from the mountains of Kashmir in the north to just south of the port of Karachi. Almost four thousand years ago, this was where the religion first took root in a mix of traditional and imported cultures brought by Aryan migrants from the Mediterranean basin to the northwest. The resulting Vedic texts were epic hymns that provided the first evidence of a faith.

The precise influences here remain a matter of some dispute.[15] Some Indians now argue that the very notion of an Aryan origin to Hinduism was a nineteenth-century German fiction designed to posit a white an-cestral alternative to Judaism. But, of course, this argument is as moti-vated by an ethnic and political agenda as the one it criticizes. Another contested German account subject to current dispute comes from Max Weber, who indulged his sociological license to suggest that the leading figures in translating the Vedas into a religion were high status Brah-mans who assumed priestly functions and developed a social ethic that reinforced their standing.[16] Their name came from another set of early texts called the "Brahmanas"; in fact, early Hinduism was generally known as Brahmanism.

Unlike Christianity, Judaism, Islam, and Buddhism, Hinduism has no single founding figure whose charismatic stature and exploits pro-vide a focal point of the faith. Its origins sometimes appear to lie just beyond a gulf separating mere mortals from the gods who live, love, battle, scheme, and cavort throughout the poetic sagas that function for Hin-dus much as mythology did for the ancient Greeks.

But most Hindus select only a few gods and goddesses for special veneration. Hindu practice resembles the Judaism we encountered ear-lier in this chapter in that what one believes is far less important than what one does.[17] Unlike Judaism, Christianity, and Islam, Hinduism has no single doctrinal text. While this provides wide latitude and consider-able freedom, it also means that there is even less of a common core. The stories of the Hindu gods are more a source of compelling tales than strict theological tenets.

If many of Hinduism's epic sagas have found their way into the national popular culture, Hinduism's devotional rounds are highly localized. Its often elaborate rituals, or *pujas*, in search of purity, virtue, and good fortune frequently revolve around food and are primarily based in the home—often with visits from the local priest. Temples are maintained in the name of a particular god, and they range from alleyway shanties to elaborate multibuilding complexes covered with depictions of the gods either in brightly colored paintings or intricately carved reliefs. But again in contrast to other world religions, the temples do not serve as the basis for collective worship or congregational action. It is said that there is nothing religious that two Hindus do together that cannot be done as well by one Hindu practicing alone.

While most Hindus are aware that their particular gods and goddesses represent only a small corner of the larger patchwork, few would find it meaningful or possible to attempt a complete mapping of the larger pantheon. But Hindu experts are quick to protest against any implication of polytheism, insisting that all of the different gods and goddesses are but various manifestations of a single godhead with wondrously diverse dimensions. From this traditional Brahmanic vantage point, there are three major gods linked in a divine division of labor: Brahma the creator, Vishnu the preserver, and Shiva presiding over the cycle of destruction and reproduction. Each can also take various forms and incarnations, so that both the noble Krishna and the swashbuckling Rama (of Ayodhya) are only two of the many avatars of Vishnu, and there is a goddess who can assume various forms, whether as the wife of any of the aforementioned gods or as the destructive demon known as Durga or as the fiercely portrayed Kali. All of these figures have various consorts and associates, including Rama's furry companion, the impish monkey god Hanuman.

For several years in the 1980s virtually all of India—not just Hindus—came to a halt on Sunday mornings to watch the nationally televised serial of Hinduism's most popular narrative, the *Ramayana*, concerning Rama's tumultuous career. Or consider India's universally beloved god of good fortune, Ganesh, the minor deity with the body of a man but the head of an elephant. According to at least one account, Ganesh's father—the great God of destruction and reproduction, Shiva—was away during the years when the boy grew into adolescence, and when the father returned to find his wife in the presence of such a handsome young man, the jealous father quickly lopped off his head with a sword. Upon learning the truth, he looked frantically for the closest replacement head available and found it on a nearby elephant.

All of this amounts to a somewhat idealized conception of Hinduism for the textbooks. But once again there is a difference between canon and context. In addition to the gap between popular and elite religion, there are growing numbers for whom Hinduism is more of a cultural legacy than a set of binding commitments and practices. Hindu ritual remains strong in the villages of rural India and among many at both the bottom and the top of the social hierarchy. However, it has atrophied in more urban settings and among the middle class, who are exposed to Western and secular influences—though these ranks do include substantial numbers devoted to chic gurus, or *babas*, whose cults attest to their astonishing powers.[18]

In much of this, Hinduism resembles other religious traditions. But there is another aspect in which it differs strikingly. So far I have only alluded to Hinduism's most sociologically compelling component—its vaunted caste system. As the device by which Max Weber's early Brahmans were alleged to have secured their status, its logic is deceptively straightforward as an elegant theodicy explaining both good fortune and bad. Thus, we are all born into a continuing cycle of rebirths, or reincarnation (samsara), that reflects our fulfillment of the laws of ethical virtue (dharma) in previous lives. Our position at any given point reflects a destiny determined by our past actions—our karma. Just as those at the top of the caste system deserve their status on the basis of past merit, those at the bottom are equally deserving because of past demerits. However, the ultimate goal is release from the cycle, or *moksha*, so that even those at the top have a further objective, just as those at the bottom are never without hope.

Being a Hindu and being a member of a particular Hindu caste is a matter of birth, not of choice or individual action. In yet another form of cultural religion, caste identity holds even for lapsed and fully secularized Hindus. The reality of caste is socially enforced even if personally denied, and there is no mobility to be achieved in one's lifetime no matter how virtuous. Just as caste is indelibly ascribed at birth, it is released only by death. Moreover, caste involves far more than religious status. Not only does each caste have its own principal social role, or *varna*, but also its own path of virtue. Caste envelops one's entire life, from one's occupational destiny to one's arranged marriage. Just as there is a division of labor for the gods, the caste system provides one for lesser mortals.

Classically, there are four principal caste groupings, but each of these includes various names, representations, and local subgroups, or *jatis*. The highest status is accorded to the Brahmans in keeping with their traditional priestly roles of administering and interpreting the very religion that so esteems them. Yet Brahmans are not alone among the blessed. Other castes also rank among the "twice born," where the male's biological birth is followed by a sacred rebirth into adolescence when he is allowed to wear the "sacred thread" of veneration across his body from the shoulder to the hip as a symbol of his high cosmic rank.

According to classical conceptions, the twice born comprise the Brahmans or priests, the Ksahtrias who are warriors or rulers, and the Vaisyas who are the farmers and merchants. But taken together, these three comprise no more than a third of the population. There is also a large group of "once-born" Sudras whose destiny it is to serve the twice born.

Finally, almost half the population falls outside the caste ranks into that infamous social category known variously as "untouchables," "*dalits*" (the oppressed), "harijans" (Gandhi's term for the real children of God), and "scheduled castes" (originally the British phrase for those "scheduled" for reserved government jobs as a kind of early affirmative action program). These are the polluted and the polluting who are literally out-castes and yet imprisoned within the caste system. For some very strict high castes, the untouchables are also unseeables, since even visual contact can be contaminating. To the untouchables falls the lot of cleaning and sweeping, dealing with human waste, and handling leather goods as the defiling product of a fallen sacred cow.

Again I have provided a textbook summary, and such canonical conceptions can be at odds with contextualized realities. While the logic of caste and its basic distinctions apply generally everywhere, the details are intricate and varied. Outsiders tend to think of caste as a single, societal-wide system that operates the same throughout India—and, indeed, the ruling British added a substantial measure of systematization in order to use caste as an administrative network. But as with other aspects of Hinduism, particular caste definitions and boundaries remain highly localized, and caste relations vary from region to region—even village to village. This is one reason why in practice there are almost as many castes as gods. It is also why some people can "pass" upward and escape their caste identity, although this is rare and risky and requires leaving their home regions where their original caste markers and mannerisms are permanent and unmistakable.

While matrimonial ads in the personal columns of local newspapers will often state "caste no problem," a variety of euphemistic codes indicate a continuing status concern. These include the desirability of "convent education" (or private schooling), women with "good knife and fork skills" (indicating the more Westernized manners of the elite), "fair complexion" (since higher castes are generally lighter in color), and "decent marriage" (meaning a substantial dowry). "Dowry murders," when a bride is married only for money and later killed, are a rising crime category. Some families sell even prepubescent daughters into marriage—often to wealthy Middle Easterners. As this suggests, gender in India (as elsewhere) has qualities of a caste distinction in its own right. Both poverty and illiteracy are considerably higher among women than men, and the lot of the widow helps one understand the once common custom of suttee, whereby the wife joins her husband on his funeral pyre.

While individuals seldom attempt to move from one caste into another, castes themselves do jockey for collective enhancement and mobility. Over time many have undergone "Sanskritization," or the process of adopting the traditional Sanskrit language and culture of the traditional Brahmans.[19] There is often a discrepancy between a caste's public position and its private self-conception. Many low castes and groups of untouchables have private "origin tales" that involve falls from grace through the perfidy of others. There are even groups whom untouchables won't speak to; for example, the Kadhars of India's poorest state, Bihar, are so low they were not even "scheduled" for the compensatory considerations of the reservations program that began with the British.

There is now considerable debate whether the caste system remains (or was ever) as strictly static or hierarchical as it has sometimes been portrayed with such pernicious majesty.[20] The question of caste's relation to class and occupation is also complex. Westerners generally think of Brahmans as invariably rich and untouchables as inevitably poor. While this pattern is by far the most common, the reverse also occurs—especially in urban areas and more Westernized occupational settings. Caste no longer dictates occupation ruthlessly. Insofar as caste remains hierarchical, this is increasingly because it is loosely tied to the stake of secular rank distinctions that holds it up like a sagging plant.

Meanwhile, not all of India is Hindu, and the question of just who is a Hindu deserves more attention. Earlier I began with a geographical and historical answer in terms of the descendants of the Indus River basin. The Indian government's definition is not much different. According to the Indian census, anyone is a Hindu who is a member of any religious group that is indigenous to India. This excludes India's almost one hundred million Muslims, plus some eighteen million Christians.

Significantly, Muslims constituted around 40 percent of the population prior to independence and the partitioning of Pakistan, but even at their current reduced proportion, they make India the third largest Muslim nation in the world. Roughly half of India's Muslims fall below its poverty line, compared to a third of the Hindus. But India's Muslims— like its Hindus—are a varied community and have never constituted a single united political constituency or "vote bank" even under crisis conditions.

If official Hinduism excludes Muslims and Christians, it includes three other religions that would prefer to be regarded separately even though they did emerge out of Hinduism. It is not surprising that Hinduism has been so fertile in producing other faiths. If one were to rank religions on a scale of pure randy lustfulness, Hinduism would soar off the chart. As part of its celebration of the life force, its mythology sometimes approaches the pornographic. Phallic symbols abound in its iconography, and it is not uncommon for paintings and temple carvings to feature a male with full erection and hands clasped over the melonlike breasts of a nubile female—both of whose smiling faces seem on the verge of lewd winks. And, of course, where sex emerges, fertility is apt to follow.

Jainism and Buddhism were born in the sixth century B.C.E., partly in reaction to Hinduism's earthiness, as well as to its gods and castes. This was a time when Hinduism was undergoing formalization and codification under the influence of a new set of texts, the Upanishads. It was also a period of general uneasiness and ferment that produced myriad leaders of change and opposition, including the Jain founder, Mahavira, and Buddhism's founder, Gautama Buddha.

The Jains have a double distinction as one of the world's few explicitly atheistic religions and perhaps its most severely ascetic faith. It is a religion of extraordinary self-discipline and self-renunciation. Its expectations of chastity, nonmaterialism, and mental discipline through yoga are legendary. Its objectives include not only the self-improvement of the practitioner but the protection of nature and its innocent minutia so vulnerable around us. Monks wear masks to avoid inhaling amoebas when breathing; they also carry brooms for sweeping the path ahead of them to avoid stepping on insects and other organisms. The principal difference between Jainism's two amicable divisions concerns whether monks need to go naked to protect creatures from being crushed in the folds of clothing. Given such onerous restrictions, it is scarcely surprising that the faith has only some four million adherents and remains largely restricted to India.

Buddhism's different story is the primary text for the next chapter. Although Buddhism broke with Hinduism only slightly after the Jains, it commended a less demanding "middle way." Buddhism now accounts for fewer than six million Indians, but we shall follow its widespread growth to the east in countries such as Thailand, China, and Japan.

A last religion to emerge out of Hinduism is Sikhism in the early sixteenth century, with Islam as an assisting midwife. Like the Jains and the Buddhists, the Sikhs had strong objections to the Hindu caste system and what was perceived as its pantheistic idolatry. Not an otherworldly religion, much of its character was shaped by persecution at the hands of the sixteenth-century Muslim Moguls. It was at this point that the Sikh leader Gobind Singh molded the faith into a militant force. He gave his five closest aides his own name of Singh (lion), and he set forth the law of the five k's, that Sikh males would henceforth follow.[21] These included beards and unshorn hair (*kesh*) gathered in a turban with a steel comb (*khanga*), a warrior's shorts (*kucha*), a steel bangle on the right wrist (*kara*), and an omnipresent sword (*kirpan*). These identifiers continue in one form or another, as does the original asceticism that is now largely channeled into the pursuit of individual honor, occupational achievement, and political power. Today nineteen million Sikhs account for about 2 percent of the country's population. Concentrated largely in the north and specifically in the northwest area known as the Punjab, Sikhs are occupationally concentrated in farming, the military, and transportation. As we shall see shortly, a recent effort by Sikh extremists to secure an independent state of Khalistan produced another of India's tragic episodes of religio-political violence, which took the life of one of India's most prominent political leaders in 1984.

Buddhism, Jainism, and Sikhism all involved reactions against Hinduism, but none were able to completely sever ties with it. This was partly Hinduism's own doing. In what some might see as a co-opting embrace, many Hindus consider Buddha a member of the Hindu pantheon as an avatar of the god Vishnu. Caste itself continues to resonate within many of these religious communities despite their formal preferences otherwise. Caste even occurs in some Muslim communities, and there is a strange reciprocity in rates of polygyny, which may actually be higher in some Hindu communities than among Muslims for whom multiple wives are religiously legitimate.

Ruling India: The Road to Independence and the Present
One question I asked people all over the world was what makes their country a whole greater than just the sum of its parts. In India I soon began to ask whether such a whole existed and if it was likely to endure. The yeas just barely outweighed the nays on both counts. Although native insiders tended to be more optimistic than outside observers, insider pessimism is growing among Indian politicians, religious leaders, journalists, and intellectuals, many of whom recall Jawaharlal Nehru's frequent reference to India's "fissiparous tendencies." As many point out, it is one thing to have confidence in India's endurance as a "civilization" but quite another to predict its persistence as a nation. Even the Indian national anthem refers more to the land than to the state. The anthem's rarefied language is intelligible to only a fraction of the populace, and it ends on a single note in a minor key that—to a Western ear—seems to need resolution into a major chord. So far the resolution has never materialized, musically or politically.

Prior to the mid-nineteenth century there was little sense of a unified India. The South Asian subcontinent was instead a mixed bag of religious, cultural, ecological, economic, and political diversities presided over by a varied lot of local maharajas and outside powers. The first great Indian ruler was the Buddhist convert Ashoka in the third century B.C.E. A series of lesser Hindu domains followed, and it was not until 1526 that anything resembling an ordered political empire materialized—and this involved an almost three hundred-year succession of Muslim Moguls, beginning with the invading Babur and progressing through Akbar to the end of the line in Aurangzeb.

Muslims had come to India before, beginning as early as the seventh century. This time, however, they came in force and to stay. Not surprisingly, most Hindus now recall the period as a dark patch in Indian history. However, not all of the Moguls were autocratic. Some like Akbar actually incorporated Hindus into their regimes and sought an intellectual synthesis between Islam and Hinduism—an idea that still has some abstract appeal for combining Hinduism's nature-centered pantheon with Islam's ascetic activism on behalf of humanity's ethical lot in the world. Ironically, the Moguls not only gave India its first sense of a cohesive society but also left a legacy that includes many of today's most popular tourist attractions—elaborate and exquisite monuments, forts, and palaces, including the majestic Taj Mahal in Agra, south of Delhi.

By the time the Mogul dynasty had run its course, another outside force was making its mark. Western traders were no strangers to India. The Portuguese had established a colony on the southwest coast in Goa as early as 1510, but British traders were to have the greatest impact, especially with the arrival of the East India Company in 1600. Over the next 250 years, this long arm of the British Empire consolidated its position through a mixture of economic blandishments and coercive measures with British power at its side. Finally, after a series of insurrections, the British government took full control of both the trading company and the subcontinent in 1858. The fabled and infamous British Raj was to remain in command for almost another hundred years.

A full evaluation of the British occupation of India is beyond me here. It is even hard to assess Britain's own ledger sheet, since recent economic assessments suggest that the benefits of the empire may not have exceeded its costs. But then India also experienced benefits and costs. The British rallied a loosely bound society into a full-fledged nation, providing a new infrastructure of communication, transportation, higher education, and government administration and bureaucracy, much of which remains today. The British built the current capital, New Delhi, just south of (old) Delhi in the 1930s, and its graceful government buildings continue to serve the country well. Much of downtown Bombay and especially Calcutta have a stately colonial influence, though most of the latter's buildings now reflect the ravages of a tropical climate and accumulated disrepair, and Bombay's name has officially, if not collo-quially, reverted back to the indigenous Mumbai.

The English language became the lingua franca of the subcontinent's elites, and this also continues today. Even though less than 3 percent of the population speaks English, it is the one language spoken and read by upper castes and classes across the country and the one common sec-ondary language in the schools—although India's adult literacy rate is still below 50 percent. As for the country's thirteen major indigenous languages, they are all highly regionalized, and only Hindi in the north-west accounts for as much as 30 percent of the country's population while others such as Urdu, Bengali, and Tamil claim 10 percent or less.

With British power and language came English culture. While it is not hard to find summary judgments of the Raj's heavy-handed admin-istration and arrogant exploitation, assessments of its seeping cultural influence are more ambivalent. This is particularly true of the hotly de-bated legacy of Western secularism and the British response to Hindu-ism itself. British insensitivities were legion and legendary, and yet it was the British who first banned suttee and who first developed the in-novative policy of reserving government jobs for untouchables, even as the British also gave caste distinctions new and broader significance as a way of keeping track of their subjects.

The ultimate assessment of the British presence came from the In-dians themselves. Undercurrents of resistance were apparent from the outset, and they erupted periodically. The British government's take-over from the private East India Company was occasioned by an 1857 mutiny in the army, where Indian enlisted men served under British officers. The triggering incident remains unclear, though rumors had spread that bullets were coated both in pigs' fat and beef grease, which would be a profanation to Muslims and Hindus respectively. Of seventy-four battalions, forty-seven mutinied, twenty were disarmed, and only seven (largely Sikh) units remained loyal and in order. The British took massive if unofficial revenge. But they also began to democratize the military and the civil service. Still, their subjects continued to chafe, and temperatures continued to rise.

In 1915 a very slight forty-seven-year-old came home to India from South Africa where he had put into practice a legal education received in England some twenty years earlier. The son of a successful tradesman and member of a Vaisya caste—the lowest group among the "twice born"—the man was Mohandas Gandhi, or Mahatma (great soul), as he was soon to become known for leading the world's first and most suc-cessful nonviolent movement. Working with the Congress Party that had been formed in 1886, his first large action against the government ended in tragedy in the city of Amritsar in 1919. Thousands gathered in a space with only one narrow exit for what was to be a silent symbol of protest. But when some grew restless and unruly, British soldiers opened fire and killed or wounded more than fifteen hundred. This only cemented Gandhi's nonviolent resolve (satyagraha). For almost forty years, this tiny giant in a self-woven *doti*, or loincloth, lived a life of spartan asceticism and sexual abstinence as he led an unrelenting pursuit of independence by brilliantly deploying fasts, strikes, and his own radiating personal integrity. The cause was finally rewarded in 1947. Following World War II, Britain decided to cut its economic and geopolitical losses and grant India the freedom and autonomy that had been so long in coming.[22]

But what kind of India was to emerge? The first and most important choice was whether a separate Muslim state would be partitioned off. The idea was initially broached by Mohammed Ali Jinnah, the Oxford-educated and essentially secular Muslim leader who raised it as a possible bargaining chip for negotiations. Other principal figures in the negotiations—including the British representative, Lord Mountbatten; the great untouchable intellectual B. R. Ambedkar; the Cambridge-educated secular Hindu Jawaharlal Nehru; and Gandhi himself—opposed the idea. Even Jinnah was privately cool to it, but once he had proposed it to his party, the Muslim League, and within the Muslim community, the idea took on a life of its own, and Jinnah could not back down.[23] This ailing but stiffly erect man over six feet tall but less than ninety pounds finally carried the day reluctantly on behalf of partition. As noted earlier, East Pakistan (now Bangladesh) and West Pakistan (now simply Pakistan) were granted separate national status. But with partition came tragedy. Close to half a million lives were taken in the savage and seemingly senseless conflict between two armies of refugees relocating to their new homelands.

As a chilling punctuation to the violence, Gandhi himself was assassinated on January 30, 1948—not by a Muslim but by a Hindu whose co-conspirators believed that Hinduism had been betrayed as Gandhi reached out to India as a whole. The assassin Godse was hanged, but every year the Godse family commemorates the event and reaffirms their unchanged position. The irony that Gandhi was killed by a fellow Hindu rather than a Muslim was compounded because, of the four statesmen deciding India's fate, Gandhi was by far the most religiously committed, only to be killed by one who found his faith wanting.

Meanwhile, there were other questions to be resolved concerning the new Indian state, and Nehru assumed the position of primary leader of both the nation and its dominant Congress Party. The country adopted a parliamentary system much like the Britain's. But unlike Britain, India was to have a constitution, which was finally adopted in 1950 after three years of negotiation and writing. The constitution's religious clauses had a double-edged quality. On the one hand, they reflected the U.S. Constitution in providing for a neutral state that would respect the "freedom of religion" in all of its diversity. On the other hand, there were also measures that made some religious exceptions. The constitution permitted the continuance of the British "reservations" policy of setting aside government jobs for untouchables and "other backward classes"; it regulated Hindu temple administration to prevent sacred prostitution and to allow greater access on the part of lower castes; and it retained the ban on the practice of suttee. In return for these reformist measures, many Hindus sought freedom and affirmation for more traditional practices concerning the treatment of women and of cattle. However, Nehru finessed the former on early feminist grounds, and he justified his opposition to a Cattle Preservation Bill as consistent with the Congress Party's position since the 1880s that this was a purely religious issue not appropriate for secular legislation.

But if Hindu privileges were rebuffed, Muslim prerogatives were endorsed. Largely as a political gesture toward a minority Muslim community ravaged by partition, Nehru and his associates permitted the continuance of a Muslim Personal Law that allowed Muslims to be bound by their own Sharia in such matters as marriage, divorce, and inheritance rather than be subjected to a single state code that would apply equally to all citizens regardless of religion. This later became a sty in the eye of traditional higher-caste Hindus who saw the Muslims receiving special dispensations denied Hindus. Many Hindus saw themselves as singled out for reformist meddling. Although Article 44 recommended further work toward a uniform civil code that would apply to all religions in the indefinite future, this provided little solace to the Hindus.

Nor did it appease the secularist Ambedkar, for whom such a uniform code was essential to the new state. He not only resigned from the Congress Party but from Hinduism. After publicly considering the religious alternatives, Ambedkar led his followers to Buddhism. In fact, a significant fraction of India's Muslims, Christians, and Buddhists are converts from low-caste and untouchable Hinduism. This is another factor that rankles Hindu traditionalists, who see their closed cosmic system ripped open.

Any government that favors freedom of religion but then initiates religious reforms and exceptions would certainly seem inconsistent. At the time, commentators on the enacted Indian Constitution were aware of the problem, even though outside experts played down their concerns for the sake of cross-cultural diplomacy—what the philosopher Charles Taylor later referred to in a New Delhi lecture as "obligatory hypocrisy."[24] India's constitutional treatment of religion suggested a fundamental

problem in the womb of the new state. The good news is that the gesta-
tion period was more than thirty years. The bad news is that when it
ended, violence was very much in attendance.

Reapproaching Ayodhya and India's Future

By 1980 the proudly independent democracy of India was in the
hands of a second generation of leaders. Jawaharlal Nehru had died, and
the mantle of party and national leadership had fallen to his daughter,
Indira Gandhi. But troubles once deferred had begun to resurface. There
was still no resolution to the dispute over Kashmir, the area in the north
jointly controlled by China (15 percent), Pakistan (35 percent), and India's
state of "Jammu-Kashmir" (50 percent), where most of the conflict has
been focused. At the time of independence and partition, it was agreed
that negotiations would occur later to adjudicate the conflicting claims
once and for all. But the border between these areas has been policed by
Indian and Pakistani troops for fifty years, and the region has experienced the equivalent of five wars, two full scale.

Kashmir was only one of several parts of India where movements
threatened secession. Virtually every corner of the society was being
nibbled on from the inside. As a pointed instance, the Punjab also borders Pakistan to the southwest of Kashmir. This is the area of greatest
Sikh concentration—where a group of Sikh insurgents led by Sant (priest)
Jarnail Singh Bhindranwale pressed for an independent nation. Prime
Minister Indira Gandhi sought to head off the impasse by befriending
Bhindranwale so as to better reason with him. However, in 1984 she
sent troops into the sacred Sikh Golden Temple of Amritsar, where—
just as in 1919—tragedy leaped from the barrels of military guns. This
time the dead were Sikh militants, including Bhindranwale himself. In
light of Indira Gandhi's earlier overtures to the Sikhs, this was seen as an
act of betrayal, and she was assassinated by her own Sikh bodyguards
later that same year.

Like the murder of her unrelated namesake, the Mahatma, Indira
Gandhi's death illustrates again what can happen when a political moth
draws too close to the religious flame. She was ultimately succeeded as
prime minister by her son, Rajiv Gandhi, an engineer and commercial
pilot who never shared the family's political enthusiasm or experience.
Meanwhile, interpreters of the Sikh insurrection differ. Some portray it
as a deeply religious cause, but others see more secular wolves dressed
as sacred sheep.[25] The Sikh militancy has been at least temporarily
quashed by canny and forceful police action—leading some to suspect
that forceful measures are an ultimate rather than proximate answer.
Yet some rebuttal is provided by the continuing insurgent violence in
Jammu-Kashmir in the face of strong Indian military measures.

Consider also a very different case that had already been working its way toward another sort of national convulsion. In 1975 in the central India district of Indore a relatively prosperous Muslim man expelled the first of his two wives from his household following forty-three years of marriage and five children. In 1978 the wife, Shah Bano, filed a criminal complaint asking for the equivalent of $38 per month maintenance from her husband's annual income of $4,600. At this point, the husband availed himself of Muslim personal law to effect a "triple divorce" by saying "I divorce you" three times. Although he had paid $15 a month for the two years following separation, he argued that this ended his liabilities— again according to the Sharia. Normally a Muslim wife would relent, but not Shah Bano. To simplify a complicated chain of legal actions and appeals, she pursued her case to the Indian Supreme Court, insisting on her rights not just as a Muslim but also as an Indian citizen. In 1985 the court held that the husband was indeed liable according to an Indian criminal statute concerning acts that may produce vagrancy and that his wife's Muslim treatment had involved misinterpretations of both the Sharia and the Koran. Accordingly, Shah Bano was awarded a continued monthly allowance. Not surprisingly, the traditional Islamic community was furious, and the mullahs quickly began to mobilize politically. While there were some lower court precedents for the decision itself, Muslim traditionalists were especially affronted by the impertinence of a Hindu court arrogantly instructing mullahs on how to interpret the Koran.

Over the next several years the new and inexperienced prime minister, Rajiv Gandhi, took two actions that mollified conservative Muslims. First, he spearheaded a bill through Parliament that effectively reversed the Supreme Court action and restored Muslim authority in matters of divorce. Second, he buckled under another wave of traditional Muslim pressure and banned the novel *Satanic Verses* by Salman Rushdie, the Indian ex-patriot living in London whose work was perceived as so betraying and defiling of his Muslim heritage that Iran's Ayatollah Khomeini had put a price on his head.

Both of these actions met with widespread Muslim approval but were greeted contemptuously by traditional Hindus, who saw them as just more evidence that the supposed secular neutrality of the Congress Party and the Indian state was bogus. Far from being neutral, they were actually pro-Islamic. Rajiv Gandhi became quickly aware of his political miscalculation. He needed to make amends with the Hindu right, and one possibility involved the contested mosque and Rama's birthplace in Ayodhya. The dispute dated back more than a century to the late 1880s. However, in 1947 Hindus had broken into the mosque, where they placed an idol of Rama and claimed a miracle. At this point, the local judge locked up the mosque, idol and all. While a Brahman was allowed in to conduct periodic puja, all others—Hindus and Muslims alike—were denied access.

This bruise had continued to ache among Hindus. After the government's concession to the Muslims in the Shah Bano case, there were many demands for corresponding concessions, especially from those identified with "Hindutva"—a term coined in 1923 by its founder, the atheist scholar-demagogue, Vinayak Savarkar—which has become an umbrella for all sorts of right-wing Hindu nationalist groups, ranging from the Rashtriya Swayamsevak Sangh (RSS) youth brigade and the vitriolic Shiv Sena to the BJP. Under pressure from other Hindus—and, it is rumored, Rajiv Gandhi as well—a local judge ordered the gates to the Ayodyah mosque reopened in 1996, and Gandhi participated in the ceremonies.

Like his mother, Rajiv Gandhi was also assassinated. In 1991 a woman approached him in the crowd at a South Indian political rally and killed both him and herself with explosives she had wrapped around her body. She represented a group of Tamil Hindu extremists seeking to overturn Buddhist power in neighboring Sri Lanka. Here is yet another religious flame that continues to take its toll.

Meanwhile, the BJP keyed its 1992 political campaign to Rama and Ayodyah. Rama's birthplace was even more compelling as a result of the popular television series depicting his exploits. The BJP launched a massive caravan across northern India featuring the party leader in a jeep decorated as Rama's chariot. The campaign climaxed with the massive rally in Ayodhya that dissolved into the one-day destruction of the Babri masjid in 1992. While it is estimated that religious strife or communalism had already taken some seven thousand lives during the 1980s, Ayodhya unleashed another spasm of violence—mostly Hindu on Muslim in the Bombay stronghold of Hindutva.

What has happened since? Despite initial pledges and a Supreme Court order to rebuild the mosque and produce a joint Hindu-Muslim site, the matter has become entangled in the political and bureaucratic underbrush. The Supreme Court has been perhaps deliberately dilatory in hearing an appeal of the bill that overturned its Shah Bano decision. However, there is some indication that lower courts are increasingly following the Supreme Court's example in many such cases. There is even some hope that the courts can provide what Parliament cannot, namely, a uniform civil code. To the extent that such a code requires a compromise between Hindu and Muslim codes that are themselves internally contested, it is a political impossibility. But such a code may have a chance if it is interpreted less grandiosely as simply a set of minimum national standards to which all citizens are held and entitled but beyond which they may freely invoke religious customs and rituals.

Muslim-Hindu conflicts will continue to simmer and erupt throughout India. Some suggest that there are mollifying developments at work within the Muslim community. Here as elsewhere in Islam, women like Shah Bono are increasingly mobilized for change, and a new generation of cultural Muslims has filled the leadership void left by partition half a century ago when so much of the Muslim elite concentrated in Pakistan. Many seek to avoid the trap of tit-for-tat violence while pursuing now new forms of accommodation. But a still younger generation of Muslims is quicker to inflame.

Meanwhile, the march of Hindutva continues and is directed as much at secular reformers as at Muslims and adherents of other faiths. In 1990 the government accepted the recommendations of a study concerning caste and the reservations policy. The Mandal Commission had urged that an even greater number of government jobs be set aside for untouchables, a proportion that would approach 60 percent in some South Indian states. This not only further riled the Hindutva movement but provoked large and unruly demonstrations of high-caste university students who saw both their religious and economic status threatened.

The Mandal Commission's recommendations were not restricted to Untouchables. They applied more broadly to "SC/ST/OBC," or "scheduled castes, scheduled tribes, and other backward classes." The "tribes" referred to are isolated communities in remote areas of India beyond the reach of conventional categories. But the Supreme Court faulted the commission for its nonreligious interpretation of "backward classes"—an interpretation that stressed not religious status but broader cultural and economic disadvantagement. In sociological terms, this marked a shift from "ascribed to achieved" status, and it was partly a response to what Indians know as the "creamy layer" problem, that is, guaranteeing jobs to untouchables who are in fact quite well educated and economically well-off.

Partly as a result of these controversies, the BJP looms ever larger on the national political scene. A series of corruption scandals has exacted a major toll on the long-dominant Congress Party and left many wondering who will succeed leaders now in their seventies and eighties. Congress Party leadership has fallen to Rajiv Gandhi's Italian wife, Sonia Gandhi—perhaps en route to their daughter, Priyanka. But there is a pervasive sense of "regime decay."[26] National pride in this independent democratic state has corroded over the past half century. There has even been a secularization of the very concept of state secularity as an ideal that has lost its luster.

At the same time, the BJP faces problems of its own. Various regional parties have won important victories in local state elections. As the BJP has begun to play down its religious agenda to reach out to a larger constituency with a broader agenda, there is an emerging rift between the BJP and the more extreme wings of the Hindutva movement. Some of the BJP's local parliamentary candidates now rarely even mention religion.

Still, the BJP overall is retaining its religious stamp, and the issue of Hinduism in politics and the Indian state is undergoing reassessment even from professedly secular Hindu intellectuals and social scientists. For many, secularism is an ideology imported by Western-educated leaders such as Nehru, one that runs counter to India's dominant Hindu culture. There were times during my visits when I felt the cold shoulder of avoidance as a contaminating representative of this alien imperialism and hence someone who could even be blamed for Ayodhya itself. The argument is that secularism has placed religion so much on the defensive within India that Hinduism has been forced to resort to extreme actions in reclaiming its rightful place within the country and the state. According to one eminent scholar, "The marginalization of faith . . . permits the perversion of religion," though the reverse proposition is also credible.[27]

Many Indian intellectuals agree with the BJP that it is time for the government to fall in step with Hinduism as the country's dominant culture. One hears the hope in some quarters that once Hinduism is restored to its rightful place, Hindutva will recede. Many assert that India's historical Hinduism was once a great and benign faith with a surpassing tolerance for other religions. One scholar points out that India's religion suffers from a double bind in that it experiences the worst of religion without being able to draw upon the best, though here it might be added that the government has its own double bind in that it is charged both with not being religious enough and being too religious.[28] Some contend that a national government can only be successful when it mirrors the surrounding culture instead of countering it, although others concur with a major theme of this book that the state must set the rules for cultural conflict and assure an equitable framework for religious diversity.

Certainly advocates of a secular state remain. Without disputing the right or even the wisdom of a flourishing Hinduism (or any other religion) in the society at large, a number of public figures have rallied to the defense of the Indian state as constitutionally chartered in 1950.[29] Such a state is intended as a neutral referee in the struggle of religion against nonreligion as well as in the conflicts within and between religious communities themselves.

It can even be argued that some of the state's alleged partisan meddling in religious matters—whether Hindu or Muslim—is simply a neutral effort to guarantee the basic civil rights of the citizenry.[30] Just as
Shah Bano had a civil right to a more generous divorce settlement, so do
Hindu untouchables have a civil right to improved employment. But
there is a catch-22 involved. The Indian Constitution does not include a
codified system of civil rights that has clear priority over competing religious claims; this is largely because competing religious claims have
made it virtually impossible to agree on what such civil rights should
entail. While any effort to specify a fully comprehensive code that would
adjudicate Hindu versus non-Hindu traditions is doomed, it remains
possible that a consensus might develop around a few basic principles
redolent of our own "life, liberty, and the pursuit of happiness." Beyond
these any religion could follow its own customs.

In all of this, perhaps the most pungent question came recently from
India's President R. D. Narayanon—the first Untouchable to hold this
largely ceremonial position. On the eve of a BJP move to open up the
constitution for amendments, this old Congress Party veteran asked,
"Is it the constitution that has failed us, or have we failed the
constitution?"

But semantics here can be confusing. In 1976, almost as a last gasp,
India's independence leaders amended the constitution to refer to a "Secular Democratic Republic." This was widely interpreted to signify secularism as official state policy. Yet there are subtle differences between
secularism as an explicit ideology of nonreligion, secularity as a policy
of neutrality concerning religion, and secularization as a historical process by which religion loses its sacred claims and urgency, sometimes to
be replaced by new forms of the sacred and countervailing processes of
sacralization. The ideology of secularism may characterize politicians
but rarely an entire society. Secularity may well apply—and apply well—
to the state but not to whole societies. Secularization characterizes all
societies in all of their cultural dimensions, religious and nonreligious,
but it never reaches the point of actual religious demise.

Finally, a distinguished Indian historian has taken keen exception
to the new revisionist portrayal of Hinduism as a once monolithic and
sweetly beneficent religion.[31] This image qualifies as another of the constructed fictions that underlie every nation, for every country is an "imagined community" to some degree.[32] Each is built as much out of articles
of faith as bricks and mortar.

Historically, Hinduism has long been a pluralistic patchwork of diverse devotees and divided castes. The internal variation among Sikhs,
Muslims, and most especially Hindus is a major reason why the country
has not been drawn into one massive communal war. Hinduism has

known both tolerance and intolerance. Though lacking an activist pros-elytizing impulse or the dominant leadership and organizational coher-ence required for such a task, it is the one major world religion that has not sought to conquer others. Insofar as Hinduism can be found in places such as Nepal, Indonesia's Bali, or the United States, this has been more a function of migration than conquest.

Precisely because Hinduism lacks such an organizational core, how-ever, some of its adherents are vulnerable to the appeal of a never-ceasing array of religious gurus and political mobilizers who promise more im-mediate gratifications. A number of my informants described friends in the leadership of Hindutva and the BJP as basically secular men whose mission is more political than religious. While it would be too strong to suggest that Hinduism has been hijacked by Hindutva, this is a possibil-ity that always lurks when power is at stake, especially when an entire national government seems to hang in the balance.

On the first anniversary of the destruction of the Ayodhya mosque, I happened to be leaving India, and on my taxi ride to the airport, we went under a bridge that carried a large banner reading: "Forget the BJP. The People's Movement for Secularism." Since then, however, the BJP has been anything but forgotten. In 1996 it finally attained sufficient parliamentary power to put its own prime minister—Atal Behari Vajpayee, a longtime veteran member of Indian politics—in office at the head of a somewhat precarious multiparty coalition. The coalition escalated Hindu-Muslim conflict to a larger plane with far greater stakes. The gov-ernment conducted nuclear weapons tests that sent a shiver around the world, not to mention through its neighboring Muslim rival, Pakistan, which has a nuclear capacity of its own. As more than one observer has noted, the world now has both "Hindu" and "Muslim" nuclear weapons in addition to the long-standing "Christian" and "atheist" storehouses in the United States and Russia. This is hardly a comforting religious parity.

A nuclear standoff across a shared border is especially discomfiting in light of escalating tensions and military engagements in Kashmir. It remains difficult for India to rebut Pakistan's moral claim to the entire area on the basis of a common Muslim religion, though there is now considerable sentiment among Kashmiris on behalf of independence rather than affiliation with either India or Pakistan. This is a religious and political stalemate that may well require outside pressure and adju-dication.

Yet outside pressure does not always work. The West has recently been drawn into India's religious conflict in still another way. Several Indian states—notably Orissa and Mohandas Gandhi's own Gujarat—have been the sites of attacks on poor Christian churches and communities. Insofar as Christian missionaries and evangelicals have proselytized disproportionately among the poor scheduled castes and tribes, some Hindus see them as interfering with the cosmic social order. Nor has the BJP government been quick to condemn the attacks or seek out the perpetrators. But the U.S. Congress's recent passage of legislation authorizing sanctions when religious rights are denied around the world is unlikely to have a major effect. The bill was largely intended to make places like India, Russia, and China safe for proselytizing Christians. Perhaps the best that can be hoped is that it does not backfire.

Conclusion

Time-honored struggles continue in both of these timeless societies. India shares with Israel a contested religious pluralism whose short-run conflicts carry enormous long-range consequences. Disputed sacred turf does indeed become a "mindfield" with explosive potential. As different as both countries are, they share a problematic future where many more lives are destined to be lost in the name of religions intended to be life enriching.

No two countries better illustrate the seductions and the subversions inherent in religion's struggle for power. In each setting, one finds more of an uneasy religious diversity than the tolerant principles of religious pluralism. In each, religious faiths and factions not only compete for political purposes but actually collide in the quest to control the state itself. While state secular neutrality is formally provided for in both Israel and India, it sometimes seems to hang by a hair. Once again, religion in politics can be valuable as well as inevitable, but a religious state is a prize whose gaudy wrapping hides a ticking bomb.

5

Tracking

Buddha

through

Thailand,

Japan, and

China

No Eastern religion has won greater respect in the West than Buddhism. As a faith based more on spiritual self-discipline than divine religious authority, it adapts relatively easily to new settings with a minimum of alien cultural baggage. Of course, Buddhism has its own canons and traditions, but as we follow it into the three countries of Thailand, Japan, and China, we will see that it is different in each case, as is its relation to power, politics, and the state. In Japan and especially China, it has come to share the religious mantle with other faiths—both sacred and secular.

Buddhism and the Middle Way

The founding figure of Buddhism, Siddhartha Gautama, was neither the first Buddha nor the last. After all, the term "buddha" originally meant "enlightened one" with no implication of a singular divinity. The Gautama family was Hindu and of the Kshatriya rather than Brahman caste. They lived in north India, where the father was a wealthy raja, and Siddhartha was a young prince raised to privilege. He was married and had a son at the time of his epiphanal revelation under the legendary "bodhi" tree concerning the ills of the world and his responsibility to them.

Responding to the example of a local guru, he is said to have left home and family in the dark of night to join the company of senior divines who could instruct him in the ways of renunciation. When the recommended pattern of extreme asceticism and self-punishment left him spiritually and ethically unfulfilled, he sought a "middle way" between indulgence and mortification and between the needs of the self and assistance of others. He is said to have begun his "preaching" in the village of Sarnath, only a few miles from Benares, Hinduism's most sacred city on its most sacred river, the Ganges. This was the area where Gautama concentrated his lifelong teaching until he died of an intestinal disorder at approximately eighty years old. His last words to his disciples are recorded as, "Decay is inherent in all compound things. Work out your own salvation with diligence."[1]

As this suggests, Buddha regarded salvation as more of a personal matter than the result of a divine or ecclesiastical intervention. Buddhism's beginnings seem anything but incandescent and perhaps even a bit shy of religion itself. But this was part of the point of the middle way. Buddha was suspicious of the supernatural and the transcendent. He rejected the notion of an omnipotent God, counseled monks to never claim magical powers, and broke sharply with the Hindu conception of a transmigratory soul that moves through successive reincarnations to a final nirvana released from the cycles of rebirth. Although Buddhists could aspire to rebirth and nirvana, these were possible in this life as well as the life beyond. Buddhism's conception of nirvana as ultimate salvation was less a realm apart than a stage of spiritual self-fulfillment.

Buddhism's commitment to the reasonable middle might be seen as both a blessing and a curse. On the one hand, it is responsible for a good deal of its recent appeal to those Westerners who are in retreat from the mystifications of Christianity but seek a commitment that will lift them out of a spiritually wanting and all-too materialist lifestyle. On the other hand, members of more otherworldly religions might wonder where the magic lies in Buddhism. It is true that, like most other faiths, Buddhism's contemporary variants have strayed from its classical origins, and many have added mysterious components despite the founder's injunctions. But it is also arguable that, because Buddhism itself renounces magic, magic tends to flourish outside the faith. Every Buddhist country hosts a flourishing marketplace of superstition ranging from astrologers and fortune-tellers to amulets and sacrifices—none of which are commonly regarded as religious.

At the same time, Buddhism has its own versions of the compelling, charismatic core that every successful religion requires. The faith offers a three-fold refuge—traditionally called the "three jewels." The first is the charismatic figure of Buddha himself, as augmented by succeeding Buddhas and Bodhisattvas—those destined for elevation to Buddha-hood who choose to remain with the needy to do good works. There are diverse scriptural accounts of the Buddha and his life in various languages, including both Pali and Sanskrit. There are also various relics of the Buddha that receive high veneration, including sacred footprints, strands of hair, and even a tooth now enshrined in Sri Lanka. Burial stupas provide domed encasements for venerated ashes. There are also the sculptured representations of Buddha in various sizes, ranging from the minute to the truly immense, and in various poses, whether reclining or seated with specific hand and arm postures representing specific religious states, including meditation, teaching, and praying. All of this is despite Buddha's own admonitions against any such images—admonitions that lasted a millennium or so before representations began to emerge in 500 C.E.

The second jewel is that of dharma, or the doctrine of the faith. Here Buddha's teachings left a deceptively simple but systematic legacy that is more ethically didactic than mythically inspirational. They include both the *dhamma*, or general ethical principles of life conduct, and the *vinaya*, or particular guidelines for monks. The former include the Four Truths concerning the reality of pain and suffering, the myopia of craving, the elimination of suffering through the elimination of craving, and the importance of following the Eight-Fold Path. This in turn involves the right view, the right thought, the right speech, the right action, the right livelihood, the right effort, the right mindfulness, and the right concentration. It is tempting for Westerners to compare these eight injunctions with the Ten Commandments of Judeo-Christianity. While the latter emphasize how one should not behave, the Buddhist path is more positive and more oriented to inner states than outward actions. Indeed, it is this emphasis on the individual's inner melding with the forces of the world that leans Buddhism toward inward spiritual equanimity rather than outward social reform. It has usually been more world renouncing than world conquering.[2]

Finally, Buddhism's third jewel involves the *sangha*, or the religious order of the original disciples and current monks. At first, the monks had only the most meager personal property—an undergarment, two robes, a belt, a knife or razor, a sewing needle, a water strainer, and perhaps most important of all, a bowl for receiving alms or daily food donations. Monks fasted from noon to the next morning, when they silently made their rounds to beg food for breakfast. But begging was really construed as an altruistic gesture to afford their followers an opportunity to "make merit" by donating provisions.

Buddhism began to change almost immediately following Buddha's death. Initially, the faith expanded and flourished in India for almost a millennium, where it was aided considerably by Emperor Ashoka, a Buddhist convert who played a legitimizing role somewhat similar to that of Constantine as a convert to Christianity some five hundred years later in the West. Ashoka ruled in northern India from 274 to 232 B.C.E. and sent emissaries to carry the religion to the island society of Ceylon (now Sri Lanka) off the subcontinent's southern tip. Still a major religious force in India in 500 C.E., Buddhism then began to ebb. Its accommodating spirit left it vulnerable to a resurgent Hinduism, which reappropriated it as simply another Hindu sect founded by yet another incarnation of Vishnu. Moreover, from a very early point, the sangha's ecclesiastical indifference created a vulnerability to new movements within the faith. Thus, Buddhism's decline was abetted by the rise of a new Tantric development whose ritual was almost anti-Buddhist in replacing asceticism with conspicuous sensuality—even sexuality.

But as Buddhism began to decline in India, it was on the rise elsewhere—spreading by cultural diffusion rather than the political conquests more characteristic of Christianity and Islam. For instance, Tantric Buddhism moved north and into Tibet where it curbed its indulgence and became known as the Diamond Vehicle, Vajrayana, or Lamaist Buddhism. It subsequently split into two branches known by their head wear as "red hats" and "yellow hats." The latter represents the more reformed Tantrism and is presided over by the Dalai Lama, now in exile from Chinese political authorities.

Meanwhile, Buddhism's two much larger branches had taken distinct forms within a century of the Buddha's passing and began to spread out of India to the east and northeast. Each form had developed a different interpretation of all three jewels. On the one hand, Theravada Buddhism is closer to the original ascetic faith of the Buddha with its focus on the great Gautama Buddha, his teachings, and the sangha with its "begging" monks. This strand of Buddhism is now dominant not only in Thailand—where I will examine it more closely—but in neighboring Myanmar (formerly Burma), parts of Cambodia, and in Sri Lanka.[3] In the latter case, the controlling Sinhalese Buddhists have been locked in a protracted civil war against insurrectionist Tamil Hindus from nearby southeast India. However, scholars now hold that Sri Lanka's Buddhism took on a more Western and aggressive emphasis after it was codified and translated by a nineteenth-century American Protestant missionary.

It is at least arguable that Sri Lanka's tragic cycle of violence might have been obviated altogether without Henry Steel Olcott's well-intended intervention.[4]

If Theravada Buddhism can be likened to Christianity's Catholicism, a second branch emerged with parallels to Protestantism. Mahayana Buddhism puts less emphasis on the monk-laity relationship and allows lay followers more hope of being favorably reborn on their own merits. At the same time, it has developed a more transcendent conception of the realm beyond death and a more richly variegated array of Buddhas and Bodissatvas who benefit this world. Mahayana Buddhism moved north and east to China, Korea, and Japan. Because of its wider embrace of the laity and less restricted sense of a spiritual elite, it depicts itself as the "greater vehicle" while referring to the more traditionally constricted practices of Theravada as the "lesser vehicle," or Hinayana. The divisions are now some two thousand years old and so geographically separated that they generate little hostility or competition.

Thailand: Buddhist State or State Buddhism?

Greetings and entrances are always hard on foreign ground. In Thailand, it is hard for a Westerner to master the graceful bow, or *wai*, with the proper position of one's peaked fingertips—whether at the forehead for royalty or monks, at the nose for the elderly and the venerated, or at the chest for peers and others. After removing my shoes before entering a temple, I would set my sturdy size thirteens aside like Gulliver's boots among the sandals of Lilliput.

Thailand's Buddhism beckoned warmly. The saffron-robed monks made their morning "begging" rounds to provide the rest of us an opportunity to accumulate virtue through our contributions. Gold seemed omnipresent, as many *wats* (temples) have glittering golden spires, and all offer other ways of *bun*, or making merit—either by buying small bits of gold foil to apply to religious icons or by purchasing live sparrows in small basket cages for the privilege of releasing them. Most of the iconic representations are small and easily grasped, but certainly not the fifty-yard-long reclining Buddha inside a vast shed, propped on his elbow with an air of supreme repose.

By most historical reckoning, Thailand was preponderantly Buddhist by the time of its first unification as the Sukhothai kingdom in the late thirteenth century. However, there have always been strong Hindu elements, and it was not until 1782 that Thailand formally shucked off formal Hindu control when King Rama I took power, consolidated the capital in Bangkok, destroyed the many phallic lingam symbols of Shiva, and proclaimed Buddhism the official religion. Although Thai Buddhism still carries Hindu "brahmanical" traces, most regard them with disdain as archaic elitism. In the meantime, Rama's monarchical progeny solidified the Buddhist state, especially King Rama IV (1851–1868) and the beloved King Rama V, or Chulalongkorn (1868–1910), who presided over sustained modernization under the threefold aegis of the king (*phramahakasat*), the state (*chat*), and religion (*sasana*).

Thailand is a country that projects a comfortable sense of cultural homogeneity with a relatively trouble-free history devoid of the scars of conquest and colonialization.[5] More than 90 percent of Thais are at least nominal Buddhists. Overall, Buddhism seems as well established in Thailand as the country's popular monarchy, though neither could be described any longer as politically dominant. The king—currently Bhumibol Adulyadej—is held in reverence as a sort of cultural symbol. But even he must show deference to the monks by performing the ritual wai before, say, a twelve-year-old novice. His deference to the secular prime minister is less ritualized but no less real.

It is also possible to overdraw Thailand's homogeneity and Buddhist hegemony. Not only do elements of Hinduism remain, but observers are now keeping a wary eye on the small but growing numbers of Muslims in the south near the border with Islamic Malaysia. Forms of Chinese magic such as fortune-telling through stick casting are evident in all but the elite Buddhist wats, and various strains of an indigenous animism in small "spirit houses" dot the country, especially among the hill tribes to the north around the Golden Triangle—an area originally named for the gold trade with the British across the border in Myanmar to the west and with the French across the border in Laos to the east but now carrying the name more cynically for an equally lucrative trade in opium.

As we shall see momentarily, Buddhism's relation to the state is also problematic. But then the state has problems of its own. Despite the Japanese invasion during World War II, Thailand is proud of having never been conquered—though the real exception may be its own military which has "conquered" the country from within many times. The current constitutional monarchy was first established in 1932 with a symbolically reigning king reined in by an elected parliament and prime minister. Since then, there have been seventeen military coups as interregnums between sixteen constitutional revisions and twenty-two prime ministers—many of whom have been ex-generals.

The country has been tossed between the reef of military rule and the riptides of political corruption. The military seems always lurking, and its last outright takeover occurred in 1991, ousting Thailand's first popularly elected prime minister since 1976 despite his considerable parliamentary majority. However, the military regime lasted little more than a year, when a virtually unprecedented round of middle-class protest demonstrations led to a restoration of democracy. But this democracy soon became an embarrassment in its own right owing to brazen vote buying and other more traditional forms of "money politics," including lavish free lunches for voters and conspicuous donations for Buddhist temple constructions, new robes for monks, and outright bribes. Not all of these blandishments are successful; some monks openly encourage their followers to vote for anyone they want and take the politicians' money to buy themselves more *nam pla*—the fermented fish sauce that is a staple in Thai cooking.

The embarrassment over corruption has been compounded by the country's recent free fall from the heights of economic prosperity to the depths of a sudden economic depression. The value of its currency dropped by almost 40 percent in the fall of 1997, a plummeting that sent shock waves throughout Asia and the world economy at large. It also had major internal consequences, including a constitutional revision that mandated a political cleanup by ad hoc outside commissions designed to curb corrupt electioneering and other practices. However, the ultimate outside commission is the military, and its hovering shadow lengthens as the possibility of yet another coup looms.

In all of this, Buddhism provides more symbolic capital than actual political clout. In the midst of the country's recent economic crisis, the supreme patriarch of the nation's central Buddhist organization called a massive prayer service in Bangkok outside of the king's palace. Adherents arrived barefoot, by *tuk-tuk* (the omnipresent three-wheeled autorickshaw), and by Mercedes. As one participant commented to a radio reporter with the realistic equanimity associated with Buddhism: "I don't think this solved the problem, but at least it cleared my mind."

Thai religion has had a seemingly inconsistent relation to the Thai government. It is one thing to describe Thailand as primarily a Buddhist culture but quite another to portray it as a Buddhist state.[6] The state exerts far more control over religion than does religion over the state. This is partly because of qualities inherent within Buddhism itself. Whereas Koranic Islam knows no distinction between religion and power, Buddhism bears the less politicized marks of its Hindu roots. Buddhism's original ideals included an arm's length relation to power and its contaminants. In contrast to Western religious traditions of activist asceticism and prophetic charisma, Buddhism is characterized more by passive mysticism and anticharismatic humility.

As noted earlier, Buddha himself issued strictures against monks claiming magical powers. Monks are also encouraged to avoid involvement with the mundane and the impure while pursuing more elevated virtue. Because Buddhism is not only otherworldly but individualistic in its praxis, it is poorly equipped for secular power struggles. Monks have little power over the laity on whom they are immediately dependent for food and resources. Certainly there is little theological basis for exacting sanctions on lay Buddhists who stray from the fold. They must contend privately with any violations of their dharma as these affect them according to the laws of karma. As one watches shaved-headed and saffron-robed monks offer the citizenry merit-making opportunities through what is ostensibly begging, it is hard to imagine the development of an independent religious power base—especially since so many monks serve only for a few months as a kind of religious rite of passage for young men.

In addition, there is a widely acknowledged distinction between the Buddhism of the temples and the "folk" Buddhism of the villages. Both stand in contrast to what might be called the "cultural Buddhism" of the urban middle class, a form of faith that is often manifest in religious indifference. These various forms of the religion inhibit the development of a system that is autonomously powerful.[7] Thai Buddhism has rarely been a source of contested cultural identity or an alternative basis of political mobilization for the alienated and disadvantaged. In offering an umbrella over the whole, it has largely thrown its lot in with the political status quo, though we shall shortly see some aggressive exceptions.

It is true that Thai Buddhism has a central ecclesiastical structure, or sangha, as created by the Sangha Act of 1902 and modified by the revolution against the monarchy in 1932 and subsequent legislation of 1941 and 1962. This national administrative structure parallels that of the civil government and, as we have seen, even has a supreme patriarch. In theory, this formal apparatus encompasses all of the country's two hundred thousand monks and thirty thousand temples—many of them quite wealthy. In practice, the results fall short of what might be envisioned. While the sangha's structure should allow religious authorities to monitor government actions at the same level, the direction of control has actually been the reverse. The government—specifically its secularly led and staffed Religious Affairs Council—has the power of appointment to religious posts, is represented in Buddhism's own councils, wields an effective veto power over religious decisions, and retains the right to intervene in internal religious disputes.

In all of this, the plum for the state is religious legitimacy, and recently legitimacy of any sort has been in scant supply. Religious sources raise the broader issue of what I shall examine in part 2 under the rubric of civil religion. Samboon Suksamran describes a generalizable dilemma here for developing nations:

> In a situation where people were divided into a secularized ruling
> elite and a largely traditional religious-oriented mass, the political

leaders were confronted with a cruel dilemma. To keep up with the socioeconomic and political changes of the modern world, and to live up to the expectations of modernized communities, certain aspects of the traditional culture had to be secularized. This is a process which is totally foreign to the traditional masses. Conflicts and tensions often escalated when social and political as well as cultural secularization were imposed on them. This inevitably led to a legitimacy crisis. . . . In these circumstances, the leaders . . . had to turn once again to religion and society's religious-based values for assistance.[8]

Still, the government purchases religious legitimacy at a bargain price. True, it provides a variety of religious stipends for temple maintenance and religious instruction in the schools. It also helps enforce the sangha's own standards for its monks and wats. But the overall deal has been struck on the government's own terms. The central sangha has been effectively left with neither much political weaponry nor a self-conscious political ideology. It has become more an appendage to the state than a source of power itself.[9] In light of recent instances of financially corrupt and sexually predatory monks, the government is now considering a national registration system with identification cards for monks. Even the supreme patriarch is specifically enjoined from speaking out directly on worldly or political matters, though he is no doubt a source of indirect counsel and support.

Recently Thailand's mainstream Buddhism has suffered its own crisis of legitimacy. This is partly a result of the widely publicized miscreance of a few prominent monks, *phras* (teachers), and abbots. In addition, Buddhism shares with every other religion a vulnerability to fission and differentiation.[10] Thailand has hosted a long-standing, if generally muted, competition for control of the sangha itself between two groups of monks—the elite Thammayut and the antiaristocratic Mahanikay. And over the last twenty-five years, Thailand has generated a wide range of movements that have outflanked and out-mobilized the sangha on every side and corroded its traditional influence.[11]

Communism was a critical issue during the early 1970s. As the Vietnam War raged nearby, the Thai military justified its own incursions into domestic politics as necessary steps to prevent a Communist takeover within Thailand itself. Buddhist movements emerged on both sides of the issue.[12] Some monks argued that killing Communists preemptively was not necessarily bad; others rallied around a particularly prominent abbot who was deposed by the government on suspicion of being both pro-Communist and homosexual. He was finally restored to his position following one of the largest demonstrations of monks in Thai history.

It is important to distinguish between rural and urban areas in virtually any account of Thailand, and this is certainly true of its religious movements. Rural wats are more involved in receiving campaign largess during political races. There is a group of Dhammajarik monks who are agents of the state in bringing Buddhism to members of the animist hill tribes in the north—originally as a bulwark against Communism. But there are also rural monks who take on environmental issues and aid in social development projects by helping to build up community infrastructures. Some of these monks are assisted by political parties and the state itself as the equivalent of government extension agents; others avoid any suspicion of co-optation by cultivating a strident political independence.

These "development" monks and movements have their urban counterparts, but here there are also other groups with different agendas. For example, the Santi Asoke is often described as a fundamentalist movement despite its predominantly middle-class support. Championing an austere lifestyle in the midst of what was then Thailand's economic engorgement, Santi Asoke also opposed some of the Brahmanic Buddhism of the national elite, not to mention the corruptions of politics-as-usual. Neither the sangha nor the state was pleased. The songha denied the group's leader, Phra Bhodirak, the traditional saffron robes (whereupon he turned to brown); the state sought to imprison him for six years, but the case continues to languish in the appeals process. Meanwhile, the movement had developed ties to the new Palang Dharma Party (PDP)— a Buddhist party led by a popular former general who had turned pacifist vegetarian and celibate and served two terms as governor of Bangkok between 1985 and 1992. The PDP finally foundered on the shoals of "money politics" when it sought to compete in national elections.

Quite apart from such organized innovations within Buddhism, there are countless aberrations on a smaller scale. For everyone who pursues a social agenda, there are others who take a more mystical turn, including a famous "magic monk" whose followers comply with an older Hindu-Buddhist tradition in seeking to drink his saliva and his urine.

From the standpoint of the mainstream, these movements are more short-term irritants than long-term sources of renewal. The country's recent economic and political crises and the sense of a cultural malaise at its core may lead to a broader religious resurgence—at least for a time. But the pattern of state-controlled religion is not likely to give way to a religious-controlled state. The myriad relations between religion and society offer another illustration of how a religious culture may be in tension with a secular power structure.

Japanese Religion: Oxymoron or Cultural Core?

On my first trip to Japan, I arrived wearing my standard summer travel garb—a photographer's vest over a polo shirt atop rumpled khakis—plus one shoe with a flapping hole in the sole that badly needed patching. I was wholly unprepared for the express train from Narita Airport into Tokyo. After inspecting a carpet clean enough for surgery, much less eating, I looked up to discover a conductor in a spiffy white linen double-breasted suit, with razor-sharp trouser creases and a handsome striped tie. This was only the first of many occasions during the next three weeks when I was to feel like the rude country bumpkin come to visit his city betters.

However, I did have the advantage of considerable space to myself on most public conveyances. This was partly because of the normal distance accorded a stranger, partly because Caucasians (*gaijins*) have a reputation of being unclean and malodorous, and partly because most Japanese are wary of being drawn into a conversation in English. Even though most speak English far better than their Western counterparts speak Japanese, the interaction is understandably uncomfortable. And the difference in language is only one of many cultural contrasts.

Consider the word "religion." Ask most Japanese if they are religious, and the answer is apt to be a clear "no." However, ask most Japanese if they participate in ritual observances, and the answer is likely to be "of course." A major source of the confusion is that the Japanese term for religion, *shukyo*, combines a first syllable meaning religious sect or organization with a second syllable meaning some form of codified doctrine. Since neither of Japan's two principal faith traditions—Buddhism or Shinto—qualifies on either count, the results are predictably inconsistent.

Recent public opinion polls show that only 8 percent claim "membership in a religious organization," and 87 percent "have never considered it." Only 26 percent say "religion is important to living a happy life," and 33 percent feel it is "essential to their life." Some 36 percent "believe in God," while 45 percent "believe in Buddha." At the same time, 54 percent report that their "house has a Shinto Shrine" and 59 percent "a Buddhist altar." Finally, 56 percent "visited a temple or a Shrine on last New Year's Day," while 81 percent "visited family graves during a designated holiday day in the past year."[13] It is little wonder that the noted Japanese scholar Ian Reader entitled a recent article on the vagaries of Japanese religiosity "Lies, Damn Lies, and Japanese Religious Statistics" to indicate that one can find support for almost any conclusion from the morass of figures available.[14]

There is a similar ambiguity regarding identification with major religious traditions. Some three-fourths of the Japanese identify themselves as Buddhists, but almost all have an affinity for the more indigenous Shinto rituals. Using the distinction that I first noted in Poland, many of these affiliations are more cultural than religious. However, both Buddhist and Shinto traditions have multiple strands. As we will see, Japan's Mahayana Buddhism has grown out of and grown apart from the Theravada Buddhism of India, Thailand, and South East Asia. There are also important differences between folk Shinto, shrine Shinto, and especially the state Shinto that developed around the emperor to become culturally and politically dominant from 1868 to 1945.

The most active religious groups in Japan today are based more on the model of a congregation than a temple or shrine. Formally, Christianity accounts for less than 1 percent of the population, though some 10 percent of the nation's schools and colleges are Christian affiliates. Far more important are a series of Buddhist and Shinto offshoots with the artless designations of "new" and "new-new" religious groups, depending on whether they were founded and spread before or after 1900. As we shall see, the most infamous movement is the Aum Shinrikyo responsible for an attack on the Tokyo subway in 1995; the largest is the Soka Gakkai.

Each of these aspects of the current Japanese scene is critical to the relations between religion, politics, and the state. But then the current scene can only be understood in historical context.

The Past as Religious and Political Prologue

As rich and enduring as Japanese culture may be, there remains some doubt about when Japan first cohered as a unified society or nation. There are three prime historical periods that are candidates for the honor, some 1400, 500, and 130 years ago, respectively.

Prior to the sixth century C.E., Japan was a congeries of fiefdoms loosely bound by a series of common cultural practices. Many involved forms of folk Shinto as a highly localized set of animistic customs, cleansing rituals, and propitiations that was more polytheistic than monotheistic and lacked a formal scripture, a system of formal ethics and sanctions, and an ecclesiastical hierarchy. Enter Buddhism. Coming from China over the next several centuries, various branches of Buddhism made special marks in Japan, including the Tadaiji, Kohukuji, Shingon, and T'ien Tai. These Buddhist movements brought more sophisticated organizational linkages, and they produced the first semblance of a Japanese political gestalt.

Buddhism was not Japan's only cultural import from China; other new patterns of language, art, and domestic life made the trip as well. Buddhism was not even the only quasi-religious system to arrive across the China Sea. The ethical and educational traditions of Confucianism arose in China at roughly the same time that Buddhism emerged in India, and it, too, has been influential in Japan, although its political impact as a centralized and elitist philosophy was limited in Japan's early decentralized, nonelitist structure.[15]

After half a millennium, fragmentation began to set in among the Buddhists, and the sense of nationhood recessed. Beginning in the twelfth century, a different sort of Chinese Buddhism began to play a more centrifugal role. This is known as the period of the Buddhist "schools." One of these was the more aristocratic and cultivated Zen Buddhism; another was the more populist Pure Land Buddhism, which was later transformed into the powerful Jodo-Shin sect; still a third was Nichiren Buddhism, an aggressively evangelical movement that was ultimately linked to the widespread Soka Gakkai in the twentieth century. The various twelfth- and thirteenth-century monasteries flourished not just religiously but economically—so much so that they have been depicted as a source of an early Japanese capitalism that parallels the European variety that Max Weber linked to the "Protestant ethic."[16]

But economic development was one thing and political development another. The next great period of state unity was the fabled period beginning in 1600, when Tokugawa Ieyasu won the Battle of Sekigahara and established his shogunate and lineage as Japan's dominant political force for the next 268 years. Again Buddhism became a major rallying device and administrative control mechanism, and a form of neo-Confucianism had a great influence on the samurai, or warrior, class through the popular movement Shingaku. Shinto was formally (if not informally) relegated to the cultural closet, and Christians were actually persecuted. According to Robert Bellah's somewhat different Weberian account of later Japanese capitalism, this was the period in which a social ethic occurred in Japan whose effect was most akin to that of Western Protestantism at about the same time.[17]

For some, however, these developments were not enough because they were insufficient to prod Japan to compete with Western powers on world terms. In 1868 Emperor Meiji emerged to take over direct rule. As preparation for this event, a small group of Japanese leaders behind the throne had gone to Europe and studied German and British political conditions. Especially impressed with German constitutionalism and the British Anglican monarchy, they adopted a combination of the two in proclaiming the Meiji Restoration. This was the advent of state Shinto, which grafted a form of emperor worship onto folk and shrine Shinto roots in order to provide a unified nationalistic system of collective consecration and commitment. Buddhism was now the frowned-upon faith. Over the next seventy-five years, a number of its temples were destroyed, its once half-million priests and nuns were considerably reduced, and its affiliated lay religious organizations were constrained not to stray from the national course. The short-term result of this sacred Japanization was a major spurt in Japanese industrialization; the longer-term effects culminated in what the Japanese knew as the Great East Asian War, including Pearl Harbor and what those in the United States referred to ironically as the "Pacific theater" of World War II.

With the war's end in 1945, state Shinto was disgraced by Japan's defeat, and public religion in general was discredited. The U.S. occupation force prescribed a new Japanese constitution that involved a de-deification of the emperor, a formal end to state Shinto, and a separation of religion and state that involved a more explicit version of the U.S. Constitution's First Amendment's strictures against a religious establishment. Article 20 is generally translated into English as "religion shall have no position of political authority." Presumably, the tragic saga of state Shinto was now over and left in the bloody dust of history. But the stroke of a constitutionalist's pen has less power over cultural conventions than over government actions. For many Japanese, the question of nationhood remained an aching but unacknowledged and untreated wound.[18]

The Current "Religious" Scene

According to government statistics, Japan now has some 180,000 "religious corporations." These include many Shinto "shrines" connected to the main branch of Shinto known as Jinjahoncho and many Buddhist "temples" representing the country's twenty-six branches of Buddhism. In Japan, unlike Thailand, Buddhist temples often resemble family businesses, and families occasionally outwit the government and succeed in using temples as tax shelters for regular commercial ventures. Temples may remain under a single family's control for generations, and the family maintains the temple, its grounds, and, most important, its cemetery. It takes a parish community of roughly two hundred families to support a priest in tending to the funeral rituals and ancestor rites that are a temple's principal focus. There is no prescribed worship, and one priest told me, "If a person comes more than once a month, I get worried because it indicates she may be lonely."

Again unlike the monks of Theravada Buddhism in Thailand, many priests not only have families of their own but secular occupations. Some use their income as doctors, lawyers, academics, or businessmen to compensate for the losses they incur from temples maintained as a family legacy and community responsibility. But in other cases, fees from the funeral practices constitute the priest's primary income, and there is increasing popular resentment over the rising prices charged for burial sites and for the ritual names "sold" for the dead. Naming prices may range from the equivalent of less than $3,000 to more than $20,000, with higher prices exacted for afterlife names of greater virtue, hence greater assurance of bliss to come.

Temple-owning families find it increasingly difficult to persuade their younger generations to assume the mantle. For those willing, there is some degree of priestly training but not always a sense of a higher calling. Even those who do take on the responsibility do not necessarily regard it as a matter of religious devotion. As one priest commented after interrupting our conversation to don his priestly garb and dash off to greet a parishioner who had rung the bell at his temple's entrance: "Oh, I regard the basic Buddhist beliefs as fictions but lovely fictions."

The parishioner at the temple door was unlikely to be exclusively Buddhist. If he invoked Buddhist ritual for death and family convocations, he probably relied upon Shinto rituals to cleanse away ill fortune in seeking a good future for his newborn daughter, good blessings for each new year ahead, good results on an examination, and even good performance of a new car, computer, or corporate venture. Shinto rituals and festivals pervade the culture and the calendar, with petitions to the *kami*, or spirit forces, of local shrines or the great Supreme Sun Kami, Amaterasu. But there are hundreds of other Shinto divinities, including some deified as a result of particular accomplishments such as winning grand champion status in sumo wrestling. One of the latest of these enormously rotund Shinto "gods" is an Hawaiian, Akebono, whom one of my informants was amused to observe crossing himself before a bout in good Catholic fashion.

But then Christian ritual is another increasing Japanese presence. It would not be at all surprising for our Buddhist parishioner's daughter, once grown, to be married in a Christian ceremony. Traditional Shinto bridal costumes are so elaborate as to be exorbitantly expensive, and Christian weddings have a special cachet derived from widely watched American television. In all of this, a Westerner may wonder about form without content, but from a Japanese standpoint, form is often content. A Westerner may also wonder about a single individual's seemingly indiscriminate embrace of so many different ritual traditions. But as we have seen, this sort of internal pluralism would be far less surprising to many in India and especially Indonesia.

In one sense, however, this is all a layer removed from Japan's real religious action occurring within the "newer" religious groups whose combined memberships may account for as much as a fifth of the Japanese population, though precise figures are elusive. Autonomous and syncretic lay organizations began to develop in the eighteenth century. The Shingaku movement founded in the 1730s by Ishida Baigan was a meld of his early Shinto and later neo-Confucian and Zen Buddhist influences.[19] Similar movements came in greater numbers after the turn of the nineteenth century. Some were affiliated with the Shinto and Buddhist priesthoods, but others were independent. Many of these "new" religious groups founded prior to and just after the 1868 Meiji Restoration persist today. Tenrikyo was formed by a woman with an aversion to worldly possessions and status distinctions, whose healing powers led to a ritual of ecstatic dance. Today Tenrikyo's more than two million members attend centers all over the country, though they often make haijlike trips to the headquarters in Tenri City.

The more numerous "new-new" religious groups were primarily founded in the 1920s and 1930s. Again, many were independent of the major traditions, but several of the most successful were explicitly lay organizations associated with particular Buddhist schools. This is true of Reiyukai Kyodan and its own subsequent offshoot, Risshokoseikai—the second largest of these religious groups with some five million adherents.[20] It is also true of the largest, the Soka Gakkai (SG), whose own perhaps overgenerous estimates involve some twelve million members, or almost 10 percent of the entire Japanese population.

The SG began in 1930 and became a lay affiliate of Nichiren Buddhism—the twelfth-century "school" that was far more active and extreme in its proselytizing than its contemporaries, the Zen Buddhists or the Pure Land sect. SG adopted the Nichiren's Lotus Sutra as its mantra and became devoted to spreading its vision of Buddhism as a national faith. However, like many of the "new-new" religious groups, SG's real growth did not begin until after the World War II because of dampers applied by the government. During the war, SG's two primary leaders were imprisoned for their pacifism and their objections to state Shinto. One died in prison, but the survivor emerged to lead a mobilization that competed with a third wave of still newer groups that has gone virtually nameless, perhaps because there seems to be little enthusiasm for "new-new-new."

The SG competed very strongly but not without considerable controversy.[21] There is little question that the SG offered solace, support, and a sense of community to the many postwar Japanese who moved from rural to urban settings or experienced other forms of personal turmoil. Unlike conventional temples and shrines, it offered a network of small, local, communal organizations that provided anchor points, especially for women who were relatively neglected by more traditional religious institutions. But there were other factors involved in SG's phenomenal postwar growth. The SG was unique in having its own political party, Komeito (clean government). In addition, following the aggressive legacy of Nichiren Buddhism, SG utilized a coercive form of recruitment known as "shakubuku." Stories are legion of how its agents would move into a neighborhood or a household and simply refuse to leave until the residents joined. Once someone joined, there were financial as well as social obligations. In 1969 a popular professor and television personality, Fujiwara Hirotatsu, published an account of these matters called *I Denounce Soka Gakkai*. The work created a national sensation and only added to the movement's unsavory reputation among more sophisticated Japanese.

SG began to change. Its young, ambitious, and organizationally adept new president, Daisaku Ikeda, sought to detach himself from the movement's early practices. While the movement's growth began to level off, it also took on new activities and a new sophistication. By the time of my first contact with the group in 1993, its membership had become increasingly middle class; its daily newspaper, *Seikyo Shimbon*, claimed the nation's third largest circulation; its Soka University had a large Tokyo campus with an impressive art museum and burgeoning enrollments; its ties with the Komeito Party had been publicly loosened (though not severed) to avoid criticism; and its Soka Gakkai International pursued a "Buddhist" agenda of world peace, nuclear disarmament, environmental conservation, and enlightened tolerance around the globe, with growing membership organizations in countries such as India, the United Kingdom, and the United States.[22]

As an outsider who had given a few lectures and participated in several seminars sponsored by the SG in Tokyo and Cambridge, Massachusetts, I was not at all clear on how to interpret such organizational change. Did it reflect the common Western religious process whereby rebellious "sects" ultimately become so institutionalized and established as to resemble the very "churches" they had rebelled against in the first place? Or was it more a case of the familiar corporate saga of organizational differentiation in which the initial core remains but other new and relatively autonomous undertakings are added? Still another possibility is that there was less actual change than met the outsider's eye and the highly touted new developments were really a public relations gloss on an internal program that had changed very little.

As is so often the case, the truth may span all of the above and more.[23] But while I was in the midst of this interpretive quandary, a more recent and dramatic development added to the mystery. In 1992 the SG was effectively defrocked. The chief abbot of the small surviving group of Nichiren Buddhist monks decided to end sponsorship of the SG as its lay organization. There are various accounts of the action—some based in personalities and others rooted in organizational misunderstandings, financial asymmetries, public notoriety, and conflicting agendas. The SG has made no formal action in response and appears to be waiting for the abbot's retirement to resume relations.

Current Crises of Religion, Politics, and National Identity

Despite the country's recent affluence and the understandable pride in economic and technological marvels at the heart of what some describe as "new Japan theory," many Japanese have a gnawing sense of spiritual emptiness, cultural erosion, and national vacuity.[24] There are a wide variety of palliatives, including the aforementioned newer religions.[25] These movements have assumed various forms reminiscent of a family household, a parent-child relationship, Protestant-style congregations, a consumer model offering help in one's occupational tasks, and avowedly nationalistic movements separate from either Buddhism or Shinto.[26]

While Japan's politicians often speak out against religion publicly, some political leaders privately hunger for a return to a nonmilitaristic state Shinto. Formally, the state continues to be separated from religion of any sort. But in 1985 then Prime Minister Nakasone provoked a major controversy by leading his cabinet in a public visit to Tokyo's Yasukuni Shinto shrine that honors soldiers who fought for the emperor in World War II but not civilians who died as a result of Allied bombing. This is one of several cases that have made their way to the Japanese Supreme Court as possible infringements of the Constitution's Article 20 separating religion from "political authority"—or more accurately, the government. In most cases, the court has found no violation, though its reasoning has varied from holding that Nakesone was acting privately to ruling that Shinto is not actually a religion in the first place.

There have been more recent evidences of state Shinto's seeping return. For example, the central Ministry of Education exerts uncommon power over religious matters, especially in the schools. By 1989 ministry officials had grown so concerned about the centrifugal tendencies in Japanese society that they sought to enact a centripetal counterforce. The ministry engineered legislation that required singing the national anthem (*kimigayo*) and displaying the national *hinomaru* flag of the rising sun at public school graduation ceremonies. Since both of these contain Shinto images, several of my interviewees suggested that they might well mark the first step down a slippery slope toward a renewed religious state. The ruling Liberal Democratic Party (LDP)—the ironically named conservative power in Japanese politics since World War II despite periodic scandal and corruption—has recently filed legislation to enact both provisions formally. While most of the considerable opposition comes from pacifists objecting to a symbolic return to Japan's militaristic past, the religious overtones have not escaped attention. Nor did the recent remarks of Prime Minister Mori before a gathering of conservative politicians that Japan remains a "divine nation" that is "centered on the Emperor." Still, Japan is a country where many politicians are not only critical of religious organizations but campaign against them before an electorate that shares their suspicions.

Politicians were afforded a special opportunity by the 1995 nerve-gas attack on the Tokyo subway at rush hour by the followers of the "new-new" religion, Aum Shinrikyo. The attack killed eleven commuters and sent some five thousand more retching to the hospital. The resulting "trial of the century" of the movement's leader, Shoko Asahara, could take up to ten years. Its surrounding publicity has been a trial in its own right for many marginal religious movements who have been tarred by the same stereotypes and sanctions applied to the Aum cult. This guilt by association is especially true of the SG and its long-standing relation to the aforementioned Komeito as one of the largest opposition parties in Japan. It is true that Komeito and SG have not been legally linked since 1970, but there are enough perceived affinities and public contacts between the two that discrediting one goes far toward besmirching the other.

Given these circumstances, it is scarcely surprising that the LDP should take advantage of the opportunity to constrain Komeito as a sometime political thorn in its side. This was a principal motivation behind its successful amendments to the Religious Corporation Law in 1996 giving the government tighter reporting requirements, greater monitoring vigilance, and vague new standards of political propriety over all religious organizations.

It is a testament to Japan's political flux that the "New Komeito" subsequently joined the LDP's ruling parliamentary coalition. As is perhaps perversely predictable, the Aum Shinrikyo has revived and persists. In 1999 the Japanese Diet passed much sterner "anticult" legislation providing that groups such as the Aum "suspected of mass murder" are not only subject to strict government constraints but may be banned. Komeito actually supported the recent bills when it joined the LDP coalition government. But SG and other religious observers fear the current mood may mark a potential sea change in state policy toward religious groups of all sorts, especially those that are somewhat off center. Certainly the party in power has greater resources with which to root out its opposition. This might seem consistent with a secular state in the antireligious sense of the phrase, but it is a departure from a secular state that is neutral concerning religion in general and religions in particular.

On my last visit to Japan in May 1996, I elaborated some of these concerns in a public lecture and in several seminars and interviews. All of these were at the behest of the SG. Their representatives had heard me give a scholarly paper on the general topic of religion, politics, and the state at meetings in Quebec the previous summer. Because my general position seemed to address their specific plight, they asked me to repeat the message in Tokyo. As in similar relations with other religious groups, I encountered no pressure to change or tailor my message in any respect—though I was vexed when an SG journalist asked my opinion of the organization, and my response of "fascinating" later appeared in print as "wonderful." Presumably this was only an innocent casualty of cross-cultural communication.

Indeed, President Ikeda and his staff were generous almost to a fault. It is sometimes hard for a Westerner to accept the full brunt of Japanese gratitude and its attendant etiquette without wondering about ulterior motives. I accepted the invitation, however, because I had an ulterior motive of my own in wanting to learn more about an organization that is notoriously defensive and difficult to penetrate. To use a metaphor I have deployed differently in this volume, I sometimes had the sense of resembling a research moth drawing too close to its subject's flame with the danger of becoming too warmed by co-opting praise.

The SG is hardly the first religious group to flatter its observers. Some years ago I received an invitation from a comparable group in the United States to attend an enticing conference of scholars in Greece. When afforded an opportunity to ask Harvard's distinguished social theologian Harvey Cox how he responded to similar opportunities, he replied with complete innocence: "I generally turn them down because I think they may want to use my name for legitimacy. But, Jay, I don't think you have anything to worry about." Of course, he was right, but I didn't go anyway. When religion becomes politically embroiled, it deserves a wary eye.

China: The People's Republic as a Secular Bastion?

Arriving in China is like entering a time warp that hurls one alternately toward the future and the past. Under the tight control of an omnipresent Communist Party since 1949, the nation resembles an astonishingly successful experiment in managing the world's largest population before it breeds to death. At the same time, traces remain of one of the world's most ancient and sophisticated cultures. And nowadays one sees a society shifting from self-imposed isolation to an all-out sprint to catch up with economic, technological, and political developments elsewhere.

No event so captured the tensions of contemporary China than the demonstrations in 1989 that ultimately brought millions to the streets in cities throughout China, though it was the high drama of tanks versus students in Beijing's Tiananmen Square that captured world attention through its fatal denouement. This was more a campaign for reduced corruption and greater accessibility to the government than a demand to replace the government or install Western electoral democracy.[27] Some of its demands have been met in the years since, but several thousand participants remain in prison.

China is a high-volume society in both senses of that term. The sheer number of people and activities can be intimidating, as I discovered when I rode my newly rented bike into one of the most congested intersections in Beijing, only to discover it had no brakes—or when on hot and humid buses and trains I stood vertically compacted in a space that two Chinese would have considered commodious and felt like a very large, very white dim sum dumpling. But the noise volume can also be daunting to a Westerner—whether the din of new construction, the high and piercing nasal singsong of the Peking Opera, the loud slurping sounds that accompany noodles being scooped with chopsticks from a bowl held chin high, or the tendency of many conversationalists to talk with fortissimo gusto and assume that my own halting Chinese was like a balky engine that would finally roar to a start after repeated ignitions at increasing decibels. Alas, no such luck.

All of this was the setting for my effort to gain firsthand acquaintance with Chinese religion in a mammoth society controlled by an aggressively secular state. But which Chinese religion? Suddenly a host of distinctions loomed. Did I mean the seemingly inchoate welter of folk superstitions or the more circumspect and codified elite traditions? Was I primarily interested in rural or urban practices, and what about those centered in the family versus more institutional settings? Did I refer to the ancient indigenous traditions of Taoism and Confucianism or the imported faiths of Buddhism, Christianity, and Islam? And what about the surrogate "religion" of Marxism as it is embodied in the rituals and beliefs of the Communist Party and its sprawling state apparatus?

Of course, the answer was all of the above. Yet I was especially drawn to the clash between religious traditions and state secularism. Although China was not quite the last society I visited, I have saved its treatment for last because it poses what may be the ultimate questions concerning religion and society: just how necessary is religion to a people and a nation, and is it possible to imagine a successful society without religion in its conventional sense?

Introducing the Religious Chorus
In 1949 Mao Zedong was successful in a revolution that was not only political but cultural—he later even used the phrase "Cultural Revo-

lution" to describe an effort to break with the past by first denouncing and then repressing it altogether. Few Chinese today know much about events and developments prior to the twentieth century. Still, it is hard to turn off culture at a political spigot. Many Chinese still engage in practices that are rooted some three thousand years ago. Many have a social ethic and turn of thought that are themselves carried on ancient winds.

Today two indigenous religious strands survive from the distant past.[28] "Taoism"—or as it is always pronounced and often spelled, "Daoism"—has its origins in the dawn of prehistory just as it continues to survive within the gloaming of the Communist regime. A major victim of the Communist's campaign against "superstition," it now survives as part of a widespread but uncodified form of Chinese popular or folk religion, which penetrates all regions and levels of the society. This loose collection of ancestor rituals, healing practices, and household shrines pivots around local deities and combines odds and ends from all of China's faith traditions with no organizational structure or political presence.[29] Still, Taoism has continuing influence within a traditional medicine that still flourishes in many hospitals that are divided into Western and traditional wings. It is also reflected in the art of *qigong,* or the early morning, slow-motion exercises of the elderly in public parks all over the country that we shall encounter later in its more organized political manifestation as the Falun Gong (Wheel of Law). In addition, Taoist traces are discernible in the renewed vibrancy of a variety of other public festivals and importuning rites, though the line between these occasions and the ancient faith is often faint.

If Taoism has always been a folk tradition, Confucianism was more of an elite enterprise whose history and doctrines are much better preserved. Confucius himself was born in approximately 551 B.C.E., only about a dozen years after Gautama Buddha in India. But if Buddha was a prince who sought the middle way through worldly renunciation, Confucius was from a low-status family—or more accurately, a once elite family down on its luck. Confucius achieved mobility through education and later commended the same path to others. He codified the moral life and the requirements of presiding over it administratively. He specified the propriety of the "five relationships" between ruler and subject, father and son, husband and wife, older and younger brother, and friend to friend—all in descending order of importance featuring the different ideal virtues of loyalty, kinship, difference, order, and faith, respectively. Among Confucius's many ethical injunctions is not doing to others what you do not want done to yourself—a parallel to Christianity's "Golden Rule" that some argue is a more practical life guide.

Confucius's legacy includes writings such as the famed analects that became the basis of a civil service cadre whose appointments and advancements were by examination. In the sixth century c.e. this system became the backbone of Chinese governance under the emperor of the Sui Dynasty. These official national examinations persisted in one form or another until early in the twentieth century. Confucianism also involved more than an early version of bureaucracy. In emphasizing the moral virtues to be pursued in all human relationships, it represented a far broader way of life. But despite an early emphasis on heavenly intervention in human affairs, there has always been doubt about whether Confucianism is a religion.

Somewhat less doubt applied to Buddhism, which arrived in China from the southwest about the same time that Confucianism was becoming established. "Go to the West to seek truth" has become an ironic set phrase in Chinese culture because it has nothing to do with the current West but refers to the ancient practice of following the silk road west to India in order to consult the original Buddhist texts. But Buddhism was a successful import partly because it lacked a rigid set of doctrines and practices that required forced compliance and hence was able to work with rather than against indigenous practices. It was also because of the East's spirit of cultural accommodation in contrast to the West's tendency toward cultural compartmentalization. Buddhism came in several varieties, including the Tantric, Therevada, and Mahayana strands. Overall Buddhism has influenced a great many cultural forms, such as the qigong. It now has more adherents than any other religious tradition in the country. Many—but no means all—Buddhists are concentrated within the annexed territory of Tibet, where their victimization by Chinese authorities has become a continuing matter of international tension and dispute.

Islam arrived in China with Arab traders in the eighth century c.e., within a hundred years of Muhammad's death. It never became a pervasive part of the Chinese cultural fabric, but it has survived among several ethnic groups that exist outside of the 94 percent Han majority. China's Muslims are overwhelmingly Sunnis and are concentrated primarily in the northwest, where Islam is at the core of many communities. However, there are also small Muslim enclaves in major cities around the country.

Finally, Christianity arrived first in China as a Catholic presence that dates continuously from Jesuit missionaries in the sixteenth century.[30] Protestant missionaries did not arrive in force until 1842. Over the next century, both liberal and conservative Protestant groups expanded their influence. Episcopalians and Presbyterians had a disproportionate educational influence on Chinese professionals, but the Assemblies of God and Seventh-Day Adventists also developed niches. Foreign missions, missionaries, and internationally connected institutions had become important aspects of all these denominations before they were cut off first by the Japanese occupation up to and including World War II and then by the internal revolution that followed.

Official and Unofficial Religions under an Antireligious State

In 1949 the triumphant Mao proclaimed China a Marxist state on the path to a religionless society. But over the ensuing fifty years, state policy toward religion has ranged from severe suppression to strategic tolerance. As continuing accounts of China's human rights abuses emphasize, religion has often been a major target of state coercion.[31] Beginning in the early 1950s, foreign sources of support for all religions were cut off, and foreign religious representatives were evicted. Policy toward the Tibetan Buddhist movement was particularly harsh, in part because its roughly hundred thousand monks were seen as parasites in a struggling economy, its more than six thousand monasteries had vast land holdings that could be redistributed to a landless peasantry, and its many mobilizable followers constituted a major power threat to the new political system of Communism.

Religious suppression was a major motif of early state policy, but the period of the Cultural Revolution from 1966 to 1976 was especially devastating to all representatives and remnants of the old order under the ruthless actions of Mao and the Gang of Four. From the standpoint of many long-established institutions, these were the "lost years" in which whole infrastructures were decimated. Religious leaders were arrested or "reassigned" to menial labor far removed from their normal rounds. Major churches and temples were appropriated for grain storage or manufacturing sites.

With Mao's death in 1976, the oppression began to relent. By 1979 major changes were under way with the rise to power of Deng Xiaoping. Instead of fighting capitalism, there was an effort to join it. Instead of remaining closed to the outside world, ports and doors were opened. Instead of quashing religion, the state offered a constrained and conditional tolerance. Article 36 of the amended 1982 Constitution provides for "freedom of religious belief" and notes that the "state protects legitimate religious activities" in the context of a long list of illegitimate actions. At the same time, the state extended formal recognition to five (and only five) religions: Taoism, Buddhism, Islam, Catholicism, and Protestantism. Like much of the rest of South and Southeast Asia, but unlike Japan, China has no term for Christianity as a larger religious tradition that embraces the variations within it. Catholicism and Protestantism are seen as two entirely distinct religions, and this is increasingly the case for denominations within the Protestant tradition itself.

The more remarkable omission among legitimate religions is Confucianism. While the overwhelming majority of Chinese would consider themselves as at least cultural Confucianists, the tradition poses problems for the state. Its ethical system was patriarchal and prerevolutionary; its exam-based civil service system presented a threat because it relied more on merit than party loyalty; its education was only for males and ignored the new arts and science curriculum; finally, whether as a reason or an excuse, it can be argued that Confucianism is not really a religion at all. Since party officials are now casting an increasingly suspicious eye toward the superstitions of Taoism, there is a sense in which both of China's two indigenous faith traditions are in special disfavor.

As to the imported religions of Buddhism, Islam, and Christianity, the state developed three criteria of acceptability, known to Protestants at least as the "three-self" doctrine. Thus, any religious organization seeking government approval must be "self-supporting, self-governing, and self-propagating." The strategy here is clear enough; the government seeks to deny foreign funding and control while prohibiting the merger of small groups into larger and more threatening movements.

But there was a carrot as well as a stick. Those religious groups that complied with the three-self standard were granted "official" status. This meant not only that they were free to practice their faith publicly, but they were also eligible for some forms of government financial assistance, especially in recovering from the ravages of the Cultural Revolution.

I did not visit Tibet, but reports from various sources indicate that hundreds of temples, monasteries, and even lamaseries have been rebuilt.[32] However, the infant chief lama of one particular Tibetan Buddhist group was named only after being approved in Beijing. Meanwhile, Buddhist temples elsewhere in China have been growing enterprises. The famous Shoulin Temple in central China has drawn students and tourists alike on the basis of its ties to the kung fu heroics of media fame. The large Nanputuo Temple and its convent in the major port city of Xiamen continue to be a hub of activity, despite rumors that they helped secrete out of the country some students who had been involved in the 1989 Tiananmen revolt. However, political agents have been sent in to conduct classes on party doctrine; monks have been prohibited from begging, and certain ritual practices have been banned. The government has also actively promoted cremation as an alternative to Buddhist burials.

Much the same sort of conditional tolerance has been extended to officially recognized Islamic, Catholic, and Protestant organizations—though my firsthand experience was confined to the latter. I attended several Sunday services in Shanghai and Beijing, where I was once again struck by the double aptness of the term "volume." The parishioners were not only many but in full voice with hymn singing that would put most Western congregations to shame. In addition, I paid a brief visit to the leading mainline Three-Self Protestant Movement seminary in Nanjing. Its official status was reflected in the state salaries paid its faculty, most of whom seemed well reconciled to—if not actually pleased with—their standing.[33] When I asked one respondent about the harassment and imprisonment of clergy, he responded with apparent sincerity, "We really don't know much about that. News travels very slowly here. Anyway, the Communist Party is not all bad for us. After all, it has given us a special niche as martyrs—and that always helps. It has also pruned away some local superstitions and limited the competition—especially Confucianism. It has taken over the burden of running schools and hospitals, and now it has even made us a part of the United Front [a council of voluntary organizations serving the public interest]."

Yet state harassment and imprisonment do continue. Ideally, religious policy and directives flow from the Politburo at the very top echelon of power to the Chinese Communist Party (CCP) and then to the United Front Development Office (UFD), the regional offices of the Religious Affairs Bureau (RAB), the local police or Public Security Bureaus (PSBs), and finally the grassroots. But as one particularly knowledgeable respondent told me (during an interview in one of Beijing's major parks to avoid being taped or overheard), "religion may be on the agenda of one in a hundred Politburo meetings, and policies at the top are sometimes very different from actions at the bottom."

Arrests and imprisonment of major religious figures—especially Catholic clergy who maintain ties with the Vatican—have long been matters of top-level policy.[34] But harassment of Protestant groups and their leaders has more often occurred at the local level—so much so that there have been instances in which local authorities have been reined in from the top. Protestants are especially vulnerable since they are more involved in unofficial "house" churches, or "meeting points" that are often undercover but sometimes surface as rebellious challenges. The "house" pattern is characteristic of growing evangelical and sectarian groups, including the cult of the True Jesus Family led by the charismatic Witness Lee and the Falun Gong itself.

Not surprisingly, state policy toward religion varies with changing circumstances. As already noted, there was a major tightening of controls following the 1989 events in Tiananmen, but my visit in 1993 came during a period of relative relaxation. This was particularly evident around the Institute of World Religions in the Chinese Academy of the Social Sciences in Beijing. After many years of ideological work developing Marxist rebuttals to religion, there was a new—if somewhat hesitant—attempt to study religion more on its own terms. Caution still applied, and the nods and smiles during my lecture suggested that I was saying things publicly that my audience could not.

There has been a recent crackdown on these offices as politically wayward. But the institute's joke of the day was that party officials were now fighting China's third Opium War. The first two involved Britain's role in the narcotics trade in the nineteenth century; this one concerned whether Marx (and the institute's own 1986 dictionary) had been right in defining religion as simply the "opiate of the people." According to the largely unavailable CCP Document 6 from February 1991, some leaders had been reconsidering the possibility that religion might have more justifiable uses as a source of needed coherence and stability for its members and a possible safety valve for the state itself.

Over the last two decades, religious visitors to China have shared an excitement over new levels of religious activity, and many of their reports would suggest a major boom.[35] Nonetheless, it is difficult to assess the claim statistically. There is virtually no reliable data available for any faith. Recognized Taoism, like unrecognized Confucianism, has long ago seeped into the societal pores. It is hard to distinguish—let alone count—regular adherents and occasional dabblers among Christians and Buddhists. If one looks for regular church or temple involvement and ritual participation, the total may be in the hundreds of thousands, but if criteria are relaxed to embrace a more casual cultural influence, the numbers can reach tens of millions. Islam tends to be bracketed territorially, though it is risky to assume that residence in a traditionally Islamic province (or ethnic group) assures Muslim adherency. The figure that the state uses for Catholic membership is 3.3 million, but it has been used since 1949. Estimates of Protestant numbers range from 5 million to 100 million, depending upon whether the figures are coming from the state or from satellite evangelical offices in Hong Kong. Of course, these vagaries plague any overall estimate of the self-consciously religiously involved. Even if one accepts a figure of some 200 million, this is only a sixth of the population. Where does this leave the rest?

Communism as a Quasi-Religion

In addition to the vestiges of traditional faiths and the growth of more recent religions, there are other sacred systems that may function as quasi- or substitute religions. The family has itself been a sacred institution in China, though recent government policy has imposed a one-child norm, and the extended family has suffered from both shrinkage and separations. In a much larger familial sense, just being Chinese—especially a Han Chinese—has long conferred deep cultural pride and continuity. However, this has been both buttressed and assaulted by events over the last half century. On the one hand, China's long period of national isolation reinforced feelings of singularity; on the other, China's Communist ideology and organization have been strongly anti-traditional.

It is not simply that party members are expected to profess atheism and forego any conventional religious affiliation. Marxist Communism has offered a surrogate religion with its own sacred doctrines, sacred rituals, and even sacred congregational units. For many years, Communism has served as a national quasi-religion supported by a massive apparatus for propaganda and social control. With the "cult of Mao" at its core, Communism in China has been a kind of secular faith that took special pride in transcending the delusions of conventional religion.

However, if nonmaterial beliefs were forsworn, other religious trappings existed in profusion. Party declarations included a steady stream of hermeneutics against what Deng Xiaoping called "spiritual pollution." Party doctrine produced its own catechism in a constant flow of memorable moral injunctions such as the Four Points of Decency (mind, language, behavior, and environment), Three Ardent Loves (party, country, and army), and in what appears to combine Christian and Confucian decalogues, Ten Musts and Must Nots.[36] There was an elaborate ecclesiastical structure that cascaded down from the top party echelons to local party cells for the priesthood and local work units for the laity. These had their own rituals, including periods of self-criticism that approximate confessions.

One must be careful about giving too much credence to these parallels—and offending religionists and secularists alike. Yet there is one more similarity that bears special mention. Both religious systems and political systems involve cultural constructs subject to the erosions of secularization in a changing world. Matters once clutched to the bosom are gradually extended to arm's length for more objective scrutiny. Things once taken literally sometimes become taken for granted and later left aside. There is now much talk in China about precisely such a dynamic affecting Communism itself. It is not hard to find people who will say quite openly that Communism is being taken less and less seriously, that the work units have crumbled, and that the party itself is a sort of empty shell that retains power more through state coercion than consensual commitment.[37]

China is yet another country with concerns over a diminishing cultural core. One can imagine a long series of widespread and binding cultural systems that have had their day and gone the way of all flesh, including Confucianism, Buddhism, and now Communism. It is true that processes of secularization sometimes leave a void for corresponding movements of sacralization. But given the pervasive emphasis on China's new capitalism, there is great concern that money is at best a hollow repository of the sacred. Some hope that Communism itself may be modified and restored to good standing, though this may depend on the charisma of the next generation of national leadership that is yet to be determined. Meanwhile, a few others have clearly turned back to more conventional religions, and there are even those who still hold out hope for indigenous Confucianism. It is not uncommon for religions to undergo major alterations to hold or regain constituencies, and with a few nips here and the odd tuck there, even Confucianism could be made to fit.[38] The scenario is not unimaginable, but neither is it likely. The country's cultural and religious destiny for the twenty-first century is anything but clear. In the foreseeable future the better bet is that party officials will continue to illustrate the old Chinese proverb that warns of "scratching the boot while the foot continues to itch."

A final revealing episode concerns the qigong movement mentioned previously as combining Taoist and Buddhist elements. During my visit, I spent a pleasant early morning in a Beijing park with hundreds of older people engaged in everything from exquisitely slow martial arts routines to badminton and Western fox-trot dancing. It seemed wonderfully innocent and very communal. I was aware that the government was keeping a careful watch on its political potential even then, but I was unprepared for what later happened. Just two months prior to Tiananmen's tenth anniversary, another mass demonstration occurred in the form of a day-long vigil outside of the nation's central CCP headquarters. This one involved some ten thousand well-mannered, elderly members of the Falun Gong. The object was not to oppose Communism but to enlist the media in imposing pressures on the government for greater freedom. Although the largest demonstration since Tiananmen, the results were different. No violence ensued, and Premier Zhu Ronghi agreed to a late-night meeting with the demonstrators' leaders. At the same time, the premier was reputed to have said that he was an atheist who could not be forced to bow to their beliefs, and security across the country was tightened to make sure that nothing similar would happen again. Clearly the party was concerned that the assembled ten thousand reflected a much larger potential movement of perhaps a hundred million. As a form of venting steam to reduce pressure, there had been some liberalizing reforms after Tiananmen. But in a country where power was now dependent on an authoritarian structure without the support of a Communist cultural consensus, the threat was palpable and arrests have become a commonplace. Once again, the boot was scratched but the itching continued.

Conclusion

Given the legacy of Buddhism, it is not surprising that Buddhist countries raise perhaps the most basic of all questions concerning religion and society, namely, what qualifies as religion in the first place, and how dependent is society upon it? If religion requires deference to a supernatural authority operating through divine intermediaries embedded in some form of hierarchical structure, the indigenous cultures of the East can stake a fair claim to be religionless. If religion need only involve some sense of a sacred commitment that is both rooted in and affirming of a social community, then the East is highly religious indeed.

Of the three countries examined here, Thailand is the most conventionally religious with its tradition of Theravada Buddhism and ties to the state through the sangha. However, even though Thailand is officially Buddhist, we have seen that the state is the controlling partner in an uneasy relationship that reflects more of a state religion than a religious state.

Both Japan and China have been multireligious societies for almost fifteen hundred years. The great internal traditions of Shinto in Japan and Taoism and Confucianism in China have shared the local turf with faiths from the outside, including various traditions of Buddhism and Christianity in each country, not to exclude Islam in China. But China's enthraldom with Communism also reached sacred proportions. For more than forty years, China has belied the axiom that only countries that pray together stay together. If this is a peculiar note on which to end this religious odyssey, it is a highly appropriate note on which to turn toward home.

Part Two

Coming

Home

6

Culture Wars

and Religious

Violence

At this point, our global journey changes course in three senses. First, instead of considering countries one at a time, the analysis is more genuinely comparative. Second, instead of continuing in a descriptive mode, the focus is more on key issues that inform the relations between religion, politics, violence, and the state. Third, instead of winding farther outward on our journey, we shall be returning to the United States as both a pivot for analysis and a beneficiary of insights gained elsewhere. Comparativists are never far from home, and it is time to show how and why.

Throughout the foregoing, we have shuttled between civility and violence. The distance is often short, and the trip can be astonishingly quick. Even the most violent societies develop codes of honor; even the most civil nations know moments of brutal strife. The United States has surely had its share of political violence—from the infamous War between the States and labor strikes of the nineteenth century to the civil rights struggles and the anti-Vietnam War movement of the 1960s and early 1970s.

Where religion is concerned, Americans have tended to celebrate their diversity rather than contest it. For most of its history, the United States has been at religious peace with itself, if not always with others. But in recent years, some have perceived a shift away from tolerant pluralism toward entrenched conflict. This is a good place to begin placing the United States in comparative perspective.

"Culture War" at Home and Abroad?

The recollection was chilling. America had finally imploded, and one witness described it this way:

> It was after the catastrophe, when they shot the President and machine-gunned the Congress and the army declared a state of emergency. They blamed it on the Islamic fanatics, at the time. Keep calm, they said on television. Everything is under control. I was stunned. Everyone was, I know that. It was hard to believe. The entire government, gone like that. How did they get in, how did it happen? That was when they suspended the Constitution. They said it would be temporary. There wasn't even any rioting in the streets. People stayed home at night, watching television, looking for some direction. There wasn't even an enemy you could put your finger on.[1]

Of course, this is fiction, not history. But today Margaret Atwood's nightmarish novel of a United States taken over by right-wing religious fanatics is reflected in increasing concern over an American "culture war."

Few descriptions of American society have made a quicker transition from jargon to cliché than the phrase "culture war." Over the last decade, the term and its connotations have found their way into newspeak, political sound bites, and kitchen seminars the country over. It now seems a common assumption that the war is already upon us with mounting casualties. Recent accounts carry ominous warnings of a degree of national combat not seen in this country for almost a century and a half.[2]

The rhetoric points to another civil war—this time between liberals and conservatives, orthodox and progressives, modernists and fundamentalists. It suggests that Americans who have not yet chosen sides will have to soon. Some would even say that this is no longer a war of mere words or government policy options, since the violence has already begun.

Cassandras of division and polarization are hardly new among American pundits. Politicians have often used the theme as part of a classic "scare and unite" strategy. Survey researchers from Marx forward have noted conflicts in society's ranks.[3] While James Hunter has done more than others to promote the phrase "culture war," he is not alone in developing the theme. Other observers have also noted a growing rift in American culture that begins with religion and then threatens to spill into the political arena. Previous conflicts between religious liberals and religious conservatives were somewhat muted because they were allocated into distinct denominational camps that had relatively little to do with each other. But this new conflict transcends denominational lines and expands beyond old religious boundaries.[4]

According to this interpretation of American culture, the originating tensions between religious liberals and religious conservatives began in the theological split between modernists and fundamentalists early in the twentieth century. By the mid-1970s disputes flared over a series of social and moral controversies concerning abortion, pornography, homosexuality, women's rights, and school prayer. As these disputes moved aggressively to the center of the political stage during the 1980s, they have increasingly led to bitter politics—again not just between denominations and political parties but often within and beyond them.

Some alarmed observers stop short of envisioning a culture engulfed in flames or embroiled in war. Others are less restrained. Hunter paints increasing polarization on a much larger canvas with far more vivid colors. He describes an increasingly volatile ideological struggle between the culturally "orthodox" and the culturally "progressive" in American society. Hunter views contemporary public discourse on social and moral issues as a war between two competing moral visions that have encompassed all Americans, religious and nonreligious alike. The cultural divide between the orthodox and progressives is so prevalent that it overwhelms previous distinctions, turning them into irrelevant anachronisms. The major lines of division reflect fundamental disagreements over the sources and substance of moral truth.

Others have fanned the fire of this putative war between different ideas about who we are and who we ought to be.[5] The theme of a widespread, deep-seated, and desperate conflict is apparent in the subtitles of three recent works. Thus, Britisher Os Guinness has made a special point of America's *Time of Reckoning;* William Bennett signals alarm over *The Fight for Our Culture and Our Children;* Todd Gitlin wonders *Why America Is Wracked by Culture Wars.*[6]

As with any diagnosis of the condition of American religion and culture, second opinions are in order. It is perhaps not surprising that many of these opinions conflict.[7] What some pundits see as cultural warfare, others regard as mere cultural dustups as a form of democracy at work. It is true that religious and cultural discord has led to hostilities, violence, and even murders. As one example, few events have been more chilling than the 1995 bombing of the federal building in Oklahoma City. But while minuscule minorities have grotesquely abused the right to bear both arms and witness, one must wonder about the larger patterns involved.

Much of the disagreement between the hawks and doves of a domestic U.S. culture war hinges on the terms involved in the phrase itself: "culture" and "war." The adversaries agree on the importance of culture as a social force. But it is possible to overstate its claims and to ignore its interactions with more structural differences such as social class. It is also possible to exaggerate conflict involving whole cultural camps pitted against each other.

Regardless of how cultural a conflict may be, to what extent is it a war? Here is another source of ambiguity and one compounded by disagreement over whether the operative term for the United States is "war" or "wars." The difference is not trivial. More than one war at a time can crosscut each other and amount to no real overarching war at all. Multiple conflicts can prevent any one conflict from becoming all-engulfing. The tensions between persons of different classes, ethnic backgrounds, and gender tend to intersect and counterbalance rather than overlap and exacerbate each other.

References to "war" suggest various images and scenarios. These include the macho contests between officers in search of medals, the self-fulfilling prophesies of moral provocateurs, and the exaggerated fantasies of reporters confusing fact with fiction for lack of a firsthand view. There is no question that all of these are implicated to some degree in the current contest. Certainly there are sufficient extremists on both the left and the right to begin the action. Whether true believers or movement professionals, they have a clear interest in ginning up the conflicts. Nor do they lack complicit coverage on the part of media anxious to sell books, newspapers, and air time.

At one level, the mere acceptance of the phrase "culture war" is ipso facto evidence of its reality—at least in the eyes of the beholder. But at another level, it is worth checking on the basics. Quite apart from those proudly leading the march to battle (and those reporting on them), it is worth asking, who is following? Regardless of the sometimes violent actions of movement lieutenants, it is hardly idle to ask of the mood of citizen foot soldiers.

In many descriptions of culture war, political ideology seems to get the better of empirical inquiry. Much of the talk has the darkly pessimistic quality of a jeremiad rather than analysis. In addition to warnings of violence, there is a concern over the prospect of democracy at an end. Of course, these would not be the first social scientists adrift in the singular present with no historical anchor. There is certainly no question that the topic engages one's values and interests. This is not simply a matter of seeing one's glass half full or half empty, since it seems disturbingly likely that many alarmists would refuse a refill.

Clearly a good deal of the problem here is semantic and conceptual. Accordingly, it is worth pausing for a definition. I define a true "culture war" as a national conflict that involves widespread polarization and concerted violence over government legitimacy and control in the pursuit of noneconomic interests. Of course, every definition is an invitation to quibble, hence a bit of amplification is in order. By "widespread polarization" I mean a significant division among a population taking clear sides on the matters at issue rather than the efforts of a few to roil the waters of the many. "Concerted violence" means a strategic use of collective force on a large scale as opposed to aberrant actions that are more individualized and sporadic; neither isolated murders of abortionists nor a consensually condemned militia-type bombing qualify. The concern with "governmental legitimacy and control" is intended to distinguish conflicts where real power is at stake from other forms of violent confrontations, however tragic. Even the most extreme combatants at Oklahoma City, Ruby Ridge, and various abortion clinics have not called for an overthrow of the government, only a change in laws and officeholders. Finally, I specify "noneconomic interests" to distinguish culture wars from the more conventional forms of class conflict, though in truth even class struggles require cultural constructions and frames of interpretation.

At this point, I must resemble some Horatio at the bridge to semantic inflation. But given the above definition of a culture war, does what is occurring in the United States qualify? There are basically two relevant tests—one internal and the other external. The internal involves the extent of division in the national house. Here there is growing research based, for example, on recent surveys by the National Opinion Research Center.[8] On even the most controversial issues at the heart of our alleged "war," such as abortion and homosexuality, public opinion tends to be huddled in the middle rather than polarized at the extremes.[9] This applies not only to the society at large but also within groups often thought of as fully homogenous combatants, including various religious denominations.[10]

The internal argument for an American culture war is variously wanting. It fails to emphasize the force and forces of moderation that dampen the flames of warfare. While there is no doubt a minority of highly charged enlistees for virtually any issue, the majority is moderate in its views and moderating in its effect. The culture war thesis also exaggerates polarization by focusing too narrowly on the extreme flanks of public opinion. It relies on the testimony of the few who call to arms rather than the many who fail to respond. The antagonisms between movement elites are not necessarily reflected among either rank-and-file members or the great unmobilized public—as the elites themselves know full well.

A true culture war depends upon rival ideologies that go beyond single issues and meld a series of issues into one single dominant and dichotomous division. But this is hard to accomplish. For example, a number of Catholic bishops have sought support for a consistent pro-life ethic that opposes not only abortion but also poverty, capital punishment, and nuclear arms; the four positions include one on the right wing of American politics and three on the left. Thus the mobilized opponents of abortion have been anything but mobilized against poverty, capital punishment, or nuclear arms.

The internal evidence of an American culture war comes up short. But what about the second and more external test of the culture war thesis? This one requires comparisons with other countries. Not to mince words, applying the phrase "culture war" to the United States makes a mockery of nations elsewhere around the world that fulfill its criteria all-too well. Nor are these countries hard to find. On the same day that the nation's wire services and newspapers listed the 170 victims of the Oklahoma City bombing, they also described some two thousand bodies found in a mass grave in Rwanda. One United Nations report listed thirty-two ethnic and religious civil wars, each involving more than a thousand deaths in 1989–90 alone.[11] U.N. Secretary General Kofi Annan recently noted that the last decade of the twentieth century witnessed five million deaths as a result of intrastate conflict, and after reviewing the literature on worldwide episodes of intranational violence, Charles Tilly described the twentieth century as "the most virulently violent ten decades in human history."[12]

Culture Wars Around the World Revisited

Of the fourteen countries we visited in part 1, all but three have witnessed extensive episodes of internal warfare in their recent histories. Of course, this should not be construed as a gauge of the global proportion generally, since I tended to select countries where religion was heavily implicated in political violence. Still, only Sweden, despite the assassination of a prime minister; Thailand, despite the menacing shadow of the military in its wings; and Japan, despite the Aum Shinrikyo's nerve-gas attack on the Tokyo subway, have been relatively peaceful since the mid-twentieth century. The remaining eleven all evidence true culture wars that have been deeply engrained.

Certainly this was true of Brazil in the two decades stretching from the mid-1960s to the mid-1980s. As the military took over the reins of government and the dominant Catholic Church reflected the new developments of a Liberation Theology with its base communities, the stage was set for a protracted struggle that reflected differences of social class, religious action, and cultural understandings. Arrests, imprisonments, disappearances, and killings were commonplace. Nor have the wounds entirely healed. The conflict between landowners and land claimants continues to take a bloody toll in the Amazon watershed in the northern part of the country. While land itself is not a cultural matter, the struggle over it carries important ethnic and religious overtones.

Guatemala offers an even more grotesque case highlighted by its recently negotiated "conclusion." Estimates of the number of war deaths in Guatemala over the past twenty-five years range as high as 150,000, with uncounted others missing or in exile. Here, too, much of the conflict is economic as part of Latin America's continuing battle over land, agricultural control, and capitalist profiteering. But the struggle also has sharp cultural edges that reflect ethnic, linguistic, and religious differences. Guatemala's traditional Catholic dominance has given way to an uneasy religious tension and competition. Although the Catholic Church was officially disestablished in 1871, it took more than a hundred years to mount an effective challenge to its place at the head of the state table. Part of the challenge was internal, as Catholicism began to host both a late-developing liberationist movement and a small but stubborn faction of right-wing Opus Dei members. Meanwhile, there are also two external challengers: first, various forms of evangelical Protestantism in both affluent suburbs and underclass barrios, and second, a resurgence of traditional Mayan religion, culture, and identity. The latter is especially strong in the rural countryside and mountains to the north, particularly among members of the antigovernment guerilla movement still active there.

All of this has produced more changes in formal accords and rhetoric than in the country's day-to-day life. The indigenous movement now has a traditional cultural agenda to complement its radical thrusts on behalf of economic rights, gender equity, and relief from political terror. The recent peace accords are certainly good news, but they offer only guarded hope and circumscribed prospects for any major shifts in the country's enduring social reality.

Moving from Latin America to Europe, few countries have experienced more frequent or more devastating culture wars than Poland. This rich culture has been a longtime pawn and battleground of its rival neighbors. Focusing only on the events since the 1930s, Poland was the most deeply victimized site of the Nazi occupation and its Holocaust horror inflicted upon Jews, Romanies (or Gypsies), and noncompliant Christians, among others. While much of this was based on ethnic antipathy, ethnic differences are themselves cultural constructs.

Following World War II, Poland was forced to accept a Soviet-imposed Communist regime. By 1979 Polish resistance had begun to bubble over. Once again, the phrase "culture war" is simultaneously apt but inadequate in describing the years of civil insurrection between 1979 and 1989. The resistance was originally led by the labor movement Solidarity.

But when the new Polish pope, John Paul II, persuaded the Polish Catholic Church to join with Solidarity, the movement took on added legitimacy and a more explicit cultural dimension as it waged a struggle between godless Communism and God's own forces. Here the state itself was at stake. While violence was minimized by the constraints of a world as witness, the phrase "culture war" certainly applied.

The case of Northern Ireland virtually defines the phrase, even though not everyone agrees that religion per se is still the prime mover. With rare exceptions, neither Protestant nor Catholic churches or clergy are active antagonists; once powerful theological differences have lost their urgency after almost three centuries of hostilities, and the bulk of the Northern Irish citizenry have become more culturally than religiously Protestant or Catholic.

A broad religious and cultural chasm remains the basic fault line. But it would be misleading to portray Northern Ireland as a fully polarized public without a middle. By now most of the citizenry is weary of a war waged from the cultural margins. Violence has come from the extremists on both sides, whether the IRA on the Catholic side or the various loyalist groups among the Protestants. But to some degree the roles have reversed, as Protestants have replaced Catholics as the more frequent terrorists. As the demographic tide has turned and Catholics begin to enjoy political ascendancy, Protestant extremists are increasingly desperate. Extremists on both sides can be expected to continue a pattern of violence that is calculated to bring down the recently adopted peace agreement. The agreement is certainly welcome, but it is certainly no guarantee that harmony will always prevail in the years ahead.

All four of the Islamic societies I visited have experienced forms of culture wars, though of different degrees and kinds. Turkey's has been the most muted. The country's darkest stains have involved its suppression and scattering first of Armenians and now Kurds. The struggle of conservative Muslims to gain a political and policy voice has only rarely burst into anything akin to warfare. Kemal Ataturk's political takeover and cultural transformation in the 1920s shifted Islam from an official religion to the private realm. Although there have been efforts over the years to mount a Muslim political offensive, the military has always been at the ready to thwart the threat. In 1997 it forced the Islamic-dominated Virtue Party out of office. While grumbling is clearly audible, most of the national elite downplays an Islamic resurgence and is even prepared to support yet another military intervention to ward it off.

Both Egypt and Indonesia also illustrate the pattern of elite wariness over Islamic mobilization. Each society has had long-standing regimes in power that have controlled electoral processes with the same ruthless efficiency used to control other aspects of national life. While both countries are formally Islamic states, in each case Islamic movements have developed in opposition to the ruling parties and their leaders.

Egypt's culture war has been more open and more intense. The once radical Muslim Brotherhood has mellowed over time and deployed conventional political tactics. But the Islamic Group has used violence as a principal tactic of opposition. The violence has been directed sometimes against tourists as a calculated blow to the nation's economy and sometimes against secular intellectuals, nonobservant Muslims, and the small minority of local Christians. The government has responded with sweeping arrests and quick convictions that have led to widespread imprisonments, public executions, and another round of rekindled resentment and alienation in the population at large as well as among extremist factions.

The downfall and resignation of Indonesia's long-ruling President Suharto culminates—but does not end—a culture war of somewhat different dimensions. Suharto sought to embrace Indonesia's various religious strands through the state-administered religious concoction of Pancasila. Indonesia's pattern of intra-individual religious pluralism combines official Islam with unofficial Hinduism, Buddhism, Christianity, and animism; this pattern has inhibited the development of a militant Muslim movement as the nation's prime opposition force and facilitated the rise of a more modernist Islamic movement, whose leader is now the elected chief of state.

Still, Indonesian cultural differences remain a troubling source of local tensions. Violence has found victims among Christians in East Timor and Molucca, among the Chinese merchant class, and among some Muslim factions themselves. Members of the former ruling elite are not immune to threats, owing to the perception that they have lined their own pockets at the expense of the national economy.

Pakistan illustrates a different scenario of cultural warfare. Turkey, Egypt, and Indonesia all represent countries whose secular rulers are out of step with popular religious movements. By contrast, Pakistan resembles Saudi Arabia, Iran under the Ayatollah Khomeini, and now Afghanistan under the Taliban. Here the rulers play the religious card, often over the objections of other members of the national elite and the citizenry at large.

For more than twenty years, Pakistani prime ministers have resorted to campaigns of Islamization as a way of shoring up their legitimacy among the nation's faithful and their mullahs. It is hard to gauge the sincerity behind the pledges to return to Islamic traditions and the law of its sharia courts. The initiatives have a way of damping down mass political suspicion over corruption and conniving. But much of the rhetoric has a hollow quality, as these policies have been only selectively implemented to avoid detracting from the prime minister's power. Even this limited implementation has set off movements in opposition—for example, among middle-class women who see reversals of their hard-gained rights in education, employment, and court procedures concerning rape. Here, too, demonstrations are commonly followed by forced dispersal, extensive arrests, and quick "justice."

Israel and India scarcely need more elaboration as the sites of ongoing cultural warfare. Earlier I described both as cultural "mindfields." Many of us have seen the Israeli situation unfold on television, including the highs of Camp David and the lows of Hamas, Hebron, the assassination of Yitzhak Rabin, and the recent riots in Jerusalem and the West Bank. Negotiations between Palestinians and Israelis leaders are chronically stalemated, as they are too worried about their left and right flanks, respectively, to meet anywhere in the middle. Heated divisions within the ranks pit Jew against Jew and Arab Muslim against Arab Muslim; secularism and orthodoxy are in conflict on both sides. The violent actions of both Palestinian and Jewish obstructionists have been commonplace.

India also hosts not just one culture war but several. The central Hindu-Muslim conflict dates from the sixteenth century, and the partitioning of India and Pakistan in 1947 claimed as many as five hundred thousand lives. While the killings have never approximated that level in the ensuing half century, neither have they stopped. The rise of a right-wing Hindu political movement has provoked numerous bloody incidents, most recently in 1992 by destroying a Muslim mosque on the mythical birthplace of the Hindu God Rama in the north-central town of Ayodyah.

Finally, consider the People's Republic of China—shaped in one revolution in 1949 and forged by a different kind of revolution through the 1960s and 1970s. The latter involved a Cultural Revolution that had many of the earmarks of war. Led by Mao Zedong, the Communist Party and the state set about to expunge its rivals, including all traces of Western culture that could be regarded as counterrevolutionary.

Since the late 1970s, a country that had been turned in upon itself now turned outward again and toward the West. But the party has remained in rigid control, to the growing dismay of predictable opposition groups, especially students. The quashed Tiananmen uprising of 1989 brought another episode of China's culture wars to the world's television screens. More recently, state suppression of the Falun Gong is a reminder that wartime conditions can reappear at any time.

So much for a brief review of a series of countries that satisfy the earlier definition of a culture war far better than the United States. But despite my earlier concerns about a free-floating and all too expansive conception of "war" that covers an entire spectrum of human relations, it is also misleading to treat the phenomenon as a categorical absolute rather than a relative variable. It is true that the United States is generally less at war with itself than are many other nations, but it is also true that we have had our own cultural tensions and even our own episodes of culturally provoked violence.

So far my concern has been with the larger category of culture wars. But clearly religion itself has been implicated in the conflicts of every country we have visited. It is now time to look at religion's role in inciting warfare and the many questions about how and why this occurs.

Interrogating "Religious Violence"

Two errors are common in analyzing religion's relation to violence—or to virtually anything else for that matter. The first is underestimating religion's influence; the second is overestimating it. Finding and holding a proper midpoint can be precarious. Even the most balanced interpreters sometimes find themselves teetering to one side and then the other.

In part because of religion's association with ancient traditions in a modernizing world, many social scientists have dismissed religion as an archaic vestige on the margins of society rather than a featured player in the contemporary drama. Where civil violence is concerned, religion is now commonly tucked under the carpet of "ethnicity" as a larger but largely misleading rubric used by secular scholars. Yet today religion is undergoing a revival as a subject in its own right. This is largely because of its association with violence and politics. As I noted at the outset of the book, 1979 was a critical year for reassessment, with events ranging from the rise of the Moral Majority, the deaths at Jonestown, the pope's dramatic roles concerning Latin American Liberation Theology and the alliance between Polish Catholicism and Solidarity, the signing of the Camp David Accords concerning Egypt and Israel, and—perhaps most persuasive of all—the return from exile of Iran's ayatollah and the taking of American hostages in Tehran. Suddenly, religion seemed to shift from a curiosum from the past to an angry portent of trouble at hand.

But lest I begin to overcompensate by overstressing religion's impact, several cautions are in order. It is no more justified to treat religion as the always dominant channel in the societal stream than it is to treat it as an inevitable oxbow. There are times when religion surges and times when it recedes. In addition, it is important that social scientists treat religion not solely in its own singular terms but rather as only one of a range of sacred causes and commitments that can energize action for weal and for woe. Even the title of this section can be faulted for implying that religious violence is somehow categorically different from all other violence. Theology aside, religion shares with other cultural forces the same essential dynamics and scenarios of violence. In fact, one reason why religion is now losing some of its stigma among secularized scholars is that it is seen increasingly as part of the broader cultural panoply rather than a wholly mysterious realm apart.

But even culture itself has had its problems gaining a hearing in the social sciences. Basically, "culture" involves systems of socially constructed meanings, beliefs, and values that symbolically convey interpretations of what reality is and ought to be—some of which are sacred and some quite secular. But social scientists from Marx forward have been nervous about the evanescent quality of culture. Many have preferred to focus on more "structural" phenomena that reflect the concrete and institutionalized givens of the social world and are amenable to empirical measurement—whether, for example, economic differences between social classes, demographic matters of population size and the environment, or the organizational realities of communities, bureaucracies, and nation-states.

Hard-core structuralists are skeptical of the culture war thesis simply because they are skeptical of culture itself and regard it as too ephemeral and powerless to provoke and sustain anything so urgent. This structuralist perspective is still in vogue in some circles. But there is now increasing recognition that the phrase "cultural power" is not a contradiction in terms.[13] Culture can be a great reservoir of passion, resolve, and tactical advantages—at least under certain conditions. While culture and structure are always interlarded, culture is often a critical source and resource for social movements of all sorts. At the same time, culture without structure is no more viable than structure without culture. The real question is not which is dominant but how they affect each other.

Over the past century and more, social science has swayed first in one direction and then the other. Recent signs suggest the end of a long period of structural preoccupation that began in the 1960s. A new awareness of culture is reflected in booming undergraduate courses on the popular culture of fads, fashion, and the media. Few of these courses even mention religion as arguably the most popular cultural form of all, nor do many attend to culture's political dimensions. However, religion has begun to reappear as a dimension of culture that is too rich and revealing to be neglected. Religion provides an unmatched window into the exotica and erotica of society—a running, microcosmic illustration of life in both the mainstream and on the edge. As religion is implicated in both the best and worst of the human condition, it also reminds us continually of the ways in which culture and structure interact, intersect, and interbreed.

The following discussion defuses the loaded phrase "religious violence." Specifically, it explores four different ways that culture—and religion—can be involved in civil violence. These involve religion as trigger, religion as cause, religion as surrogate and construct, and religion's role in the way violence can become self-perpetuating.

Religion as Trigger

To the extent that religion becomes symbolically involved with any movement, it adds a potential flash point and hair trigger. Compared to other cultural forms, religion tends to play for higher stakes while plumbing deeper emotions. Even movement members who privately harbor sober second thoughts about a doctrine or ritual practice may be swept along in the collective tide of the moment or be reluctant to confess their doubts when events call their bluff. Religious conflicts escalate quickly and de-escalate slowly because of the inflammatory conflict over nonnegotiable absolutes and the tendency of secular opponents to pour skeptical fuel on sacred flames. Any leader whose charisma is flagging has only to raise a religious banner to secure full battle ribbons with a martyr's cluster. These dynamics are neither new nor newly noted. Illustrations abound in virtually every one of the countries we have examined—whether the Sikhs under Bhindranwale in India's Punjab, Egypt's Islamic Group under Sheikh Omar Abdel-Rahman, or Thailand's right-wing "kill-a-Commie-for-Buddha" monk.

But under what circumstances are religious sensitivities most inflamed and religious trigger fingers most likely to itch? Sacred time and space are critical. Religious violence is often coincident with religious commemorations—for example, Protestant and Catholic marches in small towns in Northern Ireland, Shia anniversaries in dominantly Sunni Pakistan, or Hindu celebrations in Muslim neighborhoods of India. More important, religious violence is linked to turf struggles over sacred space. Consider the contested mosque on Rama's putative birth site in India, Coptic Christian churches in locations venerated by Egyptian Muslims, military operations on sites sacred to Guatemala's indigenous Mayans, Buddhist temples in Indonesia's dominantly Muslim central Java, and Protestant and Catholic encroachments on each other's consecrated death sites in Londonderry, Northern Ireland—from the Protestants' Battle of the Boyne in 1690 to the Catholics' Bloody Sunday of 1972.

No country illustrates the violence of religious place better than Israel. Here tensions erupt even within faith communities, as in a recent fracas among the six Christian denominations that occupy parts of the Church of the Holy Sepulchre, the periodic violence occasioned by the Haredim of the Mea Shearim neighborhood whose boundary concerns lead to periodic struggles with Israeli police and construction crews, or the mounting struggles between the Hamas and Arafat's Palestinian authority. But, of course, there have been larger interfaith struggles for millennia, including the celebrated first-century martyrs of Masada whose memory has been reconstructed to serve Israel's current national objectives.[14] Parts of Israel are now held sacred by Christians, Jews, and Muslims alike. The latter two have long vied for hegemony in Hebron, over Jerusalem's Temple Mount and Noble Sanctuary, and over Jerusalem itself. Increasingly, the hardscrabble settlement areas of the West Bank and Gaza have qualified as religious sites worthy of ultimate defense.

However, contests over sacred time and sacred space rarely lead to violence without another acid added to the mix. That is power—whether sought or threatened. None of the examples cited here are without accompanying power struggles. All involve at least partial responses to political flux following periods of relative placidity when power relations were relatively stable. Power is very much at stake in the religious, ethnic, and national violence that has become a staple of the often purposefully protracted negotiations in Israel. Power is even at stake in clashes among Jews themselves—the Haredim and the Gush Emunim—in a country that has yet to decide on Judaism's political role, let alone Islam's.

In related scenarios, Guatemala's insurgents have recently negotiated a somewhat problematic truce in a twenty-year civil war with the promise of more power sharing. The purposive religious terrorism in Egypt is an attempt to destabilize a precarious economy so as to unseat a corrupt government for whom democracy has become a charade. Similar developments have occurred in both Indonesia and Thailand. Meanwhile, Pakistan's minority Shia and majority Sunni coexisted relatively amicably until the Islamization campaign called for Islam to have more state power and an inevitable rivalry sharpened over the question, which Islam? India's clashes among Hindus, Muslims, and Sikhs are clearly politically infused—whether as part of the continuing armed struggle with Pakistan over Muslim Kashmir, as part of the resurgent BJP's surge on behalf of Hindu nationalists, or as part of the Sikh independence movement's demands to transform the Punjab into an autonomous Khalistan.

In what I have referred to as the moth and the flame syndrome, a long list of assassinations attests to the dangers involved when political figures get too close to the religious flame and vice versa. Egypt's Sadat, India's Mahatma Gandhi and Indira Gandhi, the latter's son Rajiv Gandhi, and Israel's Rabin are just a few of the political leaders consumed by religious flames. Significantly, none were killed by an alien religionist; instead, all were assassinated by coreligionists or presumed allies who felt betrayed. Meanwhile, religious moths who have been drawn to the political flame and become targets of politically motivated assassins include Martin Luther King Jr., Malcolm X, and, less successfully, Pope John Paul II. Because religion's relationship to power, politics, and the state is so crucial, it is the focus of the book's next chapter. Meanwhile, if religion's role as a trigger of violence can be painfully obvious, religion's role as a cause of violence can be more elusive.

Religion as Cause

Consider three countries in our sample where religious differences have been most deeply and fatally divisive: India, Israel, and Northern Ireland—or in Protestant terms, Ulster. All three would seem prime instances where political violence is caused by religious differences. India's history has been written and rewritten from the standpoint of religious conflict—including those schismatic struggles that ultimately led Buddhists, Jains, and Sikhs to break away from Hinduism and Hinduism's conflicts with other world religions such as the Muslims from the sixteenth century on or Christianity under the British Raj. Israel and Northern Ireland are no less religiously contested.

My own interpretation of such imbroglios differs from the more doctrinally—even cosmically—focused accounts of other religiously oriented scholars.[15] Focusing on religious roots alone risks the overemphasis on religion warned of earlier. Religion is obviously important to the dynamic within each of the three countries, but the conflicts do not always involve pitched battles between devotees or primary disagreements over cosmologies, theologies, and ritual practices. Laity are at least as likely to be activist leaders as are clergy, and often the most militant antagonists are defending a broad cultural religious heritage rather than a narrow orthodoxy or orthopraxy.

What is more, the religious communities in these countries are hardly monolithic. Just as neighborhood sociability exists despite religious differences, so do major internal struggles occur despite religious similarities. Differences within these religious groups can be as conflicted as the differences between them. The latter include the sometimes violent clashes between high- and low-caste Hindus, Shias, and Sunnis; between secular Zionist and ultra-Orthodox non-Zionists; and between various communities of both Protestants and Catholics.

Finally, in all three countries, cultural and religious differences are exacerbated by ethnic and class inequalities. The Muslims of both India and Israel and the Catholics of Ulster have experienced structural grievances as beleaguered minorities. What is worse, these multiple grievances compound each other. Claims become exponentially more compelling when they are arithmetically aggregated.

What is at issue here is what might be termed "stacked grievances," which are the reverse of the crosscutting differences at the heart of American pluralism. Like the multiple culture wars discussed earlier, crosscutting divisions of class, race, region, and religion prevent any one division from serving as the dominant axis of polarization. A commonly cited reason why the United States has not experienced a Marxian class struggle is that the American "proletariat" comprises internal divisions between, for example, Irish and Italians, whites and blacks, males and females, Protestants and Catholics, and urban and rural residents. All of these differences involve suspicions and tensions that prevent people from galvanizing on either side of the class division itself.

However, the United States also has some experience with the opposite phenomenon of stacked grievances. For example, the religious right has shared concerns over secularity, poverty, political disenfranchisement, abortion, sexual orientation, and family values. For a time, this common ground unified a large constituency despite its differences. Ultimately, however, the religious right was limited by its own crosscutting diversity—Democrats versus Republicans, Protestants versus Catholics, fundamentalists versus pentecostals, north versus south, and women versus men. At this point, strictly religious mobilization becomes both less necessary and less possible. Thus, the pro-life movement no longer has to mobilize along dominantly Catholic lines—and no longer can.

By contrast, large-scale cultural divisions between aggregated cultural camps are more likely elsewhere. Stacked grievances over social class, political marginality, and cultural defensiveness have long united Northern Irish Catholics, Guatemala's Mayan indigenas, Israel's Palestinians, and India's Muslims—to cite only a few examples. A spark in one area can lead to spreading flames.

Religion as Surrogate and Construct

Even when religion seems central to episodes of violence, it is important to ask what the religion represents. The answer is not always what it seems. Not all ostensible religious causes or their participants have a primarily religious agenda. Some religious movements are surrogates and legitimating proxies for more pressing nonreligious causes.

The scenario is neither new nor newly noted. Scholars reaching back to and beyond Freud and Marx have seen their mission as interpreting religion in nonreligious terms. For Freud, religion reflected illusions based in an overactive super-ego; for Marx, it was a form of "false consciousness" and an opiate that dulled the pain of economic oppression. Precisely because religion's own claims and self-justifications lie in a plane apart from the social sciences, analysts have tended to set them to one side in pursuing alternative accounts. Because this sometimes involves a pilgrim's unacknowledged or possibly repressed needs and objectives, it leads the interpreter into cloudy waters of imputed motives and possible hypocrisy. God may speak in mysterious ways indeed, especially when God's voice is being thrown by ventriloquists among us.

Western missionaries in the Far East used the phrase "rice Christians" to describe those hungry followers who feigned the faith and attended their services for the rice handed out instead of for the religion dispensed. The phenomenon has analogies throughout the world, including the United States. It also has important implications for religion's relation to politics and violence. Some of the most dramatic episodes may say less about religion than is commonly assumed.

Examples of the sacred as surrogate abound in the countries we have visited. The relationship between Poland's Catholic Church and its Solidarity labor movement conferred important benefits on each—a trade of religious legitimacy for political saliency. Clearly the Church experienced a quick injection of vitality as part of this linkage. But now that Solidarity has left its embrace to join the government, many are wondering where the church will find its next ally and whether the current signs of declining religiosity do not portend a backslide to its earlier marginal dormancy. This is by no means the only case posing the question of whether a traditional sacred institution can thrive in an increasingly secular society without taking on secular allies in the process.

A similar Catholic instance involves the Latin American Church, Liberation Theology, and the base communities. There were ample grounds for the suspicions of both the Vatican and the reigning political establishments that liberationism was as much a political cause as a religious undertaking. Liberation Theology was not a purely doctrinal or ecclesiastical development. It reflected a brilliantly conceived alliance between a radical religious priesthood and a radical political movement seeking cover under the church's canopy. As in the case of Poland, it is hard to draw a sharp distinction between the religious and political motives of the participants, and perhaps it is overly picky to try. The point is that neither the religious nor the political agendas could have succeeded without the other.

Islam offers a series of instances in which religious developments mask political dynamics. Pakistan and Indonesia both illustrate a different sort of sacred surrogate. One of the recurring themes of Pakistani state leadership is invoking Islam during times of crisis. Virtually all prime ministers since the 1970s have turned to religion to shore up their sagging legitimacy. The country's various Islamization campaigns would place the nation's Western-derived legal system under the control of the traditional Sharia courts and the mullahs in charge of them. Several government respondents characterized one such initiative an outright "fraud." That is, it was launched primarily for political purposes, and the prime minister in question had no intention of placing his own administration under Islamic control. It became increasingly clear that an optimum strategy for a politician in office was to leave the Sharia Bill perennially pending in parliamentary limbo. That way he or she could claim credit for supporting the spirit of the law while avoiding the letter of the law.

Indonesia is a similar case with a twist. Prior to the most recent wave of demonstrations that finally unseated longtime President Suharto, political mobilization against the regime was illegal but religious assemblies were not. Hence, the two forces often melded to express their shared opposition to the regime. A number of Indonesian students who attended ostensibly Islamic rallies did so because it was the only way to voice protest without being arrested. At least in part, then, Islamic fundamentalism became a proxy for a left-wing and anti-Western political agenda. What appeared to be an entrenched religious conflict was in some significant measure a conflict over a much broader set of secular issues beyond the political pale. We saw similar instances of mixed motives on behalf of "religious extremists" in Egypt.

But there are other instances that caution against pat interpretations, namely, the Hindu-Muslim and Hindu-Sikh violence in India, the Catholic-Protestant impasse in Northern Ireland, and the bloody Muslim-Jewish standoff in Israel. There is no doubt that at least culturally religious differences help to account for the obduracy and emotionality of these conflicts. There is also no doubt that each situation includes many moths for whom religion has deep primacy in propelling them into the political flames. Nonetheless, as previously noted, I found virtually no respondent in any of these situations who argued that religion alone was responsible for the conflict. Those most centrally involved in the combat are rarely centrally involved in religion. It is precisely because these sacred identities have become infused with wider meanings and interests that they radiate into the wider community and are contested with such tragic intensity.

In some sense, considering the sacred as surrogate leads to two seemingly opposite conclusions. On the one hand, virtually all of the examples cited here show religion deriving sustenance and thrust from nonreligious concerns beneath its surface. On the other hand, even where religion serves as a surrogate, the question is why religion was chosen for the role. Clearly religion continues to command enormous symbolic power and legitimizing force. Whether because of its emotional salience, its moral centrality, its institutional durability, or its divine standing, religion continues to be compelling in its own right.

If it seems somewhat cynical to suggest that religion can be "just" a surrogate, it is important to re-state the point more positively. Religion is often a crucial way of constructing causes so as to give them an appeal and legitimacy they might otherwise lack. Precisely because religion continues to hover over the most seemingly secular landscapes, it offers a critical ethical narrative for movements that seek a wider audience. This even applies to movements in which structural grievances appear to be everything. These are especially common in a political science literature that tends to treat "the politics of deadly quarrels" as the quarrels of deadly politics, although lately there has been an increasing, if perhaps grudging, recognition of religion as at least a relatively minor subspecies of its own.[16]

Exclusively structural causes are no more common than exclusively cultural cases, and perhaps just as illusory. Finally an older and wiser Karl Marx came to understand that even the most abject structural deprivations by themselves are poor mobilizers—hence the importance of "class consciousness."[17] Virtually all inequities require some form of cultural construction, whether it is termed "framing," "discourse generated symbolic capital," or the aforementioned "cultural power."[18]

The result is not always a pure culture war. But cultural identities often provide critical symbolic fuel and moral weaponry for use with other causes, and of all cultural identities, religion can be the most urgent and intense.[19] While religion is not the only construct available for this purpose, it is both commonly deployed and uncommonly effective. Religion's lofty principles offer ready access to the moral high ground and often resonate widely among even the more secularized citizenry, recalling nobler commitments of nobler times past. In countries as disparate as Brazil, Poland, Egypt, Indonesia, and Thailand, I found ostensibly religious movements whose agendas are in considerable part secular.

Nonetheless, difficulties often await when structural grievances are given cultural constructions. One is a variation of the Marxian concept of "false consciousness."[20] There is a sense in which this concept is analytically equivalent to the more Weberian and Durkheimian tradition of "culture." Both false consciousness and culture involve interpretative depictions of "what is" in terms of "what ought to be." But while Marx disparaged the result, others have been more accepting, and some culture enthusiasts see culture as the ultimate arbiter of reality itself. In the eyes of these culture groupies, culture is always right and always holds the deep secrets in any social setting. However, the current recrudescence of culture in the social sciences entails a healthy respect for culture's mischievous qualities when it is out of kilter with structural givens. Culture may filter, romanticize, and distort social life to such an extent that it becomes more a source of problems than of reliable guidance.

This is apparent in religious movements where the search for broader

appeal and legitimacy may distort the original objectives. What was originally sought as a cultural cover may become a cultural transformation.
This may occur among a movement's audience and among its participants; cultural power can have as much impact on its wielders as on its
targets. Within virtually every one of the sites of religious violence we
have visited—not to mention others such as Iran, Algeria, and Afghanistan—one can discern cases in which religion has not only expressed
other grievances but actually displaced them.

However, the reverse is more common. Although Marxists rarely
mention the possibility that structural frames or constructions may
eclipse what were originally more cultural complaints, this is a common by-product of secularization. A number of movements that began
with such cultural objectives as enhanced religious standing, ethnic affirmation, or national identity have taken on more structural goals and
political agendas in keeping with modernity's more secular discourse.
Virtually every one of the world's major religions offers examples of groups
that have converted their otherworldly aspirations into this-worldly
terms. After all, dominion over political kingdoms in the here and now
offers more immediate and more certain gratification than dominion over
soteriological kingdoms in the life beyond. Examples include segments
of Northern Ireland's IRA, Israel's secular Zionists, and Guatemala's
Mayan guerillas. India's BJP is now caught in a tension between its
Hindutva roots and its mass political aspirations, especially as compared
with the ethnic and religious constructions of Sikhs in the Punjab.[21]

The analysis of religion is too important to be left solely in the hands
of either the true believer or the iconoclast. If the former tends to find
religion everywhere, the latter tends to find religion nowhere. Clearly
religion persists as a vital social and political force, but probing the how
and why also persists as an important inquiry. Meanwhile, there is one
last cultural scenario that relates religion and violence. It is one that
seems to run counter to the search for more conventional causes of violence and one that turns causes and consequences on their heads.

Violence As Self-Perpetuating

So far I have tried to provide an overview of factors producing
violence and how religion fits within a mix of other cultural and structural considerations. Like most other accounts, I have treated violence
as a consequence. In this last section, however, I want to examine violence
as a cause in its own right, describing how it can take on self-perpetuating
influence once it is culturally—and often religiously—constructed. David
Apter makes the point lyrically: "[V]iolence generates its own objects. It
creates interior meanings. Seeking the moral moment in the cannon's
mouth it ritualizes death as sacrifice, turns martyrdom into testimony.

When death is the measure of devotion to noble causes, even the victims become co-conspirators if they accept it as some historical necessity. It is one way for political violence to become legitimized."[22]

The point here is not just that violence can be legitimized by other considerations but that, on occasion, violence can supply its own legitimacy. Ultimate causes of violence are frequently lost in the recesses of history and the emotions of tragedy—especially when violence is tied to the often gossamer abstractions of religion. At the same time, proximate causes of violence can become perversely fertile as one act breeds another and violence is heaped upon violence through time. There is neither an opportunity nor an audience for dispassionate observers to adjudicate passionate claims. This is not to deny that other causes exist and that it is part of our responsibility to probe for them. But anyone who has spent time with both sides of a culture war knows how credible each can seem—indeed, how credible each must seem to sustain the mutual acts and recriminations that keep the spiral going.

This is another reason why so many conventionally plausible explanations of violence account for less than sideliners might suppose. To the extent that violence becomes its own cause and sustenance, people are drawn into it on grounds other than those usually imagined. Today's constructions of yesterday's violence are sometimes at considerable odds with initiating events. Communal loyalties remain even after the generations have wiped away original grievances and altered their founding circumstances. Because violence is so compelling in its own right, it often eclipses those mitigating factors that might abate it in cooler moments. The culture that emerges around violence serves to insulate it from inhibiting constraints.

These notions are well illustrated in Northern Ireland. Both Protestant loyalists and Catholic Republicans lacked clear explanations of the violence continuing between them, except for factors that pertained to the last volley of violence itself. Of course, once other considerations are suggested agreement readily follows. If it is true that the conflict is rarely seen in sectarian religious terms, it is not wholly secular either, since both communities have evolved from religious subcultures that inspire allegiance even among the unchurched. At the same time, to condition negotiations on a complete cease-fire and relinquishment of arms is to put power in the hands of the last fanatic on either side with a gun and the inclination to use it. Such absolute imperatives are out of character with the spirit of negotiation itself.

But then Northern Ireland is hardly alone in hosting a culture of self-justifying violence. India's religious conflicts are saturated with stereotypes of the way in which Hindus, Muslims, and Sikhs are violence prone. Veena Das has analyzed the future importance of survivors' accounts of past violent episodes.[23] The psychoanalyst Sudhir Kakar has commented on the identical elements in conflicting Hindu and Muslim accounts of the same riots.[24] Paul Brass has contributed a careful study of violence in Uttar Pradesh, showing how immediate accounts of a given episode serve to becloud originating causes and how different constructions of the same episode reflect different interests, with the media generally reflecting those of the elite.[25]

Certainly the violence between Israeli Jews and Muslims is not only mutually perpetuating but compounded by memories of such historical events as the Holocaust and the imposition of Israeli statehood. In both instances, burnished memories of past victimization are sometimes deployed as justifications for present preventive violence.[26] This even applies to lesser forms of violence such as forced settlements, coercive boycotts, and proactive policing. Cultural and structural differences between Jews and Palestinians are exacerbated by violent acts on both sides that serve as perception filters and ideological reinforcers.

Violence everywhere requires interpretation and attribution. Like ethnic and racial identities in particular, the religions of both perpetrators and victims are often all too conspicuous markers that set off the next round in a violent cycle. Given religion's high emotional content, it can be blamed quickly and recklessly in ways that affect violence for generations to come.

Conclusion

This chapter has sought to unpack and re-sort the complex matters associated with culture wars and religious violence. After defining the notion of a culture war more precisely than is common in popular treatments, I suggested that the present level of "warfare" in the United States falls mercifully far short of the conflict in other countries around the world.

All of this was a preamble for a more focused discussion of religious violence. In order to cool the incendiary implications of religious violence, I placed it in the context of cultural versus structural perspectives. Rather than endorse a hard distinction between religious, political, and other types of violence, I found that they all intersect. Rather than concede there is a firm separation between structural and cultural causes of violence-prone movements, I argue that neither is adequate without the other, and that the two should be regarded as complementary instead of mutually exclusive. Finally, rather than accept religion or any other set of ultimate causes as definitive, I noted that violence often takes on a life cycle of its own in which each episode provokes the next and for reasons little related to first causes or initial grievances.

In a way this entire chapter is a prologue in its own right. The next chapter focuses on religion, politics, and the state. As country after country around the globe attests, the lines between these spheres are not easy to draw and even more difficult to enforce. However, few boundaries are more important to patrol with vigilance.

7

Religious

Politics

without a

Religious State?

The most important factor in religion's relation to violence involves its relation to power and the state, and yet the possible relationships vary widely. In some cases, religion may turn its back on the state as a defiling digression from more important otherworldly concerns. In other cases, religion may be deeply implicated in either a religious state or a state religion, depending upon who is the dominant partner. In still other cases, there may be a tension between religion and the state, as each plays moth to the other's flame. Even where there is a de jure or de facto separation between the two, each has something to offer and to gain from the other. But religionists and politicians alike may go too far and suffer—sometimes fatally—for a reach that exceeds their grasp.

Because America's own separation of church and state has become such a global reference point in these matters, I begin with three ways in which the U.S. system is misunderstood, both at home and abroad. The last of these suggests that religion's relation to power may involve very different relations with politics and with the state. Four separate combinations are apparent among the countries we have visited, and it is worth exploring their straining tendencies and the frequent differences between surface appearances and deeper realities.

Three Common Misinterpretations of U.S. Separationism

"Congress shall make no law respecting an establishment of religion, or prohibiting the free exercise thereof." Since this initial clause in the U.S. Constitution's First Amendment was adopted in 1791, it has been interpreted both by an army of legal specialists and by a nation of willing believers.[1]

The two interpretive communities have not always agreed. Legalistic conclusions of the former have often been distorted or ignored by the popular will. Consider, for example, the widespread currency of Thomas Jefferson's reference to a "wall of separation" between church and state. Because Americans are proud of their constitutional heritage, many have taken the Jeffersonian metaphor to heart and tend to regard the wall as more unique and more impregnable than the facts warrant. As we shall see later, other countries have developed their own forms of separationism, though in no country, including our own, is the separation absolute. Meanwhile, three additional misunderstandings of the U.S. tradition are common not only around the world but also in the United States. Each deserves a bit of exegesis.

"Establishment" versus "Free Exercise"

The most popular view of the First Amendment celebrates its guarantee of religious freedom for religious groups seeking to avoid state interference while pursuing their inalienable rights.[2] This is certainly a noble and important aspect of the wording. But it is significant that the free-exercise clause actually follows the so-called establishment clause. A major concern at the time was protecting the fledgling federal government from religious control and insuring that bullying religious majorities would not use new federal power to make life difficult for religious minorities. This is precisely what "an establishment of religion" would have entailed, hence what needed to be prevented.[3]

Over time the establishment clause has become the one of the most distinctive parts of our constitutional tradition and one that it is still rare in other nations around the globe.[4] It is the key to some of the most important church-state litigation of the last half century. Here the complaining plaintiffs have not been those seeking freedom for religion but those seeking freedom from religion, at least in the public arena. The latter's concern has been to limit state religious endorsement of prayer in the public schools or state-supported religious interference in private matters such as abortion.

Over the last two hundred years, the definition of an offending religious establishment has also evolved.[5] The establishment threat comes not just from large denominations preying upon small religious groups but from perceived state support for the idea of religion in general as opposed to nonreligion. It was President Dwight Eisenhower who captured the limits of American religious tolerance when he said he didn't care which God citizens believed in as long as they had one. If translated into actual policy, this would have been an establishment violation because it amounted to a state official endorsing religion. However, one can also imagine an establishment violation that involves the opposite, that is, government endorsement of or support for nonreligion or what has been called "secular humanism" in the society at large. State departures from neutrality on either side of the religious fence have been judged constitutionally offensive.

Yet there are some well-accepted exceptions. Laws concerning the free exercise of religion often have explicit or implicit contingencies concerning the national interest. In the United States, there are well-established precedents for denying free exercise to practices that endanger the health and welfare of innocent victims, including the children of Christian Scientists who are protected from their parents' decisions to withhold critical medical care. There are also precedents for allowing church-state relationships that might otherwise suggest an "establishment." Basically, religious organizations may receive government funds to operate day-care centers, hospitals, and relief programs, for example, as long as both the intent and the consequences are secular. As the government's social missions have expanded, religious organizations are frequently indispensable allies in providing services. This has resulted in not a few winks and nudges over relationships that satisfy the needs of both church and state.[6]

There has always been an uneasy relation between the establishment and free-exercise clauses. From a strict legal standpoint, often the first decision to be made concerning a potential church-state case is which of the two clauses is most pertinent, since arguments from the two perspectives can be the reverse of each other. For instance, consider a recent case in which two Catholic women employed at a greyhound racetrack in Massachusetts announced that they were taking Christmas day off to celebrate with their families. When the track fired them on the grounds that they had been told in advance that this was its busiest day of the year and their work was indispensable, the two women secured a lawyer and filed for state compensation on the grounds that their religious freedom had been violated. This may seem a straightforward free exercise case. However, the claim was rejected. The lower court held that if the state had privileged a religious day off compared to other possible days off—especially a Catholic day off compared to other possible faiths and denominations—it would amount to a state religious "establishment." Subsequently, the case found its way into politics, and a dominantly

Catholic legislature passed a bill favoring such freedoms. But the last shoe has yet to drop.

One can even imagine the ultimate church-state cases in which the establishment and free exercise clauses are charged with violating each other. For example, placing limits on any religion's pursuit of becoming established by the state may be an unconstitutional constraint on its free exercise. If a religious denomination is strong enough to marshal control over a government, isn't denying this a denial of its religious rights? On the other hand, a state guarantee of religious free exercise may itself be an establishment violation. After all, doesn't it single out religion for special standing and special dispensations compared to the free exercise of other beliefs and commitments?

On rare occasions, such as those involving claims for conscientious objector status during the Vietnam War, religious rights have been granted to those who have no formal religious commitments but hold religious-like convictions. The U.S. Supreme Court extended conscientious objector status to persons who were avowedly not religious but held beliefs that occupied "in the life of that individual a 'place parallel to that filled by God' in traditional religious persons."[7] This radical allowance was precedent shattering, as it represented the nose of the secular sacred camel in the religious tent. Because its legal implications are daunting, it is not surprising that the Court has seldom referred to it since. But the suggestion that there is a thin line between formal religion and other sacred cultural tenets, rites, and associations continues to haunt strict constructionists of either law or religion.

This was recently manifest in the case of similarly broad language in the short-lived Religious Freedom Restoration Act (RFRA). Congress passed the act in 1993 in response to a five to four Supreme Court ruling in 1990 that allowed the State of Oregon to deny Native Americans the right to use peyote—an illegal psychotropic plant that has long standing in their religious rituals. Until the Court struck down RFRA in 1997, a wide variety of dispensations were claimed on the basis of personal religious practices. These dispensations included everything from drug use to conjugal visits as privately sacred rituals for prison inmates.

Clearly this is no simple matter. To the extent that religion is restricted to its conventional forms (Buddhist, Catholic, Hindu, Jewish, Muslim, Protestant), this comes close to requiring an establishment of specific religions through state certification of only recognized churches, sects, and faiths. To the extent that religion is left to the definition of each individual, this involves such wide latitude as to stretch "religion" beyond the point of credibility. The First Amendment's combination of establishment and free-exercise clauses was a brilliant exercise of statecraft that has left the nation with a vexing conundrum of interpretation and implementation. But this is hardly the only hobgoblin of inconsistency that bedevils the First Amendment.

Cultural versus Structural Separation

In large part because of the United States's heralded separation of church and state, many around the world see the country as a great bastion of secularism. After all, any country that tries to keep religion separate from its government must be a country in which religion has little influence; surely a secular state will lead to a secular society. Actually both assumptions are off the mark.[8] The reality is that religion has thrived in the United States, but this, too, is often blown out of perspective. For every observer who sees the United States as demonically secular, there is another who portrays it as a global religious beacon. The United States is singled out for both its separation of church and state and for being among the most religious nations in the world. There are several possible resolutions of this apparent contradiction.

For one thing, the early and continuing absence of a single state religious establishment or monopoly cleared the ground for a variety of religious flowers to take seed and bloom. The rise of different denominations became a defining attribute of American Protestantism, and the competition among faiths has prodded growth across the ever widening spectrum of American religious pluralism.[9]

But a different resolution of the American religious paradox involves another paradox that itself needs resolution. The United States is widely known for its civil religion as a form of national faith—and faith in the nation—that is anchored in the common denominator of the country's pluralistic Judeo-Christian heritage. Yet there appears to be a conflict between civil religion as a celebration of the nation's religious identity and separationism as a doctrine devoted to keeping religion and the state at arm's length. Three ways of bridging this conflict emerged in a study of religion and politics in a medium-sized New England city.[10]

A first reconciliation involves a tendency to give public privileges to the religious mainstream rather than to controversial religious minorities. Thus, majoritarian prayers at public events are acceptable, whereas minority rituals are not. Prayers at the beginning of each day in the U.S. Congress (and virtually all state legislatures) are led by rotating Protestant, Catholic, and Jewish clergy, but sect and cult leaders are not among them.

A second rapprochement makes separationism and civil religion mutually contingent. Thus, the country can endorse religion's separation from the state because religion is free to function elsewhere in the nation's cultural rounds, including its churches, temples, and mosques. Conversely, it is because religion flowers so luxuriantly in the society at large that separation is needed to protect the state and governance process from it. Put more pithily, having rich religious traditions, we need church-state separation; having church-state separation, we turn to other gardens for cultivating religion and can well afford them.

Finally, a third resolution of the conflict involves structural versus cultural interpretations of separationism. Many citizens would apply the rigorous canon of church-state separation to concrete structural matters of actual state policy and its implementation, while applying less vigilant controls to religion's cultural expressions. Indeed, the latter category includes many of the exceptions to a strict "wall of separation"—from such "merely cultural" practices as prayers in Congress to inscribing "In God We Trust" on the nation's money. While prayers in public primary and secondary schools are prohibited because of their possible effects on young and impressionable students, they are not banned in public colleges or universities or for that matter on general public ceremonial occasions such as Fourth of July festivities or presidential inaugurations. Public opinion supports such cultural expressions of religion even as it rejects religion as basis of actual state laws and regulations—whether these involve limits on abortion rights or blue law restrictions on Sunday shopping.

Of course, there are those who even take issue with allowing the merely cultural exceptions. After all, "mere culture" is not as trivial as the phrase suggests; culture often wields power that can lead to concrete, structural outcomes. However, it takes both a thick wallet and a thick skin to file a lawsuit against culturally ensconced practices accepted by most of one's fellow citizens. Overall, the courts have honored the exceptions despite plaintiff opposition. Even where the courts have ruled practices such as prayer in the public schools unconstitutional, it is estimated that they persist in as many as a fourth of the nation's schools, an indication that local sentiment is often a better guide to practice than is national jurisprudence.

A major trend in judicial separationism has involved widening the scope of what is at issue. Initially the First Amendment focused on churches and denominations. Gradually, free-exercise decisions expanded to include religious beliefs and practices sometimes only loosely tied to specific institutions—for example, the right to provide religious home schooling to one's children. Finally, there is the aforementioned effort to include any culturally prescribed belief or behavior that is equivalent to religion or leaves the definition of religion to the individual.

Free-exercise cases have shifted from involving churches to involving religion and then to involving the broadly but vaguely sacred. Can the same shift be far behind for the establishment clause? If there is a danger that the state may become controlled or controlling on behalf of a dominant religious interest, doesn't the same danger exist for other cultural interests? At first blush, this may extend the sublime to the ridiculous. After all, a government without a culture suggests a nation without a soul. Yet there is rich precedent for trying to keep the state separate from establishments based on gender, ethnicity, or social class. There has been a good deal of opposition mounted against the government's tendencies to reflect the interests of wealthy white males. The idea is not to expunge culture from the individual consciences of state officeholders but rather to avoid established entanglements between the state apparatus and any specific cultures and interest groups, however these are defined.

Separation from Politics versus the State

By now it has become a truism that religion and power should be kept separate in all respects. But such a standard is no more feasible than a complete separation of church and state. While breachings of the Jeffersonian "wall" have tended to be more cultural and symbolic than substantively structural, politics remains a crucial bridge between religion, on the one hand, and the state, on the other.

Over the past two decades, religion around the world has been increasingly involved in culture wars and state subversion with rising violence. Not surprisingly, there has been a corresponding increase in calls to ban religion from politics.[11] The argument has become a commonplace of media punditry and political talk shows; it is a frequent weapon used by one political party against another that seems to be deriving too much warmth from the religious flame. And one can certainly imagine its appeal. If there is any truth to the cliché that religion and power are a volatile and potentially lethal combination, the solution seems obvious.

Yet it is one thing to bar religion from state hegemony and quite another to bar religion from political partisanship and campaigns or religious candidates from running for office or even serving in office once elected. While many assume all are central to the First Amendment, the single sentence refers only to "Congress," not to individuals or agencies outside of government. The one pertinent clause in the original Constitution of 1787, as opposed to the First Amendment of 1791, states that "no religious test shall ever be required as a qualification to any office or public trust under the United States" (Article VI). Of course, the prohibition also extends by implication to any test for nonreligion.

American politics are replete with religious candidates of virtually every denominational stripe—clergy as well as laity, elected as well as defeated. Although there are periodic complaints that religion is not welcome in politics, these refer to the political mood not to the political rules, and they often amount to complaints that a particular type of religion has not been politically successful.[12] It is true that over the nation's history, members of some denominations, such as Episcopalians, have been more successful than others in gaining high office. But this is more a function of higher social class and its attendant political resources than religion per se. In any event, it is precisely at the point that an office-seeker becomes an officeholder that the First Amendment becomes a major constraint to acting on behalf of one's religion—or irreligion.

The only real penalty for American religious organizations that participate in politics is a loss of tax exemption—a penalty that the Internal Revenue Service (IRS) applies to all cultural institutions that would otherwise be exempt. However, the measure is rarely enforced, perhaps because this sanction itself could be construed as an infringement on free exercise, with the prospect of litigation to follow. The most significant recent case involved the campaigning of the Christian Coalition under the aggressive leadership of pentecostal leader Pat Robertson and his now departed political lieutenant, Ralph Reed. The case moldered for several years in an IRS file, as no administrators seemed eager to create religious martyrs to bureaucratic infringement. When the matter was finally decided, the coalition's tax-exempt status was rescinded, but quietly and with more of a wrist slap than a body blow.

There is little doubt that the founders understood politics as a necessary process of airing competing interests and ideologies. By contrast, the state is a structure of government within which successful politicians serve as temporary officeholders under the rules of the Constitution and under the sufferance of the electorate. Leaving politics open to religion while keeping the state closed involves one of the less remarked upon of the celebrated "checks and balances" in the American constitutional system. Each practice tends to be contingent on the other, much like the relationship between separationism overall and civil religion described earlier. Religion can be active in politics precisely because we are protected from its state hegemony; conversely, religion need not have a position within the state because it can air its positions politically. Religious advocates on every side of an issue should be welcome participants in the political contest. But the state's primary obligation is to insure that the rules of the contest are fair to everyone.

It is true that mixing religion and politics can lead to the kind of cultural warfare reviewed in the last chapter. But this is rare except when state power hangs in the political balance, as in the cases of Guatemala, Northern Ireland, Egypt, Israel, and increasingly India—to name only a few countries that have become battlegrounds. A politics that follows a lawful pattern in the pursuit of well-defined and constitutionally regulated state offices is quite different from a politics of winner-take-all, including the right to redefine the state rather than merely play a role within it. Similarly, there is a crucial distinction between the state as an enduring, rule-bound apparatus of government that transcends its incumbent officials of the moment versus the state as the momentary and ideologically opportunistic creation of the last conquering politician—that is, between the state as a long-term end in its own right and the state as a short-term means to more politically particular ends.

As the founders understood, because both religion and politics involve competing moral guidelines and ethical priorities, it is only natural that the two should inform—and occasionally inflame—each other. Religious visions can become political agendas and vice versa, in the time-honored dance of the moth and the flame. Even American public opinion grasps the point.[13] Neither the Constitution nor this analysis asserts that religion should or must be involved in politics; there are other issues to animate the political zoo. However, when religion does press for involvement, it is far better to allow it in than to try and keep it out. Banning religious considerations and religious leaders from politics is simply unrealistic. Moreover, the attempt to do so is apt to backfire. When religion is denied a place at the political table, it is likely to create more problems—either as an outraged victim of a repressive political system or as an unmonitored force operating in the political shadows. In short, a politics that excludes religion is no more defensible than a state that establishes religion.

So much, then, for three key misunderstandings concerning the U.S. Constitution and its First Amendment. As many Americans fail to realize, the most pressing clause of the amendment concerns establishment rather than free exercise; its heralded church-state separation is structurally tight but culturally porous, and religion has a rightful role in politics even though state entanglement is off-limits.

As constitutions go, the U.S. Constitution is the world's oldest continuing governmental charter and blueprint, save that of the Commonwealth of Massachusetts on which it was partially modeled. But what of the putative uniqueness of American separationism? Here is yet another article of faith that is challenged by heretical scrutiny. Placing American relations between religion and power in comparative relief produces some surprising results.

Global Variations in the Relations between Religion and Power

Americans pride themselves on their singular constitutional tradition regarding church and state. However, any smugness would be only half deserved at best. Where the freedom of religion is concerned, the United States is not distinctive at all. More than 90 percent of countries around the world have some constitutional equivalent of the U.S. free-exercise clause. A guarantee of religious freedom has become an obligatory shibboleth of statehood.[14] On the other hand, the U.S. prohibition of a religious "establishment" is one of our most compelling claims to constitutional uniqueness. While the free exercise of religion has become a global cliché, the establishment clause remains relatively obscure.

As we shall see shortly, it is an ironic comment on constitutions generally that many nations have a better record in avoiding establishments that are not constitutionally banned than in nurturing the free exercise that is constitutionally secured. Indeed, what may be most distinctive about the U.S. Constitution is not so much its content as the seriousness with which it is regarded. Even Americans who know little of its specifics accord it revered status. In many other countries, constitutions are a changing gloss, and there are some in which a nation's constitutional commitment reflects the sardonic line from a recent American automobile commercial, "[Constitutions] must be good; we've had six of them in the last twelve years."

Clearly constitutions themselves are unreliable guides to actual relations between religion and power, even in the United States. A different and larger net is necessary to capture the diversity of relations between religion and power in our comparative cases. Two distinctions drawn from the last misunderstanding help to make sense of this profusion. The first concerns whether religion has a legitimate role in national electoral politics; the second concerns whether religion is officially established within the formally constituted state or government. When joined, these distinctions produce four combinations: religious states with religious politics; secular states with secular politics; religious states with secular politics; and secular states with religious politics. As simplistic as these clusters may seem, all of the fifteen countries examined here—including the United States—find at least temporary homes among them.

Religious States and Religious Politics

The combination of religious states with religious politics seems an appropriate starting point because some may regard it as the starting point of Western history, not to mention the most common type among today's non-Western societies. Because such countries are so often depicted as suffused with religion in every aspect of life, a religious state would seem to go hand in hand with religious politics.

Because the combination is so volatile, however, the pattern is more the exception than the rule. A religious state faces active religious politics when there is some religious disagreement over the state's own religious direction. Under such circumstances, the state's very legitimacy is called into question, and violence may reflect preemptive actions of state control as well as the clash among contending religious parties. If there is a single pattern that lends itself to the most widespread religious and cultural violence, it is this one. While the category is rare, it is hardly nonexistent.

Among our sample of countries, several cases qualify here—at least at various points in their histories. Like most other Latin American countries, both Brazil and Guatemala were once officially Catholic states in a religious political system that involved the subjugation and suppression of indigenous religious alternatives. Formally, both countries had severed these state religious ties by the end of the nineteenth century; informally, ties have persisted in varying forms. In Brazil, the Catholic ecclesiastical hierarchy is now seeking to reappropriate and renegotiate its seat at the right hand of the state, while at the same time both Church and state are engaged in a new religious politics animated by echoing strains of Liberation Theology on the one side and an expanding pentecostal Protestantism on the other. In Guatemala, the dominant military state has shifted its ostensible religious affiliation from Catholic to Protestant in the1990s, and there is no question that its Indian opposition is partly a movement of Mayan religious revitalization.

Perhaps the clearest combination of a religious state with religious politics is Northern Ireland. There is no question that the state is perceived in Protestant terms, whether in law as a result of its inclusion within Anglican Britain or in fact because of the three hundred-year political dominance of local Protestants. Certainly there is no doubt that politics are riven with religion—at least insofar as they have involved polarized blocs that are culturally, if not always religiously, Protestant or Catholic. The recent truce and negotiated settlement signal a change in the religious politics but by no means its end. What was once a small Catholic minority may well become an effective political majority early in the twenty-first century, and Catholics have already begun to make gains through the ballot rather than the bullets of the IRA. The shift is hastened by the increased out-migration of Protestants with resources; it is compounded by the frustrations of those less-advantaged Protestants remaining behind.

Or consider the case of Israel. Many Israelis would protest its categorization as a religious state, arguing that Zionism itself can be seen as a secular movement and that the state makes ample provision for both secular practices and various non-Judaic faiths, especially Islamic and Christian. At the same time, there is no question that the Israeli state is perceived as Jewish by most Jews and non-Jews alike. Even if this were not the case, Zionism itself may be a sufficiently sacred commitment to qualify as religious on its own terms. Certainly there is no question that Israeli politics often take religious forms. This not only applies to the participation of Muslim Palestinians, including the Hamas, but also to the struggles between various Jewish groups—whether secularists on the left or contesting movements on the right such as the Gush Emunim and the ultra-Orthodox Haredim. Governing coalitions involved precarious religious balancing. As the assassination of Prime Minister Rabin makes clear, the stakes are large and the rates of violence are high.

As all of these countries attest, the combination of a religious state and religious politics has involved some of the most deeply rooted and tragic violence of the modern era. This makes it especially important to consider the alternatives. However, it is one thing to point out the dangers of this combination in the abstract and quite another to prevent countries from sliding toward it in reality. Then, too, some of the alternatives have warts of their own.

Secular States and Secular Politics

If the first combination is stereotypically non-Western, the combination of secular states with secular politics is commonly associated with an equally flawed stereotype of the now fully secularized West. In one sense, it represents a realization of the Enlightenment vision through what has been called the "secularization of public religion" or the "desacralization of the state."[15]

The secular-state and secular-politics pattern is often associated with Western Europe in particular. Apart from the now nominally Christian Democratic and Socialist parties in Germany and France, both countries fall into this category, as does Italy in the wake of its recently renegotiated concordat with the Vatican. Sweden has just joined the category by ending the state's official ties to Lutheranism.

Much the same is true if one looks functionally rather than formally at other Scandinavian countries or at Anglican England—there are active movements on behalf of religious disestablishment in all of these symbolically religious nations. These are partly efforts to revitalize religion as an autonomous political force, since many church folk now regard the relationship as an inhibiting constraint on their prophetic roles. But then the established traces that survive are often defended principally on nonreligious grounds. In Sweden, the church functions as an unofficial census bureau and burial society, and it receives state support for rendering such services. Finally, many politicians see these establishments as merely symbolic sources of cultural continuity and vestigial charm.

Europe does not exhaust the secular-states secular-politics category.

This combination also describes two additional cases: Turkey and China. Turkey had been tilting toward the West throughout the latter days of the Ottoman Empire in the nineteenth century, when there was a special fascination with the secular theology of French positivism. When Kemal Ataturk seized power in 1921, he initiated one of the most far-reaching and enduring politico-cultural revolutions in the twentieth century. Ataturk was familiar with sociologist Emile Durkheim's argument that an ethical society and effective political culture could be sacred without being religious. Partly as a result, Ataturk banned religion from both government and politics just as he banned irregular verbs and Roman numerals from everyday discourse. For the most part, the reforms have remained. There have been several instances in which the military has stepped in to preserve secularity, and there is no question that Muslim political interests have begun to mobilize recently. But it is characteristic of Turkey that critics and participants alike resist the label of fundamentalism as it is often applied in neighboring Iran and Afghanistan.

China also qualifies as a doubly secular case, again partly on the basis of an imported Western ideology—in this case, of course, Communism. Actually, the regime's opposition to religion has vacillated since the early 1980s, and Communism itself resembles a religion, not least in the recent secularization of Communism as a sacred cause. Indeed, one of the reasons why some Chinese leaders have been more accepting of traditional Christian, Buddhist, and Islamic religious communities—as long as they operate on the state's terms—is a much-lamented void at the core of Chinese society where only money has currency. While some would argue that this is a cue for the reintroduction of Confucianism, this faith is even less preferable than imported faiths because party cadres see the Confucian tradition as a feudal and anti-revolutionary anachronism, despite its considerable informal persistence. This is a time of transition in China, but not one that threatens a serious religionizing of either the state or politics in familiar terms.

Clearly, the combination of a secular state and secular politics has some empirical standing, and it is in some measure correctly associated with Western post-Enlightenment developments. But this does not mean that all cases are confined to the West or that religion is entirely absent in any instance. Indeed, the combination in pure form runs the risk of societal lassitude if not sterility. Many of the preceding cases reveal persisting strains toward some form of religion or "sacred" alternative that state administrations seek to dampen if not drown. While these new religious developments rarely represent major trends, they are also seldom dismissable. So far, then, I have dealt with the two opposing polar combinations: the doubly religious associated with violence and the doubly secular tending toward vacuity.

Religious States and Secular Politics

There are three scenarios that combine a religious state with secular politics. The first occurs when state religiousness is an empty symbol rather than a compelling commitment—more an antediluvian form than a contemporary function. I noted several such countries under the secular-states secular-politics rubric, including "Lutheran" Sweden. Even though Sweden was formally religious until 2000, it actually reflected a cultural and political scene that was highly secular. While there were occasional religious issues that drew attention, these were much more the exception than the rule.

If this first model of a religious state with secular politics suggests a certain ritualized cover for an indifference to religion, a second version involves a religion that is such an important source of state legitimacy that no alternative faith is tolerated. Religion is banned from politics precisely because it is so potentially upsetting as an emotionally charged component of the culture at large. Religious grievances against the state are suppressed, and often any politics of real substance is kept under wraps. These are theocracies represented by some traditionally Catholic Latin American states as well as a number of Islamic hegemonies in the Middle East, including Pakistan at various points in its history. In all of these cases, the state tightly regulates the political world and affiliates with religion more to control it than to submit to it.

In some ways these first two models of religious states with secular politics are opposites of each other. The first represents religious tokenism in the midst of apathy, while the second reveals an imposed religious order to quell potential religious disorder. Still a third version of a religious state and secular politics is a perverse variant on the second. This involves states that carefully construct their own religion to frustrate the political mobilization of a genuine religious alternative.

For more than fifty years, Indonesia's government has imposed the deliberately crafted syncretic religion of Pancasila to bind together Christians, Hindus, Buddhists, and animists—not to mention the 85 percent of the population who are formally Muslims. Under the recently deposed President Suharto, strict electoral rules made it virtually impossible for any one religious group to rise up against the regime, and the state's administrative apparatus (*golkar*) also functioned as a controlling political structure. In all of this, the object was to stifle the development of the so-called Islamic fundamentalists, whose actual agendas were often more secular than religious.

Thus, the combination of a religious state with secular politics makes for even stranger bedfellows than does politics alone. All three of its scenarios are somewhat Procrustean, and the latter two share a sense of unstable vulnerability as a temporary way station for cases caught in transition between the other three combinations.

Secular States and Religious Politics

As we saw earlier in this chapter, many may regard the combination of secular states with religious politics as unlikely. After all, if a society is able to sustain a government that is basically secular, isn't this because the surrounding culture is itself so secular that there is no real religious action in the first place? Put oppositely, when any society's politics become religiously infected, how can its state structures fail to follow?

Both questions are reasonable, but the logic behind a secularly neutral state with a free-ranging religious polity is that each complements and constrains the other. There need be no limits to the free exercise of religion in politics as long as there is a strict prohibition of any religious establishment within the state. Politicians as politicians may campaign on—and even vote—their religious consciences; nor is there anything to prevent them from bowing to the bidding of religious organizations. But state officials have a different responsibility. They must remain formally and functionally neutral, not only in the competition between religions but also in the larger struggle between religion and secularism. The overall result should be a contested but vital politics framed by an equitable state that rises above the fray to guarantee fairness to all.

At least this describes the constitutional theory and founding enthusiasm behind two countries that constitute the world's oldest and largest democracies, the United States and India, respectively. After India obtained independence in 1947, it took three years to develop a constitution. The result reflected a number of Western models, including the U.S. Constitution. But while the Indian form of government enjoyed a successful run of almost thirty years with its stability and legitimacy intact, this began to unravel in the 1980s.

A growing complaint within India today is that its independence leaders were too quick to apply Western secular forms of government to an Eastern cultural reality that required its own unique state response. The argument holds that a secular state may work well enough in a country like the United States, but it is discordant within an Indian society that remains so intransigently nonsecular at its core. Indeed, the very imposition of Western secularism has served perversely to fan the flames of religious extremism by forcing religious advocates to adopt aggressive measures to make their case—measures that even include communal violence. Some go on to suggest that India is not just a deeply religious country but a fundamentally Hindu society that can only be led by a Hindu government. As this argument goes, once Hinduism converts its natural hegemony into state control, Hinduism will revert back to its natural historical tolerance of the minority religions in its domain.

Yet this is only one reading of the Indian situation. By no means all Indian influentials and intellectuals have abandoned the secular state. Many continue to resist both religious and antireligious models of the state in favor of a more neutral or areligious reading of the Indian Constitution. From this perspective, the cause of the country's communal violence is not that the state is too secular but rather that it is not secular enough—not that the state should use its influence to promote or end religion but rather that the state should be religiously impartial. But from the very outset, religion was implicated in the Indian Constitution and the government it conceived. From the beginning, there were controversial religious actions, including a state exemption for Muslims to follow Islamic rather than national laws in personal matters, liberal religious reforms required of Hinduism in temple administration, and a continuation of the British reservations policy as a form of occupational affirmative action for Hindu untouchables.

These exceptions in secular state policy have festered over the years. There is an increasing tendency for state leaders to become involved in such religious conflicts as Hindus versus Muslims in Ayodyah, Bombay, and Kashmir; Hindus versus Christians in Gujarat and Orissa; Sikhs versus Hindus in the Punjab; and southern Tamil rebels mobilizing against Buddhists in Sri Lanka. As concessions made to one group require balancing concessions to its rival, constructing state policy has come to resemble shortening a chair one leg at a time: the results are never quite even, and the seat of power becomes increasingly unstable. The assassinations of both Indira Gandhi and Rajiv Gandhi offer tragic reminders of the possible consequences.

In a strange way, one's reading of India depends upon one's reading of the United States. Is America a den of constitutionally enforced secularism or a country whose high level of religiosity is partially attributable to its Constitution? Overall, the United States may be the exception that commends the rule concerning the virtues of a secular state and a religious polity. But it would be both naive and unseemly to assume that the same combination would work identically for all other nations. Nor is India the only cautionary case.

In Egypt, the nation as a whole seems a battleground between a coercive state with an antireligious ideology of secularism on one side and small bands of religious militants on the other. The scene is not uncommon, and it has surfaced in a variety of other states that have been less than fully successful in their efforts to suppress religion opposition, for example, Indonesia, Turkey, and Thailand.

Of course, a variety of factors are involved, and democracy itself is not always a panacea or always interpreted the same way. Thus, democratic elections are one thing, but a democratic state can be quite another. In addition to regimes that limit elections and their eligible parties in order to uphold a nominally democratic state governance, there are opposition movements that see electoral democracy as a means to a government takeover—a means that can be eliminated once a theocracy is achieved. The choices are not easy.

Post-1989 Poland also qualifies as a secular state with religious politics. One might suppose it to be doubly Catholic as a reflection of both its dominant cultural religious alignment and the oft-chronicled role of the Church in bringing an end to Communist rule. But Catholicism's position has already begun to shift. Many Poles are more cultural than religious Catholics, and the old pattern of opposition to ecclesiastical authority is resurfacing, especially as the Church has sought to pressure the government into outlawing divorce and abortion. While Poland currently illustrates the combination of a secular state with religious politics, it may soon join its European neighbors to the west in the doubly secular category as even its politics loses its religious flavor.

Finally, Japan is another sharp-edged peg in the round hole of a secular state with religious politics. It is especially instructive because it reminds us that my four combinations rarely fit any country exactly. Japan has exemplified all four combinations at various times in its history.

First, one reading of Japan's Tokugawa period from the early seventeenth to the latter half of the nineteenth century is that it combined religious government (shogunates) with religious politics in the jousting between various Buddhist, Shinto, and even Christian movements. Second, the Meiji Restoration in the 1860s ultimately led to a religious state and secular politics. State Shinto came to define the government, and opposing religious voices were stilled. During World War II the two major leaders of the lay Buddhist organization, Soka Gakkai, were imprisoned for their activities. Third, at least for the first three decades following the war's end and the adoption of a new constitution, the situation was more that of a secular state with secular politics. Not only was state Shinto disestablished, but there was relatively little religious presence of any sort in a political world tightly controlled by the conservative Liberal Democratic Party.

Fourth and most recently, the combination of a secular state and religious politics has begun to surface, however imperfectly. Formally, the state continues to be secular, although there are small signs of a nonmilitarist, state Shinto recrudescence. Over the last decade religious politics of a quite different sort has involved the roles of "new" and "new-new" religious movements. The Aum Shinrikyo's nerve-gas attack on the Tokyo subway in 1995 was a pivotal event, and the resulting trial has turned out to be a siege for many marginal religious movements who feel tarred by the same stereotypes and sanctions applied to the Aum. This is especially true of the Soka Gakkai and its long-standing relation to one of the largest opposition parties in Japan.

So much for a brief exercise in cataloging the range of relationships between religion, politics, and the state. As nations strain and move from one type to another, we are reminded that a variety of factors are at work—some political and some religious. Some of the considerations go beyond constitutional considerations and suggest that even America's heralded church-state separation may be less a matter of law and binding precedent than of broader social, cultural, and institutional patterns.

Nonconstitutional Factors Bearing on Religion and Power

By now it is apparent that one must probe behind any society's formalistic facade to find the true relations between its religious and governmental systems. In fact, this was a principal motive behind the larger comparative project that spawned this book. But comparative scholars invariably enter the field with predispositions, including inclinations to maximize either differences or similarities with one's home society. Raised on a liberal diet of cultural relativism with snacks of American exceptionalism, U.S. social scientists are inclined to look more for contrasts than for similarities.

And so was I in beginning my quest for official religious states in contrast to our own church-state bisection. Gradually, however, I began to realize that similarities were at least as pressing as differences. Despite the many obvious cultural differences between societies, there were a number of shared structural circumstances. Nations are increasingly united not only by their participation in a common international political economy but also by a common vulnerability to many of the same internal political and religious dynamics. A range of nonlegal influences can cause nations to both lag behind and race ahead of their constitutions. Such influences are grouped into two categories: first, those concerning the circumstances of politics and government; second, those involving characteristics of the religious sphere. Both categories suggest reasons why it is more common to find state separation from religion than state penetration by religion.

Shooting the Gap Politically

As much as the separation of church and state is ingrained in American culture, it is scarcely imaginable for any leading American politician to follow the example of a recent leading Swedish politician, who stated that he did not believe in God though he respected those who do. Over the past quarter century, religion has loomed large in American politics—beginning with Born-again Christian Jimmy Carter, proceeding through Ronald Reagan's ties to the Moral Majority and the continuing pressure of the Christian Coalition, and extending to George W. Bush's statement that Jesus is the leader he most respects and Joe Lieberman's steadfast and public commitment to his Judaism. Piety and politics have been almost passionate companions. Even liberal candidates know that finding common cause with religious groups is important because churches and temples afford important arenas for making face-to-face and hand-to-hand contact with voters. This is especially so as labor unions, neighborhood organizations, and other voluntary associations seem in fractured decline. Moreover, showing some sort of religious commitment is a time-honored way to affirm one's moral character.

But there is a major difference between religion's role in American politics and its standing within the three branches of American government. As much as politicians protest their religious devotion, the courts, Congress, and executive branch have all been criticized for being too secular in response to religious groups and issues. The separation of church and state may seem moribund from the perspective of political rhetoric, but it is very much alive within the structure of government.

Much the same situation applies in many of the countries we have visited. Although there are conspicuous exceptions such as Sweden, Turkey, and recently Poland, it is common for political figures to don at least a light religious cloak while on the stump but to doff it when enmeshed in the chores of state administration. Note, however, that there is a political dimension to state officialdom, too. Once a politician, always a campaigner—whether in or out of office. Virtually all state leaders engage in political activities to maintain their legitimacy, and these often include religious practices—whether it is an American president attending church and prayer breakfasts, a Japanese prime minister visiting the state Shinto Yasokuni Shrine to the war dead, or a Pakistani prime minister declaring support for Islamization.

But in all such instances, there is a difference between public political ceremonials and state administrative actions. For the latter, religion may be not merely irrelevant but a major liability. Absolute religious principles do not fit well in the compromise world of statecraft. Theological constraints on state actions do not sit well with officials who seek to preserve a capacity for flexible policy responses to changing circumstances. And if religion must be incorporated into law or state policy, most officials prefer very brief and very general codifications that can be variously interpreted as conditions warrant. It is true that this may leave religion as a loose canon on the deck of the ship of state, but officials at least have temporary control of the fuse.

As a result of globalization, even the smallest nation today is heavily implicated in an international political economy that requires reliability and predictability in international terms. Local religious customs such as the Islamic prohibition of financial interest introduce extraneous factors that may alienate potential partners and allies. Partly in response to this international context, Third World governments are increasingly specialized, professionalized, and bureaucratized—though not always in that order.

Iran is perhaps the single most dramatic case of a recent "religious state" that has begun to relax its strictures for these reasons. Iran's political leadership has de-emphasized the policies of the Ayatollah Khomeini as a necessary price for re-gaining regional and world standing. A similar challenge confronted India's Hindutva party, the Bharatiya Janata Party, once it rose from a political pretender to head of the nation's governing coalition. Converting recent victories into enduring and effective governance will require filing its sharp religious edges in order to broaden its appeal and legitimacy.

Even where a nation's political leadership is overtly religious, most governments depend upon a sophisticated civil service. The civil service often becomes a community unto itself, one that is frequently secular and sometimes cynical with respect to its nation's traditional religious patterns. There was evidence of this in Iran even during the Ayatollah Khomeini's reign—and with his approval.

Religious commitments made by political officials can become political liabilities that are difficult to back away from without losing credibility. In the search for legitimacy and votes, politicians frequently promise more than they can deliver. This often portends an almost inevitable fall when they are later held to their own standards.

Any politician who campaigns on the basis of religion wields a double-edged sword. Seeking legitimacy through religion risks long-term losses despite short-term gains. Moreover, once religion is introduced into politics, it can be very difficult to pull back. Not only do its absolute criteria clash with the politics of compromise, but religion tends to be emotionally hot and accompanied by its own experts who are frequently difficult to control. Finally, very few state officials relish having to publicly oppose religious considerations once they have been activated.

All of this explains why many politicians want it both ways: that is, pulling religion close for purposes of legitimacy but keeping it at a distance in the process of actual governance. Public rhetoric on behalf of religion in politics is often coupled with private efforts to stem the religious tide within government. But sometimes this is hard to manage. State leaders are often drawn into religious disputes over which they may lose their control—and possibly their lives.

Yet from the standpoint of the state, religion may be both a source and an object of administration. It is a source because it offers an institutional network whose tentacles reach deep and wide across the society. This allows a variety of administrative efficiencies, ranging from the Swedish census to Indonesia's Golkar apparatus. Perhaps the classic instance involves the British Raj in India, during which the colonial government increased the systematic rigidity of the Hindu caste system to enhance census taking, recordkeeping, and administrative control over the sprawling country.

Religion may be an administrative object when it represents a potential base of countermobilization that must be quashed. As a cultural wild card in the frequently fixed game of state politics, religion poses a threat to established policies and policymakers. As we have seen, this is a major reason why state religions are more common than religious states. Try as I did to find a country where religion was actually in control of the state, I was unsuccessful. Sweden maintained the symbols but not the substance, and even the symbols were on their way out. Iran under the Ayatollah Khomeini would have been a prime candidate, but even during his reign not all aspects of the state were religiously secured.

In contrast to religious states, state religions involve government control over religion. In a very different breach of separationism and an ironic type of "religious establishment," governments frequently keep religion under control by "volunteering" state offices and resources to "assist" with important religious functions, including religious publication and education, pilgrimages such as the Islamic hajj to Mecca, and the maintenance of churches, mosques, and temples.

Even some of the most secular nations—for example, China and Turkey—have national ministries of religion for such purposes. These alliances between government and religion generally involve some form of co-optation, and religious groups sometimes prefer to remain outside of the state apparatus to preserve their potential for autonomous power. This was a factor in the formal disestablishment of Catholicism in Latin American countries such as Guatemala and Brazil, as well as Sweden's recent decision to break with the Lutheran Church. It also lies behind the struggle for independence on the part of China's "house" churches.

The overall point here is that it is generally in the state's interest to avoid precisely the sort of power-sharing entanglements with religion that the American First Amendment would prohibit. In this respect, good survival statecraft alone may produce results similar to those of a constitutional separation of religion and the state. At the same time, it is

also important to look at a corresponding range of religious considerations in relation to the state. As we shall see, these also lean toward
separation from the state if not from politics.

Ironies of Religious Pluralism, Ideology, Authority and Secularism

Despite the emphasis so far on the state's control over religion
rather than vice versa, there is no question that religion may also exert
influence over the state. It is true that religion often lacks the political
elites' access to the conventional instruments of structural power—
whether money, coercion, votes, or networks of influentials. Nevertheless, religion may wield considerable cultural power by seizing the moral
initiative in a policy dispute and using the media to maximum advantage in shaping the public agenda.[16] The latter form of power is often
underestimated and overlooked. But as illustrated by Liberation Theology in Latin America, Poland's linkage of the Solidarity labor movement
with Catholicism, Mahatma Gandhi's nonviolent movement for Indian
independence, Martin Luther King Jr.'s civil rights crusade, and the recent overthrow of the Suharto regime in Indonesia, cultural power can
be very potent indeed, especially for issues with high moral salience. It
is particularly useful for outsiders and underdogs as a way of converting
morality and virtue into structural advantages. Without arguing that politicians are bereft of cultural power, it is especially fertile among religious movements.

However, groups that rely on cultural as opposed to structural power
tend to be limited in the kind and degree of influence wielded. Religion
is more likely to achieve some types of political outcomes than others, and
movements such as the U.S. Christian Coalition, Turkey's "fundamentalist-
lite" Muslims, Egypt's Muslim Brotherhood, Israel's Gush Emunin
and Hamas, and India's Hindutva may suffer from three particular
discrepancies between what they aspire to and what they must settle
for.

First, while religion may seek positive power, or the ability to ini-
tiate and shape change, it may have to settle for negative power, or the
independent capacity to block or veto an impending course. Second, religion may hope to exercise primary power, or the capacity to seize and
carry through a policymaking transaction as prime mover, but it is often
limited to secondary power, which entails fine-tuning from within a
shared coalition. Third, religion may aim for "public power" shaping
public policies within the state arena, but it is frequently restricted to
"private power" concerning the attitudes and actions of individual citizens outside that arena.

There are exceptions to these limits. Sometimes religion is able to
fulfill its aspirations through an alliance with the state and its structural

resources, as in the cases of Guatemala's pentecostals, Northern Ireland's Protestants, or Pakistan's traditional Muslims. But more often, religion's power is constrained by a range of religious characteristics themselves. It is worth reviewing several of these variables and the paradoxes within them.

Religious Diversity. Few countries are as religiously heterogeneous as Indonesia, India, and the United States, but fewer still are as religiously homogenous as, say, Sweden. Even where a nation is dominated by a single faith tradition—for example, Christian, Hindu, Islamic, Jewish—major differences within the tradition can be contested and divisive, as in Catholic versus Protestant, Hindu versus Sikh, Sunni versus Shiite, and Orthodox Jews versus Reform Jews. How does the degree of heterogeneity bear upon religion's relation to the state?

The answer is rimmed with irony. In the rare case of religious homogeneity, a religious alliance with the state is often structurally redundant in light of the cultural consensus. In Thailand, Buddhism is so encompassing as to reduce the urgency of its governmental ties. Even when the government itself begins to experience religious atrophy, there is little sense of alarm because there is no religious alternative waiting in the wings. Sweden's final act of religious disestablishment elicited more yawns than protests. Other European states evidence similar trajectories, including Poland's increasingly cool shoulder to the Catholicism it once treated so warmly.

But if a state alliance doesn't matter much when there is very little religious competition, it may matter too much when religious diversity leads to conflict. The very prospect of one religion or religious group gaining state favor and power may activate a bitter religious rivalry. This is part of the religious unease that now affects Brazil and Guatemala, as traditional Catholicism must contend with expanding Protestantism. The conflict between Protestants and Catholics in Northern Ireland is tragic and long standing. Earlier we saw the increase in Sunni-Shiite conflict in Pakistan as talk of Islamization escalated. India's Hindu-Muslim strife has added a tragic note to the triumph of subcontinent independence from the British and has continued to erupt over state policies ever since. These two quite different religions were reasonably tolerant and even culturally complementary until a contest for state power led to an increasingly bloody rupture.

However, there are instances in which religious diversity can result in at least a symbolic form of unity. In the United States, state occasions often invoke and celebrate a common Christian heritage, despite religious tensions that have increased throughout the twentieth century between conservative and liberal factions of virtually every faith community. In post-World War II Indonesia, Pancasila is a deliberately crafted religious common denominator under the aegis of the state that combines elements of Islam, Hinduism, Buddhism, Christianity, and animism. Such civil religions put a civil face on a potentially fractious body politic.

Religious Ideology. Ideologies filter any organization's sense of the world while guiding its responses. Ideologies are also responsible for galvanizing an organization's membership around a core set of objectives. From an ideological perspective, every religion experiences and trades upon a gap between the world as it ought to be and the world as it is. This tension is a virtual constant for religions seeking power. It underlies the paradox that a religion without a crisis is a religion within a crisis.

Insofar as religious organizations are involved in improving the lot of their adherents or changing the shape of the world around them, the task depends upon a pervasive and critical sense of need and mission that compels a response. A religious movement or organization lacking such a sense may settle into a complacency that may rob it of the vitality needed to endure.

As we have seen, some religious traditions actually spurn the contaminants of power and its ignoble pursuit, while others see involvement in state matters as their birthright and responsibility. Moreover, there are different forms of religious prophecies that lead to different types of agendas. One classic difference is between ethical and exemplary prophecies.[17] Whereas ethical injunctions involve an activist confrontation with the world in search of redress and reform, exemplary prophecy entails a more passive pursuit of personal virtue by withdrawing from the world in favor of self-discipline, mysticism, and contemplation. If the former is world conquering, the latter is often world renouncing.

Christian, Judaic, and Islamic faiths tend toward ethical action, while Hinduism and Buddhism are inclined to the exemplary. Once again, however, there is variation within each tradition. Within Christianity, conservative Protestantism in the United States has traditionally shunned politics to focus on personal otherworldly salvation—although the Moral Majority and Christian Coalition have posed recent exceptions. Liberal Protestantism in the United States has often carried its social agenda into political action, whether through abolitionism, the Social Gospel movement in the early twentieth century, or its later linkage to anti-Vietnam War activities and to movements against discrimination based on race, poverty, ethnicity, gender, and sexual orientation. Meanwhile,

Catholicism has had a strong affinity for corporate ties to the state itself, though this is an ideology whose time has largely passed in Europe and is fading in Latin America.

Similar variations occur within other faith traditions. Recall the contrast between Israel's two versions of Jewish fundamentalism: the Gush Emunim in their Zionist zealotry and the ultra-Orthodox Haredim who oppose the very concept of Israel even as they reside within it. There is a considerable difference between the state-allied Buddhism of Thailand and the state-withdrawn Buddhism of Japan. Certainly India reveals an important ideological difference between the aggressive activism of the Hindutva movement and its political party and the more ascetic and contemplative inner searches of more traditional Hindu gurus.

Finally, Islamic ideology has generally held that there can be no line between the faith and the state. At one extreme, there are Islamic movements in Egypt, Pakistan, and to a lesser degree Turkey that hold to the religion's world-reforming ethos and seek a return to state power through radical means. On the other, there are also Muslims who are wary of such a prospect and have turned to cultivating more privatized virtues.

In all of this, ideologies are as much a consequence as a cause of political change. The rise of both nationhood and secular nationalism has led some religions to reconsider their relation to secular power.[18] In responding to the bittersweet fruits of modernity, religions often mount short-run challenges followed by longer-term reconciliations. However, so-called fundamentalist movements are almost never a simple return to the past, for they typically combine past and present elements in something quite new for the future. This generally involves using modern means while rejecting modernist ends.[19]

There is no question that these ideological dynamics are the crucial stuff of continuing religious vitality and renewal. Narratives of successful religious movements can be both demonic and heroic. But only a few movements survive their initial founding stage and mature to a more successful and stable existence. Even though they adopt modernist tools, these are seldom a match for the greater array of modernist weaponry in the hands of the state and their more secular opponents.

Religious Authority. The fate of religious movements depends upon more than ideology alone. Another nest of factors involves religious authority and the extent to which it produces both clear leadership and clear control over a diverse and potentially divided religious community. The classic distinction here is between three forms of authority, or legitimations of power.[20] These are traditional authority (involving monarchs and familial leaders who are followed because that is the unchallenged custom); charismatic authority (involving an imputed magical capacity to overcome insuperable obstacles through the gift of grace as in stories of great leaders from Gautama Buddha and Jesus to Muhammad and Gandhi); and rational-legal authority (involving a systematic codification of the leaders' rights and responsibilities within a charter, constitution, or set of bylaws). Most successful leaders combine a bit of all three and so do most successful organizations. The rise of Catholicism from a struggling sect to a global church is a stunning saga of sheer organizational triumph that combines abundant elements of charismatic, traditional, and more recent rational-legal authority.

It is not hard to see why charismatic authority is associated with ethical prophets and ideologies of religious change if not outright revolution. But charisma can be as much the product of crisis and changing circumstances as the cause. When times call for charisma, groups tend to find someone on whom to bestow it. Traditional leaders are less likely to be agents of change, and rational-legal leaders are also unlikely to carry a political torch, working more within organizations than outside of them.

There are various types of authority and organizational structure that can be effective for religion. Within Christianity itself, the rise of Protestantism represented an organizational rebellion against Catholicism's massively hierarchical structure in favor of an emphasis on the autonomy of the local congregation—and indeed the individual adherent. While both religions traditions have been successful in spreading to other societies, it is not surprising that Catholicism has tended to win from the top down, using its organizational power and sophistication to concentrate on state alliances, whereas Protestantism has tended to convert from the bottom up in a more grassroots political fashion that is consistent with its emphasis on individual followers in small communal settings. However, Protestantism has had its hierarchical exceptions—for example, in the Anglican Church tradition—and today's Catholicism is host to a congeries of competing movements just beneath its surface. The contrast between the Vatican and Latin America's small base communities illustrates the church's organizational extremes.

Turning to other religions, Hinduism is more centrally organized in Indonesia's Bali than in India. Buddhism's hierarchical sangha in Thailand differs from the more differentiated model of competing schools in Japan. However, neither Buddhism nor Hinduism has had the kind of organizational development that would favor widespread political mobilization or state power. Within Islam, there is a fundamental distinction between the more authoritatively structured Shiites and the more locally autonomous Sunnis. It is not surprising that the Shiites have been most politically successful in developing an orthoprax state, namely Iran. While there are state-oriented movements within Hinduism and

Buddhism—for example, India's Hindutva and Sri Lanka's Buddhist majority—the initiative in each case arose more from professional politicians than professional religionists.

Consider the combinations that result from crossing the two distinctions between ethical and emissary prophecy, on the one hand, and between strict and loose organizational control, on the other. From the standpoint of sheer political potency, the combination with the greatest potential is ethical prophecy embedded within and protected by a hierarchical ecclesiastical structure—for example, eighth-century Islam or pre-Reformation Catholicism. Conversely, the least likely source of political power is emissary prophecy with virtually no organizational trappings—for example, Hindu and Buddhist communities that revolve around gurus and monks.

Ethical prophets without an extensive organizational structure rely on what I referred to earlier as cultural power. Some may be successful, but others may be spitting in the political wind—a common syndrome among messianic visionaries whose eccentricities preclude organizational cooperation and mobilization. The reverse combination of an elaborate ecclesiastical structure without an ethically prophetic spark is particularly vulnerable to internal decay and external co-optation. Control by the state virtually assures that religious leaders who make it to the top of the ecclesiastical ladder are selectively recruited, systematically socialized, and generally rewarded for their loyalty to the status quo. But this is characteristic of high religious officialdom everywhere, including the Vatican curia, the Catholic episcopates in Latin America, Islamic imams in the corridors of power, or members of the upper reaches of the Thai sangha. While there are certainly heroic exceptions in positions of high leadership in every faith, they are not the rule.

This last scenario suggests one final irony of religion-state separation: those religious groups with the greatest organizational resources to place at the disposal of a political perspective rarely fulfill their political potential. If they retain their independence outside of the government, they are likely to do so by whispering rather than shouting, for fear of being overheard. If they are taken into the halls of state, they may never be heard from again in anything approximating a prophetic voice. Having gained so much, religious leaders and organizations now have too much to lose. This is a common outcome in religion's continuing quest for power.

Secularization and Secularism

No factor casts a larger shadow over religion's relation to power than that of secularization. Secularization describes a form of adaptation to changing circumstances, and it can both hinder and help a religious institution. The hindrance is obvious in the disconnect with past sacred commitments; the help involves making room for sacralization or new sacred commitments that may be more relevant and prevent the religion from becoming an anachronism. In this sense, secularization can be a precondition of revitalization. Far from eradicating religion, the oscillation of secularization and sacralization tends to irrigate, prune, and cross-fertilize religion in a way that produces not only new varieties but new vigor. Those who deny secularization and focus only on the sacred vestiges of the past tend to be oblivious to emerging sacred forms of the future.

Since so much of this debate hinges on Western historical records and trajectories, it is significant that once again our non-Western cases are more similar than different. Every society we have visited provides firm evidence of extensive secularization. Respondent after respondent repeated the mantra that religion was just not what it used to be, either privately or publicly. At the same time, many respondents also said that this was a reason for the activism of the very religious movements I had come to ask about, since these were—in my words, not theirs—sacralizing responses to secularization. Even when these responses called for a return of religion to some central role—whether personally or societally— it was generally acknowledged that one could never literally return to the religion of one's forebears.

Every retreat into the past is inevitably a dialogue with the present. Certainly this is true of those who seek a return to some prior and purer religious alternative to the present, as in the so-called fundamentalist case. These movements generally involve persons marginal to—and not to be confused with—the cultural mainstream. Precisely because of their marginality, these groups and their leaders sometimes lack the broad political credibility necessary for full-scale mobilization. The American religious right, for instance, often constructs its own stained-glass ceiling. The strident appeals necessary to galvanize its most likely followers assure that it will alienate the much broader potential constituency on which ultimate success depends. Frequently the struggles occur between political extremes, leaving the much larger political middle unmoved. Charges of "fundamentalism" from the secular camp resemble charges of "Communist conspiracy" from the political right. Religious extremists and public secularists often occupy parallel positions in each other's demonology.

But, of course, none of this is to deny the force of many such religious movements, especially if their elemental flame burns long enough to survive the secularizing tendencies that accompany their mobility into higher-status ranks, their evolution into bureaucratized organizations, and their involvement in the ways of conventional politics. In several countries, secularism itself has become a major bone of contention and political foil. Turkey and India have both witnessed the rise to power of religious parties campaigning against secularism. Neither Turkey's Virtue Party nor India's Bharatiya Janata Party has yet become an established majority party, and both attained power through coalition juggling. Still the struggle continues. In Turkey, the almost eighty-year legacy of Kemal Ataturk's ban against religion in either the state or politics is at issue. In India, it is the half-century experience with a "religiously neutral" constitution that is being questioned. Many in the great Hindu majority see the state favoring Muslims, while those in the small Muslim minority take the opposite view. Over time there has been an ironic secularization of secularist principles themselves.

The broader relationship between the secularization and politicization of religion involves some surprises. At one extreme, a strictly traditional religion may turn its back on politics altogether or be so otherworldly and so out of touch with secular issues as to be ineffective. At the other extreme, a highly secularized religion may lack the incentive and resolve needed to swim against state and societal tides. Religious groups in the middle of the continuum are most often politically implicated. Here secularization has gone far enough to admit political concerns but not so far as to be politically enervating.

Secularization is related to the kind of politicization as well as the degree. Because secularization tends to be more pronounced among people with greater education, higher status, and more contact with the West, it characterizes those more rewarded by the status quo and hence more likely to favor it politically. This means that the forms of religion that have easier access to the state tend to be more secularized rather than less. Conversely, the forms of religion most opposed to the state tend to be more traditional but also more socially marginal, with fewer resources available for the contest. As comets flashing across a secular sky, they often burn brightly but quickly.

From the standpoint of religion and the state, then, power may sometimes become powerlessness, and religions outside the state's embrace can occasionally become very hot indeed. This is a major reason why religious movements sometimes exert disproportionate influence by refusing the path of compromise and co-optation. As is apparent from the liberation movement of Latin America, the Catholic IRA in Northern Ireland, the ultra-Orthodox Haredim in Israel, or India's Hindutva, maintaining a resolute independence can at least postpone the shift from absolute purity to strategic pragmatism that awaits every successful movement as yet another secularizing tendency.

Conclusion

In the final analysis, a religion's capital is often best optimized when it is not a capital religion. That is, while religion has a rightful and undeniable place in politics, religion functions best outside of the state nexus rather than within it.

So much for a condensed version of one of the book's central themes. But in some settings the message may be easier to say than to hear. Because it parallels a fundamental message of the U.S. Constitution's First Amendment, I am very much aware of the risk of being seen as at best unimaginative and at worst an intellectual imperialist.

Restating American shibboleths is certainly not the way to win friends, let alone influence people, abroad. Americans have long been snickered at around the globe for their naive provincialism and their arrogant tendency to judge other countries too quickly and too much in America's own terms. Those who fall into such categories often lose honor at home as well. In an increasingly multicultural world, it is increasingly incorrect to export our solutions for others' problems rather than import their solutions for our own troubles.

Anyone engaged in comparative research learns early and often to take refuge in the phrase, "all else equal." In addition, any American engaged in global analysis must be especially sensitive to America's own conceits. One of the problems of comparative work concerns the dilemma of how to handle one's own values and one's best sense of what might work for others.

The problem is exacerbated when one seeks not just to understand but to prescribe. But even here there are two possible errors. One is to blunder ahead and prescribe one's own medicine for every patient, regardless of the ailments and host conditions. But another error is to pull back into a benighted relativism that treats every society as only analyzable in its own terms and only changeable in its own fashion. The latter is especially problematic as a mere pose—what philosopher Charles Taylor once termed the "obligatory hypocrisy" and false cultural respect required by today's global diplomacy.

India offers an important example. At the end of his magisterial volume, *India As a Secular State*, published in 1963, Donald Smith noted presciently some of the evidences of a religious virus in the secular constitutional patient.[21] But Smith went on to express full confidence that India in its wisdom would soon work its way through or around the problem. One can only wonder whether that confidence was any more genuine then than it might be now. India's problems persist, and I have no illusions of offering either epiphanies or panaceas.

Lest I be seen as a mere intellectual jingoist, in the final chapter I offer a critique of one of America's most enduring self-conceptions. Our mythology holds dear our standing as the world's most religious complex society, but this status does not bear up well under comparative scrutiny.

8

Taking

Exception to

American

Exceptionalism

Every nation that endures and flourishes requires at least some sense of its own uniqueness. In the United States this has become a conviction bordering on fanaticism. To be an American is to be told repeatedly that one's country represents the best, the most, the highest, the purest. In short, to be an American is to be exceptional, and the doctrine of American exceptionalism has become a staple of the nation's faith in itself.[1]

This is certainly true of American religion. Long touted as the most religious industrialized nation in the world, the United States has nurtured the conceit of a divinely favored nation. For many, the sense of a religious mission lies at the core of the national identity. U.S. citizens take pride in levels of religious belief and participation that place it at the very top of countries around the globe. But just how exceptional is American religion? Are we as distinctive as is often claimed? Is the difference a matter of being more religious or differently religious? These are fitting questions to guide this concluding chapter. After all, the sometimes hidden objective of any comparative study is to illuminate one's own lot.

Three particular claims to uniqueness need assessment. One involves the organized world of America's congregations, churches, and denominations; another concerns levels and styles of individual religious involvement; a third centers on our national sense of an overarching civil religion that binds the country together while healing the bruises of its diversity. This last aspect of American religion needs to be placed in the comparative perspective of a world teeming with both nationalism and globalization.

The Legacy of Congregations

Few images of the stereotypical American community fail to include at least one corner church with a steeple—religious congregations dot the American landscape in profusion, whether the white frame icons of New England Congregationalism, the neo-Gothic edifices of Episcopalians and Presbyterians, the contemporary stylings of Lutherans and Unitarians, the storefront sects of urban neighborhoods in transition, or the new suburban campuses of conservative Protestant groups. These structures also loom large in the country's institutional sector. Religious organizations not only provide critical support mechanisms for their own communities, they account for the lion's share of the nation's voluntary giving and voluntary services, and they represent a major source of political influence and mobilization.

The public image of American religion reflects a longtime emphasis on the local church or congregation as the center of religious activity—an emphasis that began elsewhere. When the Protestant Reformation broke with Catholicism in sixteenth-century Europe, Protestantism did what every successful movement must, namely, stress a problem to which it had the solution. In this case, the problem lay in its new theological emphasis on the individual's direct relationship to God unmediated by priests or a church hierarchy. Catholic salvation required institutional sponsorship and intervention, but Protestant salvation was solely between the individual and an all-knowing God. Whatever attraction this new Protestant doctrine may have had, it also had a downside. Individual adherents not only gained a new religious freedom but also a new feeling of anxious loneliness, left by themselves in a theological wilderness. The solution was nothing less than the congregation itself as a source of fellowship and reassurance.

The congregation was especially important in the rural areas and small towns of Europe and America, where it was often the only gathering point. The United States's particular emphasis on frontier self-reliance and local democracy gave congregational life a further thrust that was later carried back into the new "frontiers" of urbanization. Congregations were at the heart of American communities across the land and at every status level. Churches, sects, and temples offered a range of social activities and services. In addition, they sometimes exerted an ethical influence that energized the local body politic.

The longtime Protestant focus on congregational life has few equivalents among other religious traditions, but parallels have begun to develop in recent years. Reform Judaism has a much more congregational focus than does Orthodox Judaism, whose houses of worship are more strictly devoted to sex-segregated worship and education. Gradually the American Catholic parish has taken on congregational qualities, especially as participation is less tied to neighborhood residence and individuals are allowed to select their churches.

The congregational model was at the core of the Liberation Theology movement within Latin American Catholicism. A key to this development was a move away from the patriarchal impersonality of large parishes toward the more egalitarian intimacy of base communities. These congregation-like units have been among the most successful Catholic responses to Protestant pentecostalism's own stress on tightly bonded (and highly feminized) congregations. In somewhat the same spirit in Poland, the political cells of the Solidarity movement gave the Catholic Church new contacts with the people during a decade of cooperation. Now that these contacts have largely disappeared, the Church is suffering the consequences.

Neither the Islamic mosque nor the Hindu temple functions as a congregation in the Protestant sense. With the family as the key Islamic institution, Muslim ritual life is not grounded in a wider network of social activity and support. Strictly speaking, the mosque is not one of the pillars of Islam, nor is it critical to the prayers that are essential but can be performed anywhere. The mosque is a special locus for prayer alone, and other activities within it are formally proscribed. In practice, mosques can take on educational functions and even serve as a mobilizing vehicle under the leadership of particular imams or mullahs. But traditionally the mosque lacks a sense of full-blown congregational solidarity. The Hindu temple is more a shrine to a particular god or goddess than a center of lay activity. Hindu rituals often revolve around the home in their concern for the purification of food and body. Rather than go to the priests, Hindus often have the priests come to them.

It is perhaps not surprising that other faith traditions have spawned a variety of extrareligious movements that provide more communality. Some are spiritual, some social, some educational, some economic, some political, and some all of these. Buddhism has followed several slightly different paths, depending upon which Buddhism is in question. The Theravada Buddhism of Thailand and Southeast Asia is a tradition controlled by monastic monks. Temples are centers of religious observance but not lay organization. Although there is an elaborate ecclesiastical structure in the sangha and some monks have considerable followings, the laity is afforded little by way of a congregational life.

Mahayana Buddhism to the northeast is more oriented to the laity. In China, Buddhist groups are often forced to take a sheltered congregational form as a protection against the party and the state. In Japan, the "new" and "new-new" lay Buddhist and Shinto movements have developed clear congregational forms. This characterizes both the most radical, the Aum Shinrikyo, and the largest, the Soka Gakkai, whose membership is now estimated at anywhere from 5 to 10 percent of all Japanese. The Soka Gakkai's intense recruitment has revolved around nested levels of lay organizations that once provided structured support and identity for rural working-class migrants to urban areas and that now perform similar functions for an increasingly middle-class constituency.

In settings where a communal or congregational grouping is lacking, the faithful may be especially vulnerable to aberrant movements that offer an equivalent to the congregational experience while pursuing more secular and political agendas. This is true of the various organizations within the ranks of India's Hindutva, as it is with several Muslim extremist movements in countries such as Egypt, Israel, and Pakistan.

Meanwhile, America's own organizational forms of religion are undergoing change. In virtually every Christian faith, there is a widening gap between national denominations and local congregations. Many older mainstream churches have lost their younger generations and have become increasingly geriatric in their membership and style. The new religious action occurs in new settings—whether in the world of cults, conservative evangelical churches, mega congregations that offer more community but sometimes less religion, or special- and single-issue movements that bear little resemblance to the churches of yesterday as they struggle in more secular venues on behalf of everything from a ban on abortion to extended rights for homosexuals.

Earlier while discussing religious violence, I described a scenario by which religion could become a surrogate or a construct for nonreligious agendas, both personal and organizational. Descriptions of American religion are laced with the motif. It provides one obvious explanation for how Americans can be ranked among both the most and least religious peoples. That is, we may be toward the top in religious "form" but toward the bottom in religious "function." Since the early nineteenth century, foreign observers have noted how Americans use their religious affiliation and participation to validate and elevate their social standing.[2]

Or consider two well-known recent religious movements in the political field, the Moral Majority of the 1980s and the current Christian Coalition. At the outset, this burst of right-wing activism was described as a massive religious movement that would not only elect candidates such as Ronald Reagan but control them once in office. Subsequent evidence suggests that both claims were exaggerated, and sometimes the influence ran unintentionally in the opposite direction as mainstream voters shrank from the prospect of a new theocracy. The size and impact of the religious right were often greatly overestimated, though there is little question that the period represented a major surge in its saliency and notoriety. It is not clear how much of this surge was due to a purely religious revitalization and how much was owed to the new politicization of a once marginal part of the electorate on other grounds. While there were surely those for whom religion was the deeply felt core of the movement, there were others who had more pressing objectives. Religion provided important overtones to the family-oriented, traditionalist agenda, but there were also old political and economic concerns long associated with the rural disadvantaged. It was largely the latter that the Reagan operatives used to pull the South and West under the Republican banner. Religion was often deployed as a legitimizing gloss. However, it soon became clear that Reagan himself was less interested in benefiting the nation's churches than the nation's business community.

If short-run tendencies on the religious right provide one American case, long-term developments on the religious left represent another. The decline of American liberal, or mainstream, Protestantism since the 1960s is easier to describe than explain. Again, however, there is a surrogate scenario. According to some perspectives, the liberal Protestant churches strayed too far from their sacred roles and mandates in taking on a host of more secular causes. It is also argued that American Protestantism became an early sponsor of a series of secular values that ultimately proved to be organizationally subversive. Such quintessentially American values as freedom, individualism, democracy, intellectualism, tolerance, and pluralism all have Protestant roots, but they are all centrifugal forces where church structures are concerned. After all, every church requires doses of faith, authority, and zealous commitment if it is to survive.

In sum, American religious organization continues to be distinctive in world context, and the congregational emphasis continues to be important. However, the organizational aspect of American religion is not as uncommon as it was even twenty-five years ago. The distinctive congregational model has spread around the globe at the same time that it has begun to diversify and even atrophy within the United States itself. If the new vitality on the American religious scene reflects a new politicization of religious movements, this is also more common around the world—as is the possibility that some of these sacred causes are proxies for secular agendas.

Do Pious Statistics Lie?

It is not hard to find statistical evidence of the religious exceptionalism of individual Americans. Virtually any polling of religious belief and behavior in industrial societies around the world will show the United States at or near the top in such matters as levels of church membership (close to 60 percent), weekly church attendance (better than 40 percent), belief in God (95 percent), and the experience of having encountered God (close to 75 percent).[3] Without actually bursting this balloon of national distinction, it is important to deflate it a bit. What is being compared in these studies is not just individual religious depths and predilections but the cultural expectations and forms for religion and religiosity that vary from one society to the next.

It is paradoxical that participating in some form of American religion remains a generally compelling national norm even though we lack a formally established national religion to participate within. One major reason involves our church-state separation. Expecting Americans to have some religious affiliation without specifying the brand has fostered a competition among religious groups to fill the need.

But if there is no formal national establishment, there are surely informal local establishments—whether Catholic in the urban Northeast, Presbyterian in many parts of the Midwest, Methodist in much of the South, Baptist in the Southwest, and, of course, Mormon in Utah. Scholars disagree whether religious participation is highest when there is a local religious monopoly or local religious competition.[4] However, there is little doubt that, in many circles, declaring oneself nonreligious is an antisocial act.

Clearly America's vaunted statistics of individual religiosity must be interpreted within this broader perspective. Without impugning the deep religious commitments of many American adherents, church membership does not necessarily entail regular church participation or personal religious commitment. Although this is not the place for a thorough critique of the sprawling research literature on Americans' religious involvement, a few cautionary notes are in order.

Consider the often quoted and widely accepted "fact" that "95 percent of Americans believe in God." The percentage is far higher than in any other nation in the Western world. But studies show such levels of belief strain credulity because they are vulnerable to variations in the question and the context. In general, the levels of traditional belief decline when a respondent has more alternatives to choose among, when these alternatives are given a neutral introduction and order, and when they include an equal number of reasonably phrased nonorthodox options.

A colleague and I once explored the issue by subjecting a student sample to two sets of questions concerning their beliefs about God. One set was heavily biased in the direction of traditional beliefs; the second was biased in the opposite direction of dissident nonbeliefs. The latter had some 25 percent fewer "believing" responses.[5] But even more striking were the responses to a final question that asked the respondents whether their "real" beliefs were more religious, less religious, or about the same as those they had just reported on the questionnaire. Perhaps predictably, some 70 percent of those exposed to the traditional bias answered that their real beliefs were less traditional than they had indicated. Much more surprisingly, this same pattern also characterized 59 percent who had been exposed to the dissident biases. Even with real encouragement and under conditions of questionnaire anonymity, it is hard to fly in the face of American religious norms.

There is an important difference, however, between intellectual conviction and cultural assent. Many who profess a belief are not expressing a considered opinion that is grounded in reason. Instead, they are aligning themselves with a community and its continuity over time. Mark Twain once observed that "faith is believing what you know ain't so." The very phrase "religious belief" is subject to misinterpretation because it is so often confused with cognitive certainty as opposed to cultural identity. What we actually believe—and with what level of intensity—is fraught with ambiguity and inconsistency, depending upon the social circumstances. It is hardly surprising that questionnaire responses are manipulatable.

A related point has recently emerged concerning church attendance. America's high level of worship activity is often paired with its high level of religious belief to cement its "most religious nation" status. And yet attendance, like belief, is problematic. One of the most significant, hence controversial, studies of individual religion in the last half century involved a check to see whether all of the more than 40 percent who claimed to have been in church on the previous Sunday could actually have shown up.[6] This study and subsequent replications and extensions show that actual levels of church attendance are about half of those that are so widely cited. Are people lying? Perhaps a better way to put it is that many are responding in terms of what they "generally do," "would like to have done," or know they "ought to be doing." They are anxious not to disappoint either themselves or the pollsters in what they take to be the larger aim of the question. Some respondents may also be wary of confessing nonbelief and nonparticipation to someone who may launch an evangelizing effort to enlist them within the fold. What may be exceptional about American religion is more its high expectations rather than its high delivery on them.

More evidence concerns the question of "religious switching," or changing religious affiliations and congregational allegiances, both of which have long been common in the United States. While some observers claim that religious switching has recently become the norm rather than the exception, closer analysis suggests that there has been little, if any, increase in the roughly 40 percent who belong to a religion different from the one in which they were reared. Of course, actual affiliation is different from attendance, and there is some evidence that the new religious marketplace involves increased shopping without buying.

Meanwhile, an equally significant debate concerns the motives of those who do switch religious affiliations. Some suggest that switching heralds a new wave of spiritual decision making and that switchers represent a resurgent religious sensibility on the part of participants seeking out new messages and new messengers. However, a recent study of switching motives reveals that the more common reasons for change involve secular life contingencies—mixed religious marriages; moving into new neighborhoods, cities, and regions of the country; the search for new social services ranging from day care to self-help groups; and the pursuit of new friendship circles.[7] The point here is not to deny that there are those who switch for deeply religious reasons, just as there are those who attend services faithfully and believe deeply in accepted religious doctrines. It is rather to stress again that American religious behavior is not always what it seems.

Just as context is important in America's putatively high levels of religious involvement, context is no less important in some of the low levels elsewhere. As noted earlier, the American Protestant tradition has been exceptional in its emphasis on the local congregation. This in turn has led to an exceptional emphasis on congregational participation and worship attendance as a measure of religious involvement. But other world religions have very different traditions and expectations. To the extent that ritual and worship are home and family centered in Islam, Hinduism, and Buddhism, they become more elusive and less amenable to an organized accounting system.

There are additional differences between Christianity and other religions that have implications for measuring religious devotion. Christianity is very much a religion of the word. But as we have seen, other faiths are religions of the act, where what one believes is far less important than what one does—and not merely as a matter of ritual observance but also as part of one's overall ethical lifestyle. This applies not only to Judaism in Israel and elsewhere, but also to Islam, Hinduism, and Buddhism. In each of these traditions, practice is more important than doctrine, and orthopraxy is a greater religious objective than orthodoxy.

Another problem in comparing levels of individual religiosity cross-nationally involves variations in defining religion itself. The question is especially apparent in understanding the Japanese and Chinese cases. As discussed previously, when most Japanese are asked whether they are religious, the answer is "no." But when asked if they participate in rituals at Shinto shrines, Buddhist temples, or within their home, the answer is generally a ready "yes." Many freely admit to superstitions and invocations of good luck for students taking exams, family events, or the purchase of a new car or major appliance. But being "religious" involves belonging to an actual religious group, and this is still rare despite the growth of such congregational movements as the Soka Gakkai.

Internal versus External Religious Pluralism

As the phenomenon of religious switching implies, religious variety is a central fact of American religious life. The country has been lionized for its waves of immigration and accompanying ethnic and religious diversity. There was a time when the country's fondest social recipe involved a melting pot, but instead there developed an ethic of tolerance for persisting heterogeneity, an ethic that defined the whole as greater than the sum of its enduring parts.[8] Ethnic, regional, class, gender, and religious differences waxed and waned, but they all continued to serve as the grid of social life. The stubborn facts of diversity finally produced our celebrated ethos of pluralism.[9]

By the end of World War II "Protestant-Catholic-Jew" had become an important shibboleth for American religious pluralism.[10] Of course, the terms occurred in numerical order and in order of actual social acceptance. The slogan also camouflaged increasingly important internal variations. Protestantism was divided into major denominational camps, not to mention major cultural distinctions between liberals, moderates, and conservative evangelicals, fundamentalists, and pentecostals. In addition to Irish, Italian, German, Polish, and French (Canadian) Catholics, Hispanic Catholicism was surging even as it was leaking into the Protestant pentecostal ranks. The percentage of Jews remained tiny, but the tensions between Judaism's Orthodox, Conservative, and Reform factions persisted. Meanwhile, the numbers of Muslims, Buddhists, and Hindus were also growing outside of the Judeo-Christian fold.

American religious pluralism's dominant assumption was that a person belonged in some fashion to one religious community or another. This was a pluralism that not only respected group differences but buttressed them. Once a Protestant, Catholic, or Jew, always a Protestant, Catholic, or Jew. There were melding processes at work, from intermarriage to integration of neighborhoods and schools, but this pluralism mainly continued to be external in the sense that the boundaries between faiths lay beyond the individual adherent.

By contrast, consider a different pattern of internal religious plural-ism where an individual may embrace several very different faith tradi-tions simultaneously. Here the diversity occurs syncretically within the individual adherent, and the external boundaries between faiths lose some of their sharp edges. In many U.S. cities, large numbers of Hispanics remain formal Catholics but attend Pentecostal Protestant services. Many Americans who do switch religious affiliations shop across denomina-tional and doctrinal lines to add a new membership without bothering to drop the old. In Guatemala, Catholic parishes have begun to make room in their worship services for elements of both indigenous Mayan religion and growing evangelical Protestantism.

While internal religious pluralism has begun to grow in the West, it has long been far more common in Eastern cultures. Earlier we saw that the Japanese are apt to engage in Shinto rituals concerning birth, Bud-dhist rituals involving death and ancestors, but a Christian wedding—though the latter is less a matter of personal commitment and more a function of American television and the fact that Western white wed-ding dresses and ceremonial accoutrements are far less expensive than traditional Japanese kimonos and all that they entail. This ritual syncretism through the life cycle suggests a very different form of plural-ism than is the norm in the West.

A similar pattern occurs in China, especially as Confucianism and Taoism overlap with each other and with Buddhist and/or Christian faith elements, not to mention the once reigning "religion" of Communism. In India, elements of Hinduism have pervaded other faiths, including Buddhism, Islam, and the syncretically founded faith of the Sikhs. Even Hinduism's caste distinctions have bled back into other religious cul-tures despite having been formally rejected by them. Indonesia offers a virtual clinic in internal pluralism. Here individuals claim several dif-ferent religious allegiances simultaneously. Indonesia is officially the world's most populous Muslim nation. However, many Indonesians are quick to assert that they are part Islamic, Buddhist, Hindu, Christian, and animist.

Multireligious conflict has been far less of a problem in the East when different religions are not sorted into distinctly different camps. There are exceptions, however, as in India where Hinduism's tracings are often unacknowledged and illegitimate, and recently in Indonesia, where conflict between Muslim militants, Christians, and Chinese has ethnic as well as religious roots and has been deliberately sparked by the military. But in general, syncretism works far better than segregation as a prophylactic against religious violence.

Syncretic and internal pluralism is hard to measure and harder still to compare with the still dominant pattern of externally bounded religious groups with distinct memberships in a country like the United States. Once again, American religiosity is exceptional because it is different, not necessarily because it is greater.

Variations on the Religious Flanks

So far I have focused on broad characterizations of religion in the United States and elsewhere. But what of religion at the margins of the religious continuum? Just as in the case of politics, much of the vitality of any nation's religion comes from its more extreme factions on both ends of a liberal-conservative continuum. Here is the domain of virtuosic and eccentric visionaries, innovative religious movements, and court cases challenging the status quo. After beginning with the left wing of religion associated with social reform, tolerance, and secularization, I shall take up the right wing so often identified with traditionalism and aggressive militancy or fundamentalism.

Accounting for the Religious Left

America's older, mainstream Protestant denominations form what is often referred to as the liberal tradition of American religion. The tradition includes the Congregationalists (now known as the United Church of Christ), Episcopalians, Presbyterians, and Unitarians, and it sometimes extends to certain brands of Baptists and Lutherans. The term "liberal" refers to a cluster of aforementioned values these churches share with the nation's political heritage—values such as individualism, freedom, equality, democracy, tolerance, and intellectual inquiry that are at the core of the nation's founding documents. These liberal values represent the basic principles behind the United States as a democratic experiment and experience. When the United States has been described as a Christian nation, it is largely the liberal denominations that have occupied center stage. And when liberal political causes have hung in the balance, it has been the left-leaning liberal denominations that have offered support. Historically, this has included causes ranging from the abolition of slavery, the reform of industrial labor abuses, the passage of social and economic legislation as a response to the Great Depressions, the civil rights movement, ending the Vietnam War, women's liberation, and most recently gay and lesbian rights.

Through World War II, liberal religion served as the nation's informal religious establishment. In the last fifty years, disestablishment has set in.[11] Since the 1960s many of these denominations have suffered reversals. Memberships have declined, as have rates of attendance, belief, and financial giving. This organizational decline may be due to the very liberal values these denominations hold dear. As noted earlier, values such as freedom, individualism, tolerance, democracy, and unfettered inquiry all militate against that sense of deep faith and compelling loyalty on which every religious organization depends. Still, the liberal churches continue to exercise disproportionate influence through their fiscal and human endowments. Because their lay members tend to be of higher social class with financial and educational advantages, they tend to dominate the nation's political and economic elites. This is also true on a much smaller scale of Reform Judaism.

Comparable liberal religious institutions in other world religions are rare. While there are certainly liberals in other faith traditions, there are few liberal movements that have crystallized into a stable organizational form akin to what Westerners might call a denomination—that is, an enduring institution with its own set of doctrinal perspectives, liturgies and rituals, ethical priorities, and organizational practices concerning power and authority. In most other faith traditions, liberals are seen as apostates who have strayed from the religious vortex and wandered off into a void not of God's making or liking.

It is true that it is a bit unfair to apply my criteria of what constitutes a liberal denomination to other faiths that lack comparable institutional infrastructures. Still, where traditional priests, imams, gurus, and monks have achieved a virtual sacred monopoly, liberal interpretations of a faith have difficulty accruing religious authority, and liberal religious movements have a hard time attaining religious legitimacy. Insofar as liberalism involves change and reinterpretation, it is a major threat to the authority of both the traditional text and its traditional interpreters. This is especially illustrated by Islam. There have been Muslim movements in the past with different interpretations of the faith—for example, the Sufi tradition in ancient Turkey. There are also current Muslim groups of intellectuals and women who are using the Internet to rally support for new interpretations of the faith. There is even one large-scale liberal Muslim movement in Indonesia, the Nahdlatul Ulama (NU), led by the country's new president, Abdurrahman Wahid. But such liberal movements are more lay organizations rather than divisions of the faith on a par with the long-standing Sunni-Shiite distinction.[12]

Islam's strong relationship to the Koran is one among several factors that discourages such a development. The Koran is just long enough to be situationally encompassing and just short enough to be memorized by school-age children. The sacred works of other faith traditions, including the Judeo-Christian Bible, are sufficiently lengthy and diverse to be inconsistent on specific points of behavior, which leaves interpretive options open for different communities of the faithful. But when religious injunctions are few enough to be literally memorable, they take on an inflexibility that makes it difficult for new interpretations to gain credibility.

Without suggesting that liberal religion has any corner on the truth, its presence can be a stabilizing factor in religion's broader societal relationships. Liberal movements or communities can serve as a buffer between religious extremists and those perceived as nonreligious. Liberal groups can also serve as a way station and a catchment for those who no longer feel comfortable in traditional settings but who do not want to leave the religious fold altogether. Finally, liberal religion offers an alternative source of religious and moral legitimacy in politics. To the extent that religion is dominated by one voice alone, it can be unduly strained and constrained.

Cultural Religion As a Massive But Neglected Category

There is an old joke about the person asked about his religion who replies, "Actually I'm an atheist," only to be asked again, "Yes, but are you a Christian atheist, a Jewish atheist, a Muslim atheist, or a Hindu atheist?" As I noted earlier, however, there are places where this is no laughing matter. The story took on a serious reality in many of my stops around the world, where I found people who see their religion as a passive cultural heritage rather an active, ongoing commitment.

From Northern Ireland to Sweden and Poland and on to Israel, I made many respondents uneasy when I asked about their personal religiosity. However, when I offered the category of cultural Protestant, Catholic, or Jew, they clutched at the category eagerly. Much the same syndrome was apparent outside the Judeo-Christian orbit. High-status Muslims in Egypt, Turkey, Pakistan, India, and Indonesia all showed telltale traces. So did many Hindus who were secular in most aspects of their lives but privately favored Hindutva's effort to Hinduize India's secular government—again as a matter of broad culture instead of narrow religion. Perhaps less that 5 percent of Chinese are formally affiliated with official or unofficial Buddhism, Christianity, or Islam. However, none of my Chinese respondents denied that virtually all Chinese carried strains of cultural Confucianism and Taoism, though many questioned whether either was a religion. The Japanese have a somewhat similarly distant yet close relation to Shinto.

In all of these cases, cultural religion is pervasive. Indeed, it is perhaps the world's most common form of religious affiliation and one that is hardly uncommon in the United States. Cultural religion is less a matter of present conviction or commitment than of continuity with generations past and contrast with rival groups and identities. In fact, identity is critical here, for religion has always ranked with ethnicity, nationality, and social class as a salient marker of personhood.

There is a paradoxical, even oxymoronic quality to cultural religion. It involves a label that is self-applied even though it is not self-affirmed. It is a way of being religiously connected without being religiously involved. It is a recognition of a religious community but a lapsed indifference to the core practices around which the community originally formed. It is a tribute to the religious past that offers little confidence for the religious future.

But if the conventional religious credentials of cultural religion are dubious and waning, it may have other social roles. In virtually every country there is a powerful current of past religion that continues to be reflected in contemporary laws, customs, and practices. In each case, religion continues to serve as source of cultural power. Past symbols and meanings echo well into the present and may still be called upon to mobilize the faithful and faithless alike. This is especially likely when one's cultural religion is juxtaposed against another conflicting tradition, as with Polish Catholics or Chinese Confucians in the presence of Communism or Israeli Jews and Indian Hindus confronted by Islam. Insofar as the cultural religion of Swedish Lutheranism is in decline, this may well be due to a lack of the kind of conflict that has occurred in Northern Ireland. After all, our identities are heavily dependent on a sharp sense of who we are not.

Within any religion's long-term historical trajectory—or any individual's experience of a waning faith—cultural religion represents the penultimate stage of religious decline, the last loose bond of religious attachment before the ties are let go altogether. But the point is not that cultural religion is a weed that will soon take over the entire religious garden or that it has no redeeming value of its own. Any source of personal and collective identity has sacred meanings that go beyond the mundane. If cultural religion is a penultimate stage of secularization, it may be enough to assure that the ultimate stage is rarely realized. Meanwhile, secularization is a topic on the left flank of religion that compels attention on its own.

Secularization in the Academy and in the Field

Moving farther out on the left flank of religion beyond both liberal and cultural religion, we come to secularism as an ideology, secularity as a social condition, and secularization as a historical process through which the sacred loses its special veneration and becomes increasingly ordinary as religion suffers decline if not demise. Today it is not uncommon to be upbraided for using the term "secularization" on the grounds that it is an old notion that has now been disproved. Perhaps predictably, such remarks are more likely to come from within than outside the religious ranks—that is, from people who have a vested interest in such a disproof. There is now a fierce scholarly battle going on over secularization.[13] But in many ways, it is a misconceived battle in the long misbegotten war over religion generally.

The real and proper thrust of secularization has been displaced rather than disproved. As noted at the book's outset, there are two versions of secularization that need disentangling. The first is the sweeping secularization thesis of the eighteenth- and nineteenth-century European Enlightenment intellectuals. Evolutionists, from Voltaire to Marx, Herbert Spencer, and Auguste Comte, posited a past when religion was all dominant and a future when religion would be all gone. They had a brimming sense that religion should—and therefore would—soon disappear altogether.

Such conceptions of a totally religious past or a totally religionless future are mythical rather than factual. There never was a society in which religion had no competition or chinks in its armor; there is no evidence that there will be any future society—communist or otherwise—in which religion is totally absent. The classical thesis of an "all-to-nothing" secularization is wrong, but it is uninstructively wrong. Nowadays rebutting Voltaire on religion is roughly akin to rebutting Newton on physics. In taking secularization theory back to the eighteenth century, its critics have sometimes purposely directed attention away from a much more pressing set of issues that require a more contemporary line of inquiry.

A new version of secularization is needed that is carefully nuanced, less extreme, and more "middle-range." Here the real question is not whether religion but whither religion. Instead of an ideologically driven and indefinite prediction of the end of religion, this new version of secularization examines a more complex dynamic—one that any religion or cultural element is likely to experience as it moves through changing historical circumstances. Thus, older sacred commitments do indeed become more secular as they become less relevant and more subject to scrutiny. But the sacred tends to regenerate rather than disappear. Secularization is often a precondition for a companion process of sacralization, by which new conceptions of the sacred emerge and claim veneration in their own right. Sometimes sacralization entails a return to revitalized aspects of an older faith; sometimes the process anoints new versions of religious doctrine and ritual; and sometimes seemingly nonreligious and previously secular objects take on a status that is sacred but not religious. Examples of how the secular can become sacred—at least for some people—include technology, political causes, art forms, sports teams, and new forms of spirituality, all of which involve many of the emotions of religion without the substance.

Secularization without sacralization is not a bad definition of the dubious diagnosis of postmodernity, with its hollow implications of a world that has lost its cultural and sacred bearings. Nonetheless, proclaiming secularization categorically false simply because religion persists is a bit like denying global warming because we have not yet been burned to a crisp and the nights do, after all, still get cooler. Moreover, secularization actually helps to insure that religion will persist by providing for its continued adaptation and updating. At the same time, secularization it also a reason why religion has changed, as has religion's place in society and politics.

America's religious exceptionalism is largely predicated on an imperviousness to secularization as it is conventionally understood. But once again it is necessary to take exception. As we have already seen, many of the most cited claims of America's high religious standing—including doctrinal belief and church attendance—need accompanying caveats. There are statistics on decline as well as on persistence.[14] But secularization is seen even more clearly in religion's relationship to power and politics at the community and national levels. Over the last hundred years, there is no doubt that religion has shifted toward the periphery of the public arena. Without suggesting that it has become solely a spectator, it has moved from a starting player to an important substitute. Religion can still make a difference by wielding its cultural power on issues that have religious import and legacies, but religion simply makes less of a difference today than in years past.[15]

Among the fourteen countries we have visited, there are many where secularity has become a way of life for significant proportions of the population. In most settings, it is only readily apparent among the urban elites, though it has cut a far wider swath in several others. Secularism has even become a state ideology in China and Turkey, and it is widely debated in India, where it is variously defined as state opposition to religion, state neutrality regarding religion, or state policy concerning religion that favors one while discriminating against another.[16]

No society has escaped secularization in one form or another—even those hotbeds of religious activity such as Brazil, Northern Ireland, Egypt, Israel, and India. At the same time, every country has also experienced sacralization—even such ostensibly secular nations as China, Turkey, and Sweden. It is impossible to imagine a society that persists without some sense of the sacred, religious or otherwise.

Fundamentalism and the Religious Right

It can be frustrating for any author to describe a work in progress. In my case, merely mentioning the words "religion and politics" often triggered the quick interruption, "Oh, you're studying fundamentalism." It is a natural conclusion. Studying religious extremism and fundamentalism has become a growth industry in global scholarship on religion.[17]

Yet the assumption that fundamentalism was my focus was inaccurate for at least three reasons. First, militant movements accounted for only a small part of my interest. Religion's relation to power, politics, and the state is by no means restricted to what occurs on its extreme right flank. For example, religion has been a thorn in the side of political elites in Latin America for more than a century, and Liberation Theology produced at least a temporary recrudescence of Catholicism in Brazil that is similar to Catholicism's experience in Poland when it joined with the Solidarity labor movement to overthrow Communism. Both cases involved politicized religion, but in neither case was the term "fundamentalism" employed.

Even in the turbulent religious waters of the Middle East and South Asia, religious politics covers a far wider band than religious extremism alone, and focusing solely on the far religious right is a sure recipe for misunderstanding the larger dynamics involved. The common image of movements like Egypt's early Muslim Brotherhood or the Islamic Group, Israel's Hamas or the Gush Emunim, and India's Hindutva is that they are wholly detached aberrations that bear no relation to what is occurring in their respective religious mainstreams. But even the most extreme terrorist movements are only shrill voices for feelings harbored by a broad segment of their more moderate coreligionists. It is generally the moderate's perceived oppressions that spark the militants into action.

A second reason for recoiling at the term "fundamentalism" is that it has become a misleading stereotype suggesting crazed fanatics wholly beyond any rational understanding. Virtually every serious scholar dealing with the topic is quick to qualify the word, if not jettison it altogether. Religious extremists or militants are rarely irrationally or pathologically hell-bent on terrorism or violence. Their politicization is a natural process and a continuing source of vitality. I have referred often to religious moths seeking the political flame for the heat that it provides. Such moths frequently have agendas in conflict not only with the secular world around them, but ultimately with much of the religious world as well. Their political involvement is both an intense tonic and a frustrating depressant. Many movements are martyred by the experience, and this simply intensifies their sense of being a spiritual elite embarked upon a mission to save the world and themselves. As charismatic, bizarre, and inexplicable as they may seem from an outsider's perspective, they are often coolly rational in their own terms.

Of course, it is not news that it is possible to be deeply religious without being a religious extremist or militant fundamentalist. However, it may be more newsworthy to note that it is also possible to be fundamentalist without being deeply religious. As noted in chapter six's account of religion as surrogate, significant proportions of most religious movements have primarily nonreligious objectives. Infamous terrorists such as Egypt's Abu Nidal and Saudi Arabia's Osama bin Laden (most recently living in Afghanistan) often use religion as a source of both mobilization and legitimacy even though their goals are frequently more secular. Advancing the faith can be far less important than assaulting the faithless. Anti-Western and anti-imperialist objectives are often pursued under the banner of religion. V. D. Savarkar, the founder of India's Hindutva movement, was a self-declared atheist who first mobilized his movement as an ethnic campaign against South Indians.

Just as one must distinguish between the deeply religious and the political militants, so must one distinguish between the generals and the soldiers. In country after country, religious movements are initiated or taken over by entrepreneurial zealots with distinctive agendas of their own. Some have religious bona fides, others have terrorist credentials; a few have both. Under such leadership, extremist groups such as the Hamas in Israel, the Islamic Group in Egypt, and the RSS youth brigade of India's Hindutva recruit many members who are initially drawn less to religion per se than to a tightly bound militaristic community, and perhaps its food and supplies. Just as with a Christian Sunday school, this process of socialization "takes" for some but not all.

Religion can follow extremism as well as precede it. Not a few so-called fundamentalist leaders began as basically nonreligious recruits seeking meager sustenance, personal identity, and the macho thrills of armed struggle—only to later find at least a version of the faith. But there are also those who once had the faith only to lose it. Just as a religious fever can be caught with prolonged exposure, so can it be lost under repeated secular contact. Those with the zeal of the converted often work side-by-side with those who retain or develop a private skepticism about the very cause they are promoting—thus producing fault lines within the movement itself. The internal tension between sacred and secular priorities and personnel is crucial to understanding any religious movement's developments and trajectories. The relationship between religious commitment and political activism should never be taken for granted.

Finally, there is a third reason for resisting the widespread use of the term "fundamentalism." The term was born in the United States, where it has a specific meaning that rarely applies elsewhere. It was originally coined in 1920 by a Texas newspaperman to describe a movement that had been involved in a series of doctrinal battles over the "fundamentals" of Christianity. The movement called for returning to a pure faith grounded in a literal interpretation of the Bible and a clear expectation that Christ would return in a time marked by apocalyptic upheaval.

It was this fundamentalism that spearheaded a Tennessee law against the teaching of evolution in the public schools and then pushed to prosecute J. T. Scopes, a teacher who openly defied the law to make it a test case. Although the "infidel" Scopes was found guilty, the fundamentalists may have lost more than they won, given the nation's reaction to their cause in the celebrated "Monkey Trial." At that point, fundamentalism began to take on especially unsavory connotations in more mainstream religious and nonreligious circles. The movement struggled as only one wing of the larger phalanx of evangelical Protestantism, and a wing whose stress on the inerrant word of the Bible was at odds with another wing—pentecostalism—and its stress on the Holy Spirit. If fundamentalists sought refuge and guidance in God's literal word; pentecostals sought rapture and protection in God's spirit, whether in healing, handling snakes, or talking in tongues. Jerry Falwell and the Moral Majority emerged from the fundamentalist tradition, whereas Pat Robertson and the Christian Coalition have more pentecostal roots. This is a major reason why Falwell and Robertson have never been allied, although both are politically active religious conservatives who live in the same state of Virginia.

Thus, fundamentalism represents one—but only one—form of conservative religious identity in the United States. How is it related to the fundamentalism one hears so much about around the world? It is true that both Christian fundamentalists and pentecostals are among those American evangelicals who have provoked sometimes violent reactions from the ranks of the indigenous in other nations. Christians have been "persecuted" in Guatemala, India, Indonesia, and China, to name only a few instances. Such events have led to the recent U.S. International Religious Freedom Act of 1998, which is a Congressional effort to safeguard American missionaries abroad. The initiative may backfire in its results and become more of a problem than a solution. Meanwhile, there is certainly no international collusion or conspiracy between Christian fundamentalists in the United States and the alleged fundamentalist movements of other faiths. Far from exporting their cause or tactics to extremists in other faiths, American fundamentalists are much more likely to see such movements as satanic rather than kindred.

Even the dynamics rarely follow the same pattern. With the conspicuous but somewhat momentary exception of the Moral Majority during the 1980s, American fundamentalists have been generally nonpolitical. But so-called fundamentalists elsewhere tend to gain attention because they are hyperpolitical. Insofar as the original fundamentalism involved a return to a putatively original faith, this is not always what one finds in eponymous movements around the globe today. To cite perhaps the most infamous case for Americans, Iran's Ayatollah Khomeini was much more of a progressive than regressive figure within Shiite Islam. He was perhaps best understood through his antipathy to the shah rather than his devotion to Mohammed. Khomeini and others like him across the Koran Belt have changed Shiism from a passive to an active religious force.

Still another misleading connotation of American fundamentalism involves followers who are simple, unsophisticated folk whose deep-seated religious commitments render them putty in the hands of a demagogic zealot. These images are increasingly inapt for both the United States and nations abroad. They are especially common in Western views of the Islamic Middle East, but there has been a profusion of studies on Muslim middle-class female university students and graduates who have returned to the veils of the faith.[18] Many religious revolutionaries are sophisticated young adults for whom religious appearances provide legitimate cover for political convictions. But, then, deep and conservative religious passion is by no means restricted to the elderly, the uneducated, or the underclasses.

Varieties of Civil Religions

One more important element of American religious exceptionalism involves a concept that is by now an old friend, civil religion. American civil religion involves the shared elements and symbols of the country's Judeo-Christian heritage as they are invoked on the nation's ceremonial occasions. The notion of civil religion is another product of the European Enlightenment, notably of the Frenchman Jean-Jacques Rousseau. The very phrase "civil religion" had an ironic ring. Rousseau was among those nonreligious seers who looked forward to an age without Christianity, yet many of these people saw the need for a different sort of "religion" that would compel allegiance to the state through a different sort of faith. In Rousseau's terms: "But there is a purely civil profession of faith, the articles of which it behooves the Sovereign to fix, not with the precision of religious dogmas, but treating them as a body of social sentiments without which no man can be either a good citizen or a faithful subject."[19]

Some 150 years later another Frenchman developed the idea further. Toward the end of his great work *The Elementary Forms of the Religious Life,* sociologist Emile Durkheim concluded his extended analysis of the tribal Arunta in Australia with remarks on France at the beginning of the twentieth century:

Thus there is something eternal in religion that is destined to out-
live the succession of particular symbols in which religious thought
has clothed itself. There can be no society that does not experience
the need at regular intervals to maintain and strengthen the collective feelings and ideas that provide its coherence and its distinct
individuality. This moral remaking can be achieved only by meetings, assemblies, and congregations in which the individuals, pressing close to one another, reaffirm in common their common
sentiments. Such is the origin of ceremonies that . . . are not different in kind from ceremonies that are specifically religious. . . . If
today we have some difficulty imagining what the feasts and ceremonies of the future will be, it is because we are going through a
phase of moral mediocrity. . . . In short, the former gods are growing old or dying, and others have not been born. It is life itself, and
not a dead past, that can produce a living cult. But that state of
uncertainty and confused anxiety cannot last forever. A day will
come when our society once again will know hours of creative ef-
fervescence during which new ideas will again spring forth and new
formulas emerge to guide humanity for a time.[20]

Durkheim's concluding prophecy was correct but tragically so. World
War I was just around the corner—the war to end all wars and the war
that took his only son.

Despite their eloquence, both Rousseau and Durkheim left us with
more of an idea than a concept. The concept did not really crystallize
until 1967, when Robert Bellah described American civil religion as essentially a bottom-up, emergent phenomenon in the Durkheimian tradition rather than the top-down, imposed doctrine commended earlier
by Rousseau.[21] Thus, our civil religion is a kind of religious common
denominator that bubbles forth from our long-standing traditions and
underscores the religious significance of the nation and its government.
It is more of a passive cultural legacy than the result of an activist political decision.

But there is another sense in which Bellah departed from both
Rousseau and Durkheim. They had been at pains to introduce a broader
concept of the sacred and to note that conventional religion per se need
not constitute the soul of a nation. But Bellah's version was more literally religious, if not religiously literal. Nor was this without reason, given
America's strong Judeo-Christian sensibilities—"Judeo" not so much
because of the role of the tiny minority of Jews in American life but
rather because Christianity emerged out of Judaism historically, theologically, and ethically. In Bellah's view, America is irretrievably religious, both at its roots and in its most luxuriant foliage. Indeed, this is

another part of American exceptionalism, since few other societies can boast such a natural melding of religion and nationhood.

Yet there are reasons to pause before accepting this portrayal. It is not clear whether this is an analysis of America's mythology or another contribution to it. On the one hand, our civil religion may not function quite the way it is depicted. On the other hand, other societies have their own versions of a civil religion, though some stretch the concept and its possibilities rather than merely illustrating it. Let us consider both complications in turn.

American Civil Religion in Doubt and in Decline?

At any given point, almost any society manifests enough cacophony to give even the most confirmed patriot second thoughts about whether there is a harmonious whole whose chorus is sweeter than the sum of its individual voices. Episodes of crime, corruption, and fever-pitched disagreement give ample grounds for pessimism. The putative American culture war between the orthodox and progressives over issues such as abortion and homosexuality hardly suggests a nation at peace. I argued earlier that this alleged "war" is really only a skirmish representing democracy in action compared to other nations where the war is a far more entrenched and violent reality. Nevertheless, even the United States has had reason to wonder whether a society that has grown so complex could any longer sustain or be sustained by civil religion and whether its manifestations haven't become more icing than cake. Bellah himself raised the issue of a "broken covenant" in expressing his bitter disappointment over the unfulfilled liberal expectations of the 1960s.[22]

America's civil religion and its heralded religious pluralism have also been pressured by an ever-expanding diversity that includes religious groups and traditions ranging from cults to the occult and from new forms of both spiritualism and survivalism to burgeoning numbers of Muslims, Hindus, and Buddhists. Even if we restrict ourselves to American Christians, we saw earlier that some observers suggest that America's civil religion has been split into liberal and conservative camps. As Robert Wuthnow puts it, the two have even managed to disagree about one of the great statements of the American credo, as conservatives stress "One nation under God" while liberals emphasize "with liberty and justice for all."[23] This is a major change from Bellah's overarching formulation. Indeed, from this earlier perspective, the detection of two civil religions may signal the absence of any civil religion insofar as there is no longer a single "sacred canopy" for the society as a whole.[24]

However, another reading of present-day America actually cleaves closer to Durkheim and Rousseau and their much broader and less theological conceptions of the sacred. Durkheim's formulation for France of

1911 resembled a "religion of the civil" rather than "civil religion" in its sectarian sense. That is, instead of assuming that religion produces civility, it may be that what is truly civil ultimately becomes religious—or more accurately "sacred."

This also applies to the United States. For a nation that was diverse from the outset and lacked other bases of cultural solidarity and commonality, the values and principles set forth in the Declaration of Independence and the Constitution may be more unifying than the Bible. The Constitution itself has often been described as America's civil religious scripture—a statement of political means that have since been elevated to cultural ends. Compared to other societies before us, it is striking just how rooted our common culture is in our political structures and their enabling documents, laws, and conflict-reducing procedures. If civility can be defined as the extent to which any society's behavior conforms to rather than departs from its own values, the United States should rank high, because its values derive from the very constitutional principles that govern our behavior overall. Insofar as America's civil religion is exceptional, it may be precisely because it, too, is more a religion of the civil. This interpretation gains credibility in comparison with other, more conflicted societies elsewhere.

Civil Religion in Cross-Cultural Perspective

I am scarcely the first to undertake a comparative assessment of civil religion.[25] However, periodic soundings are always worthwhile, especially since many countries abroad are increasingly portrayed in terms that suggest that the dominant syndrome is one of uncivil religion. But then religion in any given country can have both civil and uncivil consequences. There are any number of instances like the United States where civil religious traditions are straining to hold the center despite opposing pressures.

Virtually every Latin American country has a dominant Catholic legacy, albeit one in increasing competition with surging conservative Protestant movements and resurgent indigenous religion, such as Afrospiritualism in Brazil and Mayan practices in Guatemala. Poland would seem to illustrate Catholic civil religion at its best, though the Catholic Church has experienced declining influence since the Communists were overthrown in 1989 and the Church's ties to the winning Solidarity labor movement were loosened. Poland now seems on course with the rest of Western Europe where Catholicism is increasingly marginalized. This is particularly true of France, where the basic notion of a civil religion was given impetus by Rousseau and Durkheim.

Sweden illustrates the related pattern of formal religious disestablishment. Ending its long-standing status as an officially Lutheran nation was neither controversial nor traumatic. In fact, it was a final recognition of a cultural fait accompli that marked very little actual change in the country's politics or its culture. But it could be a harbinger of change in other countries. Anglican England could follow shortly; reports have already begun to circulate in Parliament. Many British now regard the Anglican Church and monarchy as alternately charming and charmless historical artifacts that are "merely symbolic." But as British Catholics and especially Muslims can attest, the symbols are hardly empty. Much of British law remains anchored in Anglican custom, not to mention the lifestyles and life choices of its still dominant elites.

The Middle East and the Koran Belt present a different set of civil religious scenarios. Islamic countries such as Egypt and Pakistan share a common theme with important variations. The theme involves a problem first confronted by the United States some two hundred years ago, namely, how can a struggling secular state keep a strong religious culture from becoming too dominant as a civil religious force? The political elites in these countries are terrified by the example of Iran under the Ayatollah Khomeini and Afghanistan under the Taliban. Some have dealt with the problem more successfully than others. In Egypt—as with its neighbor Algeria—a protracted armed conflict has resulted. Pakistan now publicly describes itself as a country undergoing Islamization, but many of its leaders privately seek separation from Islam's influence in order to operate successfully in a secular international arena.

There are also countries that illustrate the difficulties of a dual civil religion of the sort that some see developing in the United States. Recall the riddle of whether a nation with more than one civil religion can be said to have even one civil religion. Northern Ireland, Israel, and India all suggest the answer is no. Each society is riven by basic religious conflicts over the state and nation—whether Catholics versus Protestants in Northern Ireland, Muslims versus Jews (and Orthodox versus cultural Jews) in Israel, and Hindus versus Muslims, Sikhs, and secularists in India.

Another source of variety between civil religious traditions is whether they percolate from the cultural ground up into the state or whether they are imposed top-down upon the society by the state. Durkheim and Bellah tended to favor the former; Rousseau advocated the latter. Among the societies I have examined, the United States is joined by Sweden, Poland, and Thailand in illustrating the bottom-up scenario, which assumes a long tradition of indigenous religious homogeneity. Thailand's Buddhist civil religion and monarchy resemble the pattern of Britain and western Europe of a century ago and earlier.

But many other countries we have visited conform to Rousseau's more purposive and manipulative view of civil religion as a legitimating umbrella under the control of political figures anxious to sustain their own sense of the whole and their role within it. From this perspective, civil religion becomes the creature and consequence of the state rather than its facilitating and sustaining birthright. Civil religion is the result of a kind of cultural power play in which the state is the chief agent rather than a passive beneficiary.

Remember, for example, Indonesia's Pancasila. Created quite self-consciously in the immediate aftermath of World War II, it was expressly designed to serve as a cohesive cover over a highly pluralistic society. Comprising only five basic principles with very little elaboration—belief in (any) one God, national unity, guided democracy, social justice, and humanitarianism—specific interpretation is left to the government.

A different sort of Rousseauian civil religion occurs in Turkey, where it was ironically a form of applied Durkheimianism. In 1923 Kemal Ataturk created a secular Turkish Republic out of the remains of Islam's once great Ottoman Empire. After learning from Durkheim that a society could unite around an ethos that is sacred without being religious, Ataturk not only created a secular state but a more Westernized civic culture that reduced the country's pervasive Islamic faith to at best a private matter. Now almost eighty years later, Kemalism continues—though on half a dozen occasions since World War II it has taken actual or threatened military takeovers to keep the lid on Islamic ferment.

A similar pattern occurred in Japan, especially from 1868 to 1945. Like Turkey, Japan also moved purposely in a Western direction. The Rousseauian top-down civil religion of state Shinto was the product of a small but well-mobilized elite eager to move Japan along the path toward industrialization and world power. Today, in the wake of Japan's experience in World War II, there is a concern about a possible national unraveling despite sources of civil cohesion in a richly enduring and interrelated traditional culture.

China offers still another obvious case of an imposed civil culture if not a civil religion per se. Like Turkey, China returns us to the original conception of a civil religion that involves a nonreligious—in this case, even antireligious—sense of the sacred. The notion of Communism as a religion has become a widespread cliché. But just as there is a legitimate fear for many paranoiacs, there is a legitimate truth behind many clichés. Communism shares several qualities with more conventional religions, including ritualized characteristics of its weekly cell meetings where self-criticism is a form of confession. Lately Communism has also shown a decided tendency toward secularization—a characteristic of all religion, as we saw earlier.

China, Turkey, and even Sweden pose fundamental questions about just how important religion is to national cohesion. But then the United

States may also pose the issue. Insofar as any of these countries continue to cohere, it may be more a function of the secular becoming sacred than religion remaining civil. To put it another way, rather than regard traditional religion as the core of what is nationally civil, it may be increasingly appropriate to regard the politically civil as the core of what is tantamount to a national religion.

The Rise of Nationalism, "Culturism," and Globalization

One of the prime sources of disunity in countries around the world is the rising tide of nationalism. The recent breakups of the former Soviet Union, Yugoslavia, and Czechoslovakia reflect not only the external pushes against Communist regimes but internal pulls on behalf of distinct ethnic and religious groups seeking autonomous states to reflect their cultural identity. Similar pulls have been at work in the often changing map of postcolonial sub-Saharan and southern Africa. Previously, Northern Ireland, Pakistan, and Israel were direct products of nationalist movements. Israel continues to grapple with the demands of Palestinian nationalism, and Turkey, Poland, and China have had borders redrawn partly in response to nationalist currents. Indonesia has just decided to grant independence to East Timor, while India's struggles over Kashmir may yet have a nationalist denouement.

All of these are testaments to the lack of overlap between broadly defined cultures and civil religions on the one hand and politically conceived nation-states on the other. Whereas American culture is derived from and consistent with the state and its enabling documents, in many other countries, the culture and the state seem to be unrelated and often in conflict. The very notion of the nation-state is more an ideal of Enlightenment elitism than a naturally occurring reality. From the late eighteenth to the early twentieth century, many nations—including the United States—were assembled according to political convenience rather than cultural coherence. Religious, ethnic, and regional communities were cobbled together in a series of strained alliances under the mantle of statehood.

Politics and statecraft were supposed to provide the required solvent and glue. Using strategies ranging from totalitarian structures to artificially concocted cultures, some nations have been more enduring than others. While the United States offers one of the rare examples of overall success, even it experiences internal fractiousness. Many other countries are finding that their centers are not holding at all. For them, the ideal of nationhood has been rendered deeply suspect if not an outright mockery.

One hears much about the new nationalism in such settings. However, what is at issue is less nationalism than a kind of tribalistic "culturism." As ethnic, religious, and linguistic groups are making national claims of their own, they are turning their backs on the jerry-built nations of the past. If anything, there is a retreat from anything resembling the old form of nationhood as a political amalgam of culturally disparate communities. Small cultural islands are seeking to compete as if they were political-economic continents.

In all of this, religion provides powerful symbols for such divisive separatism. Civil religions often precede and goad the establishment of civil states, regardless of whether the new states have reasonable chances of survival as autonomous economic units. Religion is deeply implicated in efforts on behalf of (Catholic) Northern Ireland's independence from (Protestant) Britain, (Muslim) Palestine's independence from (Jewish) Israel, (Muslim) Kashmir's independence from (Hindu) India, and (Christian) East Timor's independence from (Muslim) Indonesia.

If one projects the political logic of such culturalism, it suggests a worldwide Balkanization into ever smaller culturally exclusive states. Yet this contradicts another important trend gaining momentum in the twenty-first century: globalization. How can the world become both more divided and more unified simultaneously? Of course, the answer is that neither trend is quite as pervasive as advertised.

Globalization has become both an Eleventh Commandment and a stock description of a new international scene. Virtually no society has been impenetrable to global invasions—whether global corporations, epidemics, political strife, or the circulation and contact among world religions.[26] The very phrase "world religion" connotes a religion that has ventured beyond a single society to become an international contestant.

In all of this, there is something old as well as new, something negative as well as positive. One person's new-fangled globalization is another person's old-fashioned imperialism. In fact, imperialism is the wave on which much of globalization surfs. Global consumerism includes the Avon representatives now plying the waters of Brazil's Amazon River in dug-out canoes; India's new McDonald's franchises selling Maharajah Macs made with mutton so as to offend neither Hindus with beef nor Muslims with pork; and the proliferation of "Christian" weddings in Japan.

There is no question that areas once isolated are now linked, and linked to a wider transnational culture in the bargain. The rural hut with a television antenna and perhaps a computer with satellite access to the Internet looms as a twenty-first-century icon. While visiting anthropologists studying a remote Manus fishing village off the coast of Papua New Guinea, I was struck by how the village had been affected by such modern incursions as the two-cycle outboard engine, World Cup soccer, and Christian missions. Although indigenous religion persists among the Manus, it does so in a broader context. For instance, the leader

of a local religion called Wind Nation asked me to set up an appointment for him "with President Clinton, because the two of us can combine our religions to save the world." When I pointed out that this would
be difficult in light of the American custom of separating religion from
the state, he thought for a moment and then replied, "That is a good
idea. Cancel the appointment."

But globalization is easily exaggerated. Although there are few out-
posts untouched by outside global influences, it is one thing to touch
and exploit but quite another to meld and embrace. Most local residents,
including ourselves, have a badly undersampled sense of what other cultures comprise. We tend to extrapolate from fragments that can be woe-
fully misleading. The United States is no more faithfully depicted by its
widely exported soap operas than, say, India is reliably represented by its
communal riots.

Much of the enthusiasm for the new globalism involves a series of
new nongovernmental organizations (NGOs) and social movements that
pursue common agendas across national borders. Ideally, these provide
an international infrastructure and civil society that undergirds the global culture and helps to implement its priorities.[27] Religion provides the
single largest category of NGOs around the world and the single largest
reservoir of cultural resources, and yet not all of these groups share the
same political valence. For every pro-environment group there are others mobilized around environmental destruction as a traditional livelihood. For every women's liberation movement, there are others that
involve coercive family planning or antiabortion measures. For every
movement on behalf of global integration, there are others posing various forms of cultural divisiveness and threats to the larger good.

Who is to pass final judgment on the merits of some movement objectives and the demerits of others? It is not always easy to decide for or
against female circumcision, a religious extremist government that is
popularly elected but theocratically administered, or indeed logging work
today versus nurtured forests tomorrow. Many might opt for a democratic decision, but democracy means different things in different contexts and often means very little at all unless its relationship to power is
both clarified and constrained.

Meanwhile, another issue involves not which movements should
survive but which movements will survive. According to recent social
movement scholars and organizational ecologists, it is a jungle out there—
especially at the grassroots level—where movements proliferate, compete, and sometimes disappear at a dizzying pace. A Darwinian "survival
of the fittest" applies to organizations as well as to biological species.
Nor can we be confident that the results will resemble butterflies and
giraffes rather than mosquitoes and three-toed sloths.

From this perspective, the rise of Christianity itself from its beginnings as a small, beleaguered cult is akin to an organizational miracle.[28] The basic difference between the many movements that die aborning and the very few that survive, prosper, and wield real influence lies in something called "resource mobilization."[29] Successful organizations are able to muster more of what it takes to sustain themselves over time. This generally entails resources of two sorts—one structural (money, members, connections to power) and the other cultural (motivational scripts, moral appeals, and media attention). Both of these requisites can be more difficult to come by in transnational settings where organizations have no natural base or constituency.

Although globalization connotes a happy homogenization of material benefits and mutual understandings, it often masks a deeper reality of cultural aggression that can provoke serious backlashes. As with the terms "civil society" and "civil religion," one must beware the hidden conceit of an exported Western conceptualization. This might include India's imported pattern of state secularism currently under attack by Hindu intellectuals as well as by the Hindutva rank-and-file or China's restiveness over a new spirit of democracy and capitalism let loose in the land.

Edward Said was right to call our attention to the dangers and distortions of Orientalism.[30] However, cultural stereotyping occurs both ways across any power difference, and Occidentalism is equally real.[31] The problem is not simply that we have (perhaps willfully) misunderstood "them." We have also led "them" to misunderstand themselves, or at least sewn considerable confusion about their traditional cultural forms, including religion.

There is another version of globalization that has a darker aura and has become a particular fear of the West. Samuel Huntington has recently argued that global conflict is occurring less and less between nations and more and more between "civilizations," which Huntington defines primarily along regional lines—for example, the West, the Middle East, and Asia.[32]

But just how likely is it that such massively coordinated global offensives will become preeminent? If this comparative survey is any guide, the answer is not very and for three basic reasons. First, while there are no doubt global influences at work representing different civilizations, these often work at different levels and with different implications. Recall, for example, Turkey's unsuccessful application to the European Union and how that logical political and economic alliance foundered on the illogic of Christian versus Islamic cultural differences. But then the European Union continues to struggle over cultural differences even within its Christian orbit. The English are both a culture and a channel removed from the Continent, the French and the Germans are merely civil, while the Poles and the rest of Eastern Europe pose still other differences.

Or consider Benjamin Barber's *Jihad versus McWorld*.[33] Barber's catchy title provides another illustration of stereotyping Islam in terms of the holy wars of its extremists, not to mention stereotyping the body of capitalism on the basis of the pimple of McDonald's. Still, the book depicts two globalizing tides working against each other. It describes what is less and less a clash between Western and Middle Eastern priorities and more and more a struggle between cultural and material forces that exist within every region.

Focusing more specifically on the cultural (and religious) "civilizations," there is a second reason to be skeptical of the globalizing potential. The very notion of a single seamless civilization sweeping whole nations under its power is far more fiction than fact. Of course, the United States has long experience with the misleading expectations of a cultural melting pot. It is true that some differences do elide and homogenize over time, but it is also true that new differences frequently rise in their stead. What secularization erodes, new forms of sacralization replace—whether one is talking of religion, language, cuisine, or the sheer pride of a cultivated distinctiveness.

While there is no question that major religious faiths occupy common ground, there is also no question that the ground can be rocky and crevasse riven. Would the Judeo-Christian tradition qualify as the core of a monolithic Western civilization? Certainly not on the basis of the Holocaust, which occurred within it. Even Christendom itself is divided, as indicated by traditional divisions between Catholics and Protestants, between liberal and conservative Protestant denominations, and even between such conservative movements as pentecostals and fundamentalists.

A major component in Western Orientalism is an increasing concern that Islam may become a globalizing force that chooses not to play by the standard (Western-originated) rules. But the specter of a united and politically aggressive Islam is also overdrawn. It is countered not just by different Islamic traditions such as Sunni versus Shia; it is also belied by the way the rivalries between these systems of religious authority become exacerbated when broader power is at stake. This is especially apparent when religion becomes embroiled with nationalities. The protracted conflicts between Sunni-dominated Iraq and Shiite Iran, and more recently between Shiite Iran and the Sunni Taliban of Afghanistan, suggest that a common religion may be divisive as well as uniting.

A third factor that militates against a cohesive religious force is the tension that arises when power is at issue within nations rather than between them. It is remarkable how few wars now occur between countries and how many are occurring within them. In fact, it is not surprising that the more of one kind of conflict, the less of the other. Countries at war with themselves can scarcely mobilize for wars with other nations; conversely, countries at war with others tend to be too highly mobilized to sustain internal conflict. Today it is not just the jousting between subreligious traditions—whether Catholics and Protestants in Latin America and Northern Ireland or Sunni and Shia Muslims in Pakistan. It is also the competing interpretations, gradations, and communities within a given tradition, whether traditional versus cultural identities, liberal versus conservative movements, or tolerant versus zealous agendas. Every major faith considered here reveals divisions of kind as well as degree within every nation surveyed.

Since members of the same religion are divided within nations, it is difficult—though not impossible—for religion to become united across nations. It is true that a common external foe can do wonders in healing internal strife. However, internal strife often makes it difficult to share external perceptions. If such suspicions and enmities are common shortcomings of any nation's civil religion, the prospects for a truly global civil religion would seem dim indeed.

Conclusion

At the end of the day, cross-cultural comparisons of religiousness leave less of a bottom line of clarity than a bottomless pit of ambiguity. They also offer a vast opportunity to indulge an interpretive license. In many countries one could justify summary statistics of religious involvement that range from a low of 20 percent to a high of 90 percent. Sometimes I have been tempted to juggle the data to produce a constant universal percentage of those meaningfully involved in religion in any society—say, for example, 24.3 percent. But, of course, this would amount to more mythmaking instead of the myth-breaking that is so important to the social science mission.

Is America exceptional? Of course. There is no question that our blending of national and religious heritages has produced a unique confection over the years. Yet the issue of exceptionalism has been miscast from the start. The very phrase "American exceptionalism" suggests a self-congratulatory aloofness that has been one of my primary targets. One can hope that at least the phrase is on its way out, dragging the substance behind.

Instead of asserting that Americans are more or most religious when compared to people of other nations, it is far preferable to probe how we are simply different. While it is true that some of our differences have eroded due to changes here and abroad, it is also true that others remain. These include our emphasis on religious congregational life, our stress on church and temple participation as a basis of individual piety, and what may be a unique gap between our normative expectations for religious belief and participation and a reality that falls short. The United States has developed distinctive patterns of everything from secularization to sacralization, from liberal religion to fundamentalism, and from civil religion to the religion of the civil, not to mention our tradition of church-state separation.

Yet all of these patterns and processes have both parallels and instructive differences around the globe, just as our perception of them is sharpened in the light of what occurs elsewhere. This is the real value of any cross-cultural kaleidoscope. In the final analysis, the United States' own religious dynamics may be seen best in a changing global perspective.

Appendix

A Multicomparativist

on the Road

Anyone who begins to compare societies at age fifty may seem embarked on a fool's errand. True comparativists generally select their "other culture" in graduate school in order to master the language and the nuances required for as close to a total immersion as possible. If trying to attend to two cultures in addition to one's own invites the label of "dilettante," one can only imagine the label for someone looking at fourteen. This represents not only a shift from the local to the global, but from the local to the loco—perhaps as a misguided overcompensation for the late start.

Today almost any claims to cross-cultural expertise have become politically incorrect if not intellectually dishonest. Comparisons are a very Western preoccupation, as is our effort to blend and combine elements rather than seek and distill pure essences. Presuming to understand another culture at any level is seen increasingly as an act of imperious—even imperialist—arrogance. This even applies to scholars who have devoted their entire careers to one and only one culture other than their own. Indeed, many such scholars now wear their self-doubt as conspicuous badges of intellectual honor. From this contrite perspective, one could argue that the difference between their work and my own is only a matter of degree, since if we are all inadequate, the real question is merely how much so. However, I find this argument wanting. Ironically, I sometimes seem to have more respect for comparative scholarship than do some of its practitioners—whether because they are privately jaded or publicly eager to shuck off the stigmatizing label of a Western investigative imperialist.

Of course, there are fundamental issues behind the growing chorus of mea culpas. We hear often of the "going native" syndrome for travelers of any sort. Becoming "more Indian than the Indians" is often thought of as a sure way to enhance one's admiration both abroad and at home. Nonetheless, there are problems down this path. Few persons are regarded with more pity or contempt than the many who try to go native but fail. The loss is all the greater when the process involves doffing one's own cultural clothing in the futile effort to appear naked before the world. In the case of scholars, the last step in the process often entails surrendering their conceptual categories and standards of assessment—perhaps a case of losing the intellectual war in a misguided effort to win the interpersonal battle.

Still, the objectivity of an outsider's analysis must be balanced against and dependent upon the revealing subjectivity of an insider's account. Students of religion know the tension full well from the long-standing but unresolved debate over whether one must be—or indeed can be—religious in order to understand religion. Insiders have access to experiences that afford both nuance and bias; external observers may find that their very distance from the culture at issue sometimes reveals patterns of meaning and behavior that have not occurred to the participants themselves.

Power differences between actors and the analysts always distort cross-cultural comparisons, and this cuts both up and down. Just as Western interpreters of the East are vulnerable to the sins of a patronizing Orientalism, so are Eastern observers of the West sometimes guilty of a cynical Occidentalism. Yet such cultural comparisons provide the basic language of intellectual discourse in a globalizing world. Comparisons may be flawed, but they are also indispensable. Arguing otherwise resembles the spurious reasoning that, because a totally value-free science is impossible, once values have a foot in the door, they might as well come in and make themselves fully at home.

As much as I respect intensive comparative research, mine was not a conventional comparative project. Instead it became an exercise in multicomparativism, or what I have come to call descriptive travelography and more analytic "travelology." Rather than trying to grasp the whole of only one or two societies, I wanted to look at the relation between religion and politics within a series of countries selected to highlight important variations in religion's relations to politics and the state. In selecting Brazil, Guatemala, Poland, Northern Ireland, Sweden, Israel, Egypt, Turkey, Pakistan, India, Indonesia, Thailand, China, and Japan, I had no illusions of some ultimate list. Originally, I sought out countries where there was an official religion, unlike our own separation—for example, Sweden, Pakistan, or Thailand. I then looked for instances in which religion and politics were embroiled in conflict and violence. I tried and failed to gain access to Iran, and if I were selecting religious-political hotspots today, I would want to add Afghanistan, Algeria, Rwanda, Sudan, and several of the former Soviet Republics to my itinerary. Unfortunately, there is never a shortage of instances where religion and politics are tragically intertwined.

The fourteen nations I visited were as much means as ends in my project. With no hope of becoming a fully marinated expert in any country, I wanted to use the full array of societies as a kind of multiple refracting lens through which to view my own. Of course, understanding one's own country has always been the comparativist's true objective, but this was especially true for me. America's long tradition of "triumphant exceptionalism" extends to many American scholars—until recently, myself among them—who have looked only at their own United States. But I was eager to put some of these claims to a more empirical and comparative test. In wanting to learn more about my own country by studying others, I stood with that devotee of comparative study Clifford Geertz: "Santayana's famous dictum that one compares only when one is unable to get to the heart of the matter seems to me . . . the precise reverse of the truth. It is through comparison, and of comparables, that whatever heart we can actually get to is to be reached."[1] However, I had no illusions of attaining what Geertz elsewhere calls "deep knowledge" of the countries involved or presenting what he would term a truly "thick description." In fact, a brief account of my research drill may be helpful.

Hitting the Ground Running

Typically I spent some three weeks in each country, with a few days less in some, a few days longer in others, and several months in India. I read and talked extensively with true experts both before going and after returning. My research assistant, Karen Straight, took full advantage of library and Internet resources to prepare materials for me. Indeed, some may wonder why I didn't simply stay home and conduct the research from a library carrel and on the Internet. The answer is that the travel helped to bring these disembodied materials to life while giving them meaning, depth, and texture they would otherwise lack.

Yet even on site, my research was more "secondary" than "primary." Before going, I sought the help of knowledgeable scholars to generate a list of beginning contacts whom I wrote in advance. Once on the scene, I used the time-tested technique of snowball sampling to generate new sources and informants. Very little of my research relied upon, much less developed, primary documents or samples. Most of it involved secondary learning from an array of academics, journalists, religious figures, politicians, and government officials. Although I occasionally used interpreters, I was generally dependent upon the English skills of my respondents. All of these concessions carry possible biases, but one does what one can to anticipate and offset them.

Contrary to the stereotype of the itinerant imperialist, my life abroad was not spent on sandy beaches sipping piña coladas, and my only experience with five-star hotels was occasionally to locate a copy of the *International Herald Tribune* or, better yet, the *USA Today* for its baseball box scores. While I sometimes stayed with friends or in special hostels, I was often at the mercy of the local hotel scene. Owing both to my meager budget and my eagerness to experience as much of the host culture as possible, I stayed in places a considerable notch below those of the Western business types and a sometimes insignificant step above the lairs of backpacking students, whose culinary courage and disdain of Western toilet amenities I came to admire greatly, if at a generational distance.

Of course, food is a cultural domain unto itself and one often related to religion and other conceptions of the sacred. Like the proverbial army, cross-cultural explorers travel on their stomachs. As with my hotels, this generally required eschewing both the five-star and the no-star possibilities. There is an international sameness to food both among the upper classes and the lower classes, whereas diverse cultural cuisines are most often available in the homes and restaurants of the working and middle classes. This is not the place for a paean to the food of my project, but I cannot resist mentioning a few of its glorious highs and occasional lows, sometimes as a result of the very same dish. The grilled sausage on a street in Bangkok, Thailand, or the mango milkshake from a roadside stand in Lahore, Pakistan, were both delicious but deadly. Lahore was also the scene of a wonderfully spicy meal in the home of friends on a very hot evening following a squash match. It was a meal that cried out for the cold beer unavailable to Muslim households or the unboiled water or ice that were intestinally off-limits to me. Somehow I suspect the sixteenth-century Moguls did not intend this food to be accompanied by a warm Pepsi.

Beer was available in neighboring India. On my first visit to India, I arrived from Pakistan on a day when the outside temperature and my fever were both well into the hundreds. I quaffed the first large bottle of cold beer I saw in near world-record time. Of course, India's own foods are legendary and increasingly available in the United States, though "Indian" restaurants in America are more often Muslim or Punjabi from the north of the subcontinent. As one moves from west to east and from north to south, wonderful breads give way to varied rices, and the lamb of the old Mogul empire is replaced by the exquisite seafood and desserts of Bengal and the elaborate vegetarian dishes of Tamil Nadu. Westerners often think of Indian food as vesuvial in its heat, but at least in my travels, Thailand's mouthwatering—and eye-watering—fare left India very much in the shade.

I remember a number of chicken dishes, including the webbed chicken feet that were a specialty of a restaurant in Beijing and the chicken head that was saved especially for me to suck its brains as the guest of honor in Jogjakarta, Indonesia. Brazilian mixed grills were a carnivore's delight but not exactly on the recommended list for a heart-bypass veteran. On the other hand, many of the Egyptian, Israeli, and Turkish delights were heart friendly, and Polish food had a sophistication quite different from the stereotyped cabbage and potatoes so often associated with Eastern European immigrants in the United States. While I had often heard that Japanese food represented the "bland leading the bland," I grew increasingly fond of sashimi and rice wine saki. However, if I staggered upon leaving a restaurant, this was due to the prices rather than the drink.

Language is always a problem in cross-cultural travel but especially in this case. English was the native language in only one of my fourteen countries, and many Northern Irish Catholics would detest the ring of that phrase. While English certainly serves as the elite lingua franca in India, there are other countries where that it is less true today than previously. English-language instruction in public schools has been increasingly sacrificed on the altar of nationalism. In some cases, whole generations have now been skipped, and so a shortage of teachers would make it difficult to resume English instruction even if budgets and politics allowed. As a result, many countries are at a growing disadvantage in the global political economy, where English is increasingly dominant.

But then this is an unseemly topic for Anglophones. After all, it is our lingua that is franca, and few of us have ever been forced to learn another language for our social survival. The Pope offers Christmas greetings in fifty-six languages, but I had only a middling academic introduction to French, a brief exposure to Spanish in Mexico some thirty years ago, and a halting ability to pronounce the Cyrillic alphabet without actually reading Russian. It is scarcely surprising that I found it daunting to learn twelve different foreign languages or even all the handy phrases recommended for tourists in each.

Happily, I can report one bit of good news. Just as total language command was out of the question, most of the recommended phrases were superfluous. I found that a dozen or so basic terms lubricate most simple interactions to the point that hand gestures and contextual meanings take over. Terms like hello, good morning, good-bye, thank-you, excuse me, how much, good, bad, large, small, very—these are the indispensables. The trick is to learn a serviceable but not overly accurate pronunciation, since the latter can sometimes give a misleading impression of fluency and unleash a bewildering conversational torrent in response.

True, one can (and many do) get along without even these few words. But host cultures genuinely appreciate some linguistic effort, no matter how clumsy. Once I provided comic relief to the entire rear section of a crowded commuting bus in Shanghai, as we all laughed in a cooperative effort to add another phrase or two to my embarrassingly skimpy stock. They were delighted to respond to the sign around my neck asking to be pushed off the bus at a destination a friend had written in Chinese.

I often wondered how I was perceived by those to whom I was such a stranger. Several hints emerged during a nonproject trip to visit a son and daughter-in-law who were doing real ethnography in a fishing village in Papua New Guinea. The locals were astonished at the whiteness of my legs and the vaguely Italian accent I apparently bring to every foreign language, perhaps just to luxuriate in its foreignness. But there the villagers actually knew who I was. What did others make of this tall, bald, and bespectacled egret stalking the streets of Cairo, Delhi, Jakarta, or Beijing? As I walked among them on busy streets, how did they interpret my moving lips as I often talked (and sometimes even sang) quietly to myself? With what Western intelligence service was I associated when seen writing in one of the thick, pocket-sized blue journals whose first half served as a daily journal and whose second was a repository for reading and interview notes?

Of course, their curiosity was more than justified as reciprocity for my own. Travelographers may provoke as many questions as they answer—even if their subjects are generally far too polite to ask them. Although I was rarely put on the hot seat as a representative of either the United States or the disunited state of sociology, I must apologize to both my compatriots and my colleagues for any occasions on which I let them down.

Notes

1 Religion in Opression, Liberation, and Competition in Brazil and Guatemala

1. Madeleine Cousineau Adriance, *Promised Land: Base Christian Communities and the Struggle for the Amazon* (Albany, N.Y.: SUNY Press, 1985).
2. Scott Mainwaring, *The Catholic Church and Politics in Brazil: 1916–1985* (Palo Alto, Calif.: Stanford University Press, 1986).
3. Cecilia Mariz, *Coping with Poverty: Pentecostal and Christian Base Communities in Brazil* (Philadelphia: Temple University Press, 1994); David Martin, *Tongues of Fire: The Explosion of Evangelicalism in Latin America* (Oxford: Basil Blackwell, 1990).
4. Alma Guillermoprieto, "Letter from Rio," *New Yorker*, December 2, 1991, 116–131.
5. Christian Smith, *The Emergence of Liberation Theology* (Chicago: University of Chicago Press, 1991).
6. Gustavo Gutiérrez, *A Theology of Liberation* (Maryknoll, N.Y.: Orbis Books, 1971).
7. Anthony Gill, *Rendering unto Caesar: The Catholic Church and the State in Latin America* (Chicago: University of Chicago Press, 1998).
8. Edward L. Cleary and Hannah Stewart-Gambino, eds., *Conflict and Competition: The Latin American Church in a Changing Environment* (Boulder, Colo.: Lynne Rienner, 1992).
9. W. E. Hewitt, *Base Christian Communities and Social Change in Brazil* (Lincoln: University of Nebraska Press, 1991).
10. Edward L. Cleary, *Crisis and Change: The Church in Latin America Today* (Maryknoll, N.Y.: Orbis Books, 1985).
11. Richard Adams, *Crucifixion by Power* (Austin: University of Texas Press, 1970).
12. Daniel H. Levine, *Popular Voices in Latin American Catholicism* (Princeton, N.J.: Princeton University Press, 1992).
13. Carol Smith, *Guatemalan Indians and the State, 1540–1988* (Austin: University of Texas Press, 1990).
14. David Stoll, *Is Latin America Turning Protestant? The Politics of Evangelical Growth* (Berkeley: University of California Press, 1990).
15. James Painter, *Guatemala: False Hope, False Freedom. The Rich, the Poor, and the Christian Democrats* (London: Latin American Bureau, 1987).
16. Susanne Jonas, *The Battle for Guatemala* (Boulder, Colo.: Westview Press, 1991).
17. Richard Wilson, *Maya Resurgence in Guatemala* (Norman: University of Oklahoma Press, 1995).

18. Rigoberta Menchú, *I, Rigoberta Menchú*, ed. E. Burgess-Debray (London: Verso Books, 1984).
19. David Stoll, *Rigoberta Menchú and the Story of All Poor Guatemalans* (Boulder, Colo.: Westview Press, 1999).

2 Troubles and Changes in European Christendom

1. Wlodzimierz Wesolowski, "The Nature of Social Ties and the Future of Postcommunist Society: Poland After Solidarity," in *Civil Society: Theory, History, and Comparison*, ed. John A. Hall (Cambridge: Polity Press, 1995).
2. A. Arato, "Civil Society against the State: Poland, 1980–1," *Telos* 47 (1981); Michael Patrick, *Politics and Religion in Eastern Europe* (Cambridge: Polity Press, 1991); Z. Pelczynski, "Solidarity and the Rebirth of Civil Society," in *Civil Society and the State*, ed. J. Keane (London: Verso Publishers, 1988); Jose Casanova, *Public Religions in the Modern World* (Chicago: University of Chicago Press, 1994).
3. Leonard T. Volenski and Halina Grzymala-Mosczynska, "Religious Pluralism in Poland," *America* 176 (February1997).
4. Eva Hoffman, *Shtetl: The Life and Death of a Small Town and the World of Polish Jews* (Boston: Houghton Mifflin, 1997).
5. Daniel Passent, "Unelected Powerhouses: Poles Seek a Catholic Democracy and Voters Rebuff Bishops," *Tiempo Mundial*, June 3, 1996.
6. Eileen Barker, "But Who's Going to Win? National and Minority Religions in Post-Communist Society," in *New Religious Phenomena in Central and Eastern Europe*, ed. Irena Borowik and Grzegorz Babinki (Krakow: Nomos, 1997).
7. Sabrina P. Ramet, *Whose Democracy? Nationalism, Religion, and the Doctrine of Collective Rights in Post-1989 Eastern Europe* (Oxford: Lanham and Littlefield, 1997).
8. Halina Grzymala-Mosczynska, "Established Religions vs. New Religions: Social Perceptions and Legal Consequences," *Journal of Ecumenical Studies* 33 (1):69–73.
9. Tadeusz Doktor, "The 'New Age' World View of Polish Students," *Social Compass* 46 (2):215–224.
10. Padraig O'Malley, *Northern Ireland: Questions of Nuance* (Belfast: Blackstaff 1990); J. H. Whyte, *Interpreting Northern Ireland* (Oxford: Clarendon Press, 1990).
11. Michael A. Poole, "Political Violence: The Overspill from Northern Ireland," in *Political Violence in Northern Ireland*, ed. Alan O'Day (Westport, Conn.: Praeger Press, 1997).
12. John Fulton, *The Tragedy of Belief: Division, Politics, and Religion in Ireland* (Oxford: Clarendon Press, 1991).
13. Chris Curtin, Mary Kelly, and Liam O'Dowd, eds., *Culture and Ideology in Ireland* (Galway: Galway University Press, 1984).
14. John O'Connor and Timothy O'Connor, "Neither Victory Nor Surrender: Toward a Political Economy of the Irish Peace Process" (paper presented at the meeting of the Eastern Sociological Society, Boston, March 1996); Liam O'Dowd, *Whither the Irish Border? Sovereignty, Democracy, and Economic Integration in Ireland* (Belfast: Belfast Press, 1994).
15. Steve Bruce, *The Red Hand: Loyalist Paramilitaries in Northern Ireland* (Oxford: Oxford University Press, 1992).

16. Padraig O'Malley, *Northern Ireland: Questions of Nuance* (Belfast: Blackstaff, 1990).
17. Frank Wright, *Northern Ireland: A Comparative Analysis* (Dublin: Gill and Macmillan, 1990).
18. Conrad Bergendoff, *Olavus Petri and the Ecclesiastical Transformation in Sweden, 1521–1552* (Philadelphia: Fortress Press, 1965).
19. Gunnar Boalt, *The Political Process* (Stockholm: Almquist and Wiksell, 1984); Eva Hamberg, *Studies in the Prevalence of Religious Belief and Religious Practice* (Uppsala, Sweden: Acta Universitatis Uppsaliensis, 1990).
20. Lennart Ejerfelt, "Civil Religion: Made in Sweden," in *The Church and Civil Religion in the Nordic Countries of Europe,* ed. Bela Harmati (Geneva: Lutheran World Foundation, 1984).
21. John T. S. Madeley, "Scandinavian Christian Democracy: Throwback or Portent?" *European Journal of Political Research* 5:267–286.
22. Chris Mosey, *Cruel Awakening: Sweden and the Killing of Olaf Palme* (New York: St. Martin's Press, 1991).
23. Ejerfelt, "Civil Religion."
24. Ronald Brakenheilm, "Christianity and Swedish Culture: A Case Study," *International Review of Mission* 84 (January–April 1995):91–106.
25. Ole Riis, "Patterns of Secularization in Scandinavia," in *Scandinavian Values,* ed. O. Riis and T. Petterson (Uppsala, Sweden: Uppsala University Press, 1994).
26. Grace Davie et al., eds., *Christian Values in Europe* (Cambridge: Cambridge University Press, 1993).
27. Danièle Hervieu-Léger, *Religion As Chains of Memory* (New Brunswick, N.J.: Rutgers University Press, 2000).

3   Four Islamic Societies and Four Political Scenarios

1. Ira M. Lapidus, *A History of Islamic Societies* (New York: Cambridge University Press, 1988).
2. Dale Eickelman and James Piscatori, *Muslim Politics* (Princeton, N.J.: Princeton University Press, 1996); Oliver Roy, *The Failure of Political Islam* (Cambridge: Harvard University Press, 1994).
3. Bernard Lewis, *The Political Language of Islam* (Chicago: University of Chicago Press, 1988).
4. Lisa Anderson, "Obligation and Accountability: Islamic Politics in North Africa," *Daedalus* 120 (summer 1991): 93–112.
5. Said Arjomand, ed., *From Nationalism to Revolutionary Islam* (London: Macmillan, 1984); Ernest Gellner, ed., *Islamic Dilemmas: Reformers, Nationalists, and Industrialization* (New York: Mouton, 1985); Bassam Tibbi, *The Challenge of Fundamentalism: Political Islam and the New World Disorder* (Los Angeles: University of California Press, 1998); Sami Zubaida, *Islam, the People and the State* (New York: I. B. Taurus, 1993).
6. Charles Kurzman, *Liberal Islam: A Sourcebook* (New York: Oxford University Press, 1998).
7. Panayiotis Vatikiotis, *The History of Modern Egypt* (Baltimore: Johns Hopkins University Press, 1991).
8. Raymond W. Baker, *Sadat and After: Struggles for Egypt's Political Soul* (Cambridge: Harvard University Press, 1990).

9. Saad Eddin Ibrahim, *Egypt, Islam and Democracy* (Cairo: American University in Cairo Press, 1996).

10. Gehad Auda, "The 'Normalization' of the Islamic Movement in Egypt from the 1970s to the Early 1990s," in *Accounting for Fundamentalism*, ed. Martin E. Marty and R. Scott Appleby. Fundamentalism Project Series, vol. 4 (Chicago: University of Chicago Press, 1994).

11. Giles Kepel, *Muslim Extremism in Egypt: The Prophet and the Pharaoh* (Berkeley: University of California Press, 1993).

12. Mary Anne Weaver, "The Novelist and the Sheikh," *New Yorker*, January 30, 1995, 52–69.

13. Arlene Elowe MacLeod, "Hegemonic Relations and Gender Resistance: The New Veiling As Accommodating Protest in Cairo," *Signs* 17 (spring 1992):533–557.

14. Ibrahim, *Egypt*.

15. Barry Rubin, *Islamic Fundamentalism in Egyptian Politics* (London: Macmillan Books, 1990).

16. Eickelman and Piscatori, *Muslim Politics*.

17. Samuel Huntington, *The Clash of Civilizations and the Remaking of World Order* (New York: Simon and Schuster, 1996).

18. Lord Kinross, *Ataturk* (New York: William Morrow, 1965).

19. Robert Olson, ed., *The Kurdish Nationalist Movement in the 1990s* (Lexington: University of Kentucky Press, 1996).

20. Binnaz Toprak, *Islam and Political Development in Turkey* (Leiden, Netherlands: E. J. Brill, 1981).

21. Ilter Turan, "Religion and Political Culture in Turkey," in *Islam in Modern Turkey*, ed. Richard Tapper (London: I. B. Tauris Books, 1991).

22. Nulafer Gole, *The Forbidden Modern: Civilization and Veiling* (Amsterdam: University of Amsterdam Press, 1996).

23. Metin Heper and Ahmet Evin, *Politics in the Third Turkish Republic* (Boulder, Colo.: Westview Press, 1994).

24. Seyyed Vali Reza Nasr, *Mawdudi and the Making of Islamic Revivalism* (New York: Oxford University Press, 1996).

25. Anita M. Weiss, "The Consequences of State Policies for Women in Pakistan," in *The Politics of Social Transformation in Afghanistan, Iran, and Pakistan*, ed. Myron Weiner and Ali Banuazizi (Syracuse: Syracuse University Press, 1994); Henry J. Korson, "Islamization and Social Policy in Pakistan," *Journal of South Asian and Middle Eastern Studies* 6 (2):71–90.

26. Hamza Alavi, "Ethnicity, Muslim Society, and the Pakistan Ideology," in *Islamic Reassertion in Pakistan*, ed. Anita M. Weiss (Syracuse: Syracuse University Press, 1986).

27. Mustapha Kamal Pasha, "Islamization, Civil Society, and the Politics of Transition in Pakistan," in *Religion and Political Conflict in South Asia*, ed. Douglas Allen (Westport, Conn.: Greenwood Press, 1992).

28. Clifford Geertz, *Local Knowledge* (New York: Basic Books, 1983).

29. Benedict R. O. G. Anderson, ed., *Interpreting Indonesian Politics* (Ithaca, N.Y.: Cornell University Press, 1982).

30. Arief Budiman, ed., *State and Civil Society in Indonesia*, Monash Paper on Southeast Asia, no. 22. (Centre for Southeast Asian Studies, Clayton, Victoria, Australia: Monash University, 1990.)

31. Donald E. Weatherbee, "Indonesia in 1985: Chills and Thaws," *Asian Survey* 26 (2):141–149.

32. Eka Darmaputera, *Pancasila and the Search for Identity and Modernity in Indonesian Society* (Leiden, Netherlands, and New York: E. J. Brill, 1988).
33. David Moberg, "Letter from Jakarta: The Puppet Play of Political Pluralism," *Newsday*, April 13, 1997, G4.
34. Howard M. Federspiel, *Muslim Intellectuals and National Development in Indonesia* (Commack, N.Y.: Nova Science, 1992).
35. Robert W. Hefner, *Civil Islam: Muslims and Democratization in Indonesia* (Princeton, N.J.: Princeton University Press, 2000).

4   *Two Multireligious "Mindfields"*

1. S. Ilan Troen and Noah Lucas, eds., *Israel: The First Decade of Independence* (Albany, N.Y.: SUNY Press, 1995).
2. Ziad Abu-Amr, *Islamic Fundamentalism in the West Bank and Gaza* (Bloomington: Indiana University Press, 1994).
3. Beverly Milton-Edwards, *Islamic Politics in Palestine* (London: Tauris Academic Studies, 1996).
4. Shlomo Deshen, Charles S. Liebman, and Moshe Shokeid, eds., *Israeli Judaism: The Sociology of Religion in Israel* (New Brunswick, N.J.: Transaction Publishers, 1995).
5. Benjamin Beit-Hallahmi, "Back to the Fold: The Return to Judaism," in *Jewishness and Judaism in Contemporary Israel*, ed. Zvi Sobel and Benjamin Beit-Hallahmi (Albany, N.Y.: SUNY Press, 1991).
6. Gideon Aran, "A Mystic-Messianic Interpretation of Modern Israeli History: The Six-Day War in the Religious Culture of Gush Emunim," in *Israeli Judaism: The Sociology of Religion in Israel*, ed. Shlomo Deshen, Charles S. Liebman, and Moshe Shokeid (New Brunswick, N.J.: Transaction Publishers, 1995).
7. Gideon Aran, "Jewish Zionist Fundamentalism: The Bloc of the Faithful in Israel (Gush Emunim)," in *Fundamentalism Observed*, ed. Martin E. Marty and R. Scott Appleby. Fundamentalism Project Series, vol. 1 (Chicago: University of Chicago Press, 1991).
8. Zvi Sobel, *A Small Place in Galilee: Religion and Social Conflict in an Israeli Village* (London: Holmes and Meier, 1993).
9. Don Peretz and Gideon Doron, *The Government and Politics of Israel*, 3rd ed. (Boulder, Colo.: Westview Press, 1997).
10. Dan Horowitz and Moshe Lissak, *Trouble in Utopia: The Overburdened Polity of Israel* (Albany, N.Y.: SUNY Press, 1989).
11. Ira Sharkansky, *Rituals of Conflict: Religion, Politics, and Public Policy in Israel* (London: Lynne Rienner, 1996).
12. Charles S. Liebman and E. Don-Yehiya, *Civil Religion in Israel* (Berkeley: University of California Press, 1983).
13. Ghada Karmi, ed., *Jerusalem Today: What Future for the Peace Process?* (Reading, United Kingdom: Ithaca Press, 1996).
14. Romila Thapar, *A History of India*, vol. 1 (Baltimore: Penguin Books, 1966).
15. John Keay, *India: A History* (Boston: Atlantic Monthly Press, 2000).
16. Max Weber, *The Religion of India* (Glencoe, Ill.: Free Press, 1958).
17. Lawrence A. Babb, *The Divine Hierarchy* (New York: Columbia University Press, 1975).
18. Lawrence A. Babb, "Sathya Sai Baba's Miracles," in *Religion in India*, ed. T.N. Madan (Delhi: Oxford University Press, 1992).

19. M. N. Srinivas, *Religion and Society among the Coorgs of South India* (Oxford: Clarendon Press, 1952).
20. Louis Dumont, *Homo Hierarchicus* (Chicago: University of Chicago Press, 1970); Dipankar Gupta, *Interrogating Caste* (New Delhi: Penguin, 2000).
21. J. P. S. Uberoi, "Five Symbols of Sikh Identity," in Madan, *Religion in India*.
22. Larry Collins and Dominique Lapierre, *Freedom at Midnight* (New York: Simon and Schuster, 1975).
23. Ayesha Jalal, *The Sole Spokesman* (Cambridge, U.K.: Cambridge University Press, 1985).
24. Donald E. Smith, *India As a Secular State* (Princeton, N.J.: Princeton University Press, 1963).
25. Mark Juergensmeyer, *The New Cold War? Religious Nationalism Confronts the Secular State* (Berkeley: University of California Press, 1993).
26. Ramesh Thakur, "Ayodhya and the Politics of India's Secularism: A Double-Standards Discourse," *Asian Survey* (July 1993).
27. T. N. Madan, "Secularism in Its Place," in Madan, *Religion in India*.
28. Ahish Nandy, "The Politics of Secularism and the Recovery of Religious Tolerance," in *Mirrors of Violence: Communities, Riots and Survivors in South Asia*, ed. Veena Das (New York: Oxford University Press, 1990).
29. Upendra Baxi, "Secularism: Real and Pseudo," in *Secularism in India: Dilemmas and Challenges*, ed. M. M. Sankhdher (Delhi: Deep and Deep, 1992); André Beteille, "Secularism and the Intellectuals," *Economic and Political Weekly* 29 (10):559–566.
30. Rajeev Bhargava, "India's Secular Constitution" (paper presented at conference on Constitutional Ideas and Political Practices: Fifty Years of the Republic, India Habitat Center, New Delhi, India, January 24, 2000).
31. Romila Thapar, "Imagined and Religious Communities: Ancient History and the Modern Search for a Hindu Identity," *Modern Asian Studies* 23 (2):209–231.
32. Benedict R.O.G. Anderson, *Imagined Communities* (London: Routledge, Chapman and Hall, 1983).

5 Tracking Buddha through Thailand

1. Ninian Smart, *The Religious Experience*, 4th ed. (New York: Macmillan, 1991).
2. Stanley J. Tambiah, *World Conqueror and World Renouncer: A Study of Buddhism and Polity in Thailand against a Historical Background* (New York: Cambridge University Press, 1976).
3. Trevor Ling, ed., *Buddhist Trends in Southeast Asia* (Singapore: Institute of Southeast Asian Studies, 1993).
4. Gananeth Obeysekere, "Buddhism and Conscience: An Exploratory Essay," *Daedalus* 120 (summer 1991):219–239.
5. Tambiah, *World Conqueror*.
6. Charles F. Keyes, "Political Crisis and Militant Buddhism in Contemporary Thailand," in *Religion and the Legitimation of Power in Thailand, Laos, and Burma*, ed. Bardwell L. Smith (Chambersburg, Pa.: Anima Books, 1978).
7. Prasert Yamklingfung, "Family, Religion, and Socio-Economic Change in Thailand," *East Asian Cultural Studies* 13:20–31.
8. Samboon Suksamran, "Buddhism, Political Authority, and Legitimacy in Thailand and Cambodia," in *Buddhist Trends in Southeastern Asia*, ed. Trevor Ling (Singapore: Institute of Southeast Asian Studies, 1993).

9. Samboon Suksamran, *Buddhism and Politics in Thailand* (Singapore: Institute of Southeast Asian Studies, 1982).

10. Christopher S. Queen and Sallie B. King, eds., *Engaged Buddhism: Buddhist Liberation Movements in Asia* (Albany, N.Y.: SUNY Press, 1996).

11. Peter A. Jackson, *Buddhism, Legitimation and Conflict* (Singapore: Institute of Southeast Asian Studies, 1989).

12. Keyes, "Political Crisis and Militant Buddhism."

13. Elizabeth Hann Hastings and Philip K. Hastings, eds., *Index to International Public Opinion, 1995–1996* (Westport, Conn.: Greenwood Press, 1997).

14. Ian Reader, "Lies, Damn Lies, and Japanese Religious Statistics," *Japan Forum* 211:57–61.

15. I. J. McMullen, "The Worship of Confucius in Ancient Japan," in *Religion in Japan: Arrows to Heaven and Earth*, ed. P. F. Kornicki and I. J. McMullen (Cambridge: Cambridge University Press, 1996).

16. Randall Collins, "An Asian Route to Capitalism: Religious Economy and the Origins of Self-Transforming Growth in Japan," *American Sociological Review* 62 (December 1997):843–865.

17. Robert N. Bellah, *Tokugawa Religion: The Values of Pre-Industrial Japan* (New York: Free Press, 1957).

18. John W. Dower, *Embracing Defeat: Japan in the Wake of WWII* (New York: W. W. Norton, 1999).

19. Bellah, *Tokugawa Religion*.

20. Helen Hardacre, *Lay Buddhism in Contemporary Japan: Reiukai Kyodan* (Princeton, N.J.: Princeton University Press, 1984).

21. James W. White, *The Soka Gakkai and Mass Society* (Palo Alto, Calif.: Stanford University Press, 1970).

22. Bryan Wilson and Karel Dobbelaere, *A Time to Chant: The Soka Gakkai Buddhists in Britain* (Oxford: Clarendon Press, 1994).

23. Daniel A. Metraux, "The Soka Gakkai: Buddhism and the Creation of a Harmonious and Peaceful Society," in *Engaged Buddhism: Buddhist Liberation Movements in Asia*, ed. Christopher S. Queen and Sallie B. King (Albany, N.Y.: SUNY Press, 1996).

24. Winston Davis, *Japanese Religion and Society* (Albany, N.Y.: SUNY Press, 1992).

25. Tsuyoshi Nakano, "New Religion and Politics in Post-War Japan," *Sociologica* 14 (12):1–29.

26. Susumu Shimuzono, "New Age and New Spirituality Movements in Japan" (paper presented at the meeting of the Society for the Scientific Study of Religion, Washington, D.C., November 7, 1992).

27. Jeffrey N. Wasserstrom and Elizabeth J. Perry, eds., *Popular Protest and Political Culture in Modern China: Learning from 1989* (Boulder, Colo.: Westview Press, 1992); Craig Calhoun, *Neither Gods Nor Emperors: Students and the Struggle for Democracy in China* (Berkeley: University of California Press, 1994).

28. Frederick W. Mote, *Intellectual Foundations of China* (New York: Knopf, 1971).

29. C. K. Yang, *Religion in Chinese Society* (Berkeley: University of California Press, 1967); Alvin P. Cohen, "Chinese Religion" and "Popular Religion," in *The Encyclopedia of Religion* (New York: Macmillan, 1987).

30. Daniel Bays, *Christianity in China: From the 18th Century to the Present* (Stanford, Calif.: Stanford University Press, 1996).

31. Kenneth Lieberthal, *Governing China* (New York: W. W. Norton, 1995).
32. Donald MacInnis, *Religion in China Today: Police and Practice* (Maryknoll, N.Y.: Orbis Books, 1989).
33. Philip L. Wickeri, *Seeking the Common Ground: Protestant Christianity, the Three-Self Movement, and China's United Front* (Maryknoll, N.Y.: Orbis Books, 1990).
34. Richard Madsen, *China's Catholics: Tragedy and Hope in an Emerging Civil Society* (Berkeley: University of California Press, 1998).
35. Arthur Waldron, "Religious Revivals in Communist China," *Orbis* (spring 1998):325–334.
36. MacInnis, *Religion*.
37. Willy Wo-Lap Lam, *The Era of Jiang Zemin* (Singapore: Prentice Hall, 1999).
38. Wei-Ming Tu, *The Living Tree: The Changing Meaning of Being Chinese Today* (Stanford, Calif.: Stanford University Press, 1994).

6   *Culture Wars and Religious Violence*

1. Margaret Atwood, *The Handmaid's Tale* (New York: Fawcett Crest, 1985).
2. James Davison Hunter, *Culture Wars: The Struggle to Define America* (New York: Basic Books, 1991); James Davison Hunter, *Before the Shooting Begins* (New York: Free Press, 1994).
3. Karl Marx, "A Workers' Inquiry," ed. Ken Lawrence. Freedom Information Service, Drawer D, Tougaloo College, Tougaloo, Mississippi, 1882 (1973).
4. Robert Wuthnow, *The Restructuring of American Religion* (Princeton, N.J.: Princeton University Press, 1988).
5. Richard John Neuhaus, *The Naked Public Square: Religion and Democracy in America* (Grand Rapids, Mich.: W. B. Eerdmans, 1984); James L. Guth, Corwin E. Smidt, Lyman A. Kellstedt, and John C. Green, "The Sources of Anti-Abortion Attitudes," in *Understanding the New Politics of Abortion*, ed. M. Goggin (Los Angeles: Sage, 1993).
6. Os Guinness, *The American Hour* (New York: Free Press, 1993); William J. Bennett, *The De-Valuing of America* (New York: Summit Books, 1992); Todd Gitlin, *The Twilight of Common Dreams* (New York: Metropolitan Books, 1995).
7. James L. Nolan Jr., ed., *The American Culture Wars* (Charlottesville: University of Virginia Press, 1996); Rhys H. Williams, ed., *Culture Wars in American Politics: Critical Views of a Popular Thesis* (Chicago: Aldine de Gruyter, 1997).
8. Paul DiMaggio, John Evans, and Bethany Bryson, "Have Americans' Social Attitudes Become More Polarized?" *American Journal of Sociology* 102 (November 1996):690–755; N. J. Demerath III and Yonghe Yang, "What American 'Culture War'? A View from the Trenches As Opposed to the Command Posts and the Press Corps," in Williams, *Culture Wars in American Politics*.
9. Michele Dillon, "The American Abortion Debate: Culture War or Normal Discourse?" in Nolan, *American Culture Wars*.
10. Nancy T. Ammerman, *Baptist Battles* (New Brunswick, N.J.: Rutgers University Press, 1990); Jackson W. Carroll and Penny Long Marler, "Culture Wars? Insights from Ethnographies of Two Protestant Seminaries," *Sociology of Religion* 56 (1):1–20.
11. U. N. Department of Economic and Social Development, *Report on the World Situation, 1993* (New York: United Nations, 1993).

12. Charles Tilly, *Coercion, Capital, and European States, AD 990–1992* (Oxford: Blackwell, 1992); Ruth Leger Sivard, *World Military and Social Expenditures, 1991* (Washington, D.C.: World Priorities Press, 1991); Ted Robert Gurr, *Minorities at Risk: A Global View of Ethnopolitical Conflicts* (Washington, D.C.: United States Institute of Peace Press, 1993).
13. N. J. Demerath III and Rhys H. Williams, *A Bridging of Faiths: Religion and Politics in a New England City* (Princeton, N.J.: Princeton University Press, 1992); Rhys H. Williams and N. J. Demerath III, "Cultural Power: How Underdog Religious and Non-Religious Movements Triumph against Structural Odds," in *Sacred Companies: Organizational Aspects of Religion and Religious Aspects of Organizations,* ed. N. J. Demerath III, Peter D. Hall, Terry Schmitt, and Rhys H. Williams (New York: Oxford University Press, 1998).
14. Eviatar Zerubavel, *Recovered Roots: Collective Memory and the Making of Israeli National Tradition* (Chicago: University of Chicago Press, 1995).
15. Mark Juergensmeyer, *The New Cold War: Religious Nationalism Confronts the Secular State* (Berkeley: University of California Press, 1993).
16. Ted Robert Gurr, ed., *Handbook of Political Conflict: Theory and Research* (New York: Free Press, 1980); Ted Robert Gurr, ed., *Minorities At Risk: A Global View of Ethnopolitical Conflicts* (Washington, D.C.: United States Institute of Peace Press, 1993).
17. Karl Marx, "The Class Struggles in France," in *Marx and Engels: Basic Writings on Politics and Philosophy,* ed. Lewis Feuer (Garden City, N.Y.: Doubleday Anchor, 1959).
18. David A. Snow, E. Burke Rochford Jr., Steven K. Worden, and Robert D. Benford, "Frame Alignment Processes, Micromobilization, and Movement Participation," *American Sociological Review* 51:464–481; David E. Apter, ed., *The Legitimization of Violence* (New York: New York University Press, 1997).
19. R. Scott Appleby, *The Ambivalence of the Sacred: Religion Violence and Reconciliation* (Lanham, Md.: Rowman and Littlefield, 2000); Mark Juergensmeyer, *Terror in the Mind of God: The Global Rise of Religious Violence* (Berkeley: University of California Press, 2000).
20. Karl Marx, "The 18th Brumaire of Louis Bonaparte," in Feuer, *Marx and Engels.*
21. Dipaukar Gupta, *The Context of Ethnicity: Sikh Identity in Comparative Perspective* (Delhi: Oxford University Press, 1996).
22. Apter, *The Legitimization of Violence.*
23. Veena Das, ed., *Mirrors of Violence: Communities, Riots and Survivors in South Asia* (New York: Oxford University Press, 1990).
24. Sudhir Kakar, *The Colors of Violence* (Chicago: University of Chicago Press, 1996).
25. Paul R. Brass, *Theft of an Idol: Text and Context in the Representation of Collective Violence* (Princeton, N.J.: Princeton University Press, 1997).
26. Zerubavel, *Recovered Roots.*

7 Religious Politics without a Religious State?

1. Anson Phelps Stokes and Leo Pfeffer, *Church and State in the United States* (Westport, Conn.: Greenwood Press, 1964); James E. Wood Jr., *Religion and the State: Essays in Honor of Leo Pfeffer* (Waco, Tex.: Baylor University Press, 1985).

2. Arlin M. Adams and Charles Emmerich, *A Nation Dedicated to Religious Liberty: The Constitutional Heritage of the Religious Clauses* (Philadelphia: University of Pennsylvania Press, 1990); John T. Noonan, *The Lustre of Our Country: The American Experience of Religious Freedom* (Berkeley: University of California Press, 1998).

3. Edwin S. Gaustad, *Faith of Our Fathers: Religion and the New Nation* (San Francisco: Harper and Row, 1987); Mark Noll, ed., *Religion and American Politics: From the Colonial Period to the 1980s* (New York: Oxford University Press, 1990).

4. John F. Wilson, ed., *Church and State in America: A Bibliographic Guide*, 2 vols. (Westport, Conn.: Greenwood Press, 1987).

5. Donald L. Drakeman, *Church-State Constitutional Issues: Making Sense of the Establishment Clause* (New York: Greenwood Press, 1991).

6. J. Bruce Nichols, *The Uneasy Alliance* (New York: Oxford University Press, 1988).

7. *United States v. Welch*, 398 US 333 (1970). See also Phillip E. Hammond, *The Dynamics of Religious Organizations* (Oxford: Oxford University Press, 2000), esp. 143–184.

8. James Reichley, *Religion in American Public Life* (Washington, D.C.: Brookings Institution, 1985).

9. H. Richard Niebuhr, *The Social Sources of Denominationalism* (New York: Henry Holt, 1928); Talcott Parsons, *Structure and Process in Modern Societies* (Glencoe, Ill.: Free Press, 1960); Rodney Stark and Laurence Iannaccone, "A Supply-Side Reinterpretation of the 'Secularization' of Europe," *Journal for the Scientific Study of Religion* 33:230–252.

10. Rhys H. Williams and N. J. Demerath III, "Religion and Political Process in an American City," *American Sociological Review* 56:417–431.

11. Ronald F. Thiemann, *Religion in Public Life: A Dilemma for Democracy* (Washington, D.C.: Georgetown University Press, 1996).

12. Richard John Neuhaus, *The Naked Public Square: Religion and Democracy in America* (Grand Rapids, Mich.: W. B. Eerdmans, 1984); Steven L. Carter, *Culture of Unbelief* (New York: Basic Books, 1992).

13. Ted G. Jelen, *Public Attitudes toward Church and State* (Armonk, N.Y.: M. E. Sharpe, 1995).

14. Samuel Krislov, "Alternatives to Separation of Church and State in Countries Outside the United States," in Wood, *Religion and the State*; Noonan, *Lustre of Our Country*.

15. Bryan Wilson, *Religion in Secular Society* (London: Penguin Books, 1966). Stark and Iannaccone, "Supply-Side Reinterpretation."

16. N. J. Demerath III and Rhys H. Williams, *A Bridging of Faiths: Religion and Politics in a New England City* (Princeton, N.J.: Princeton University Press, 1992).

17. Max Weber, *The Sociology of Religion* (Boston: Beacon Press, 1922).

18. Mark Juergensmeyer, *The New Cold War: Religious Nationalism Confronts the Secular State* (Berkeley: University of California Press, 1993).

19. Martin Riesebrodt, *Pious Passion: The Emergence of Modern Fundamentalism in the United States and Iran* (Berkeley: University of California Press, 1990); Bruce B. Lawrence, *Defenders of God: The Fundamentalist Revolt against the Modern Age* (London: I. B. Tauris, 1990); S. N. Eisenstadt, *Fundamentalism, Sectarianism, and Revolution: The Jacobian Dimension of Modernity* (New York: Cambridge University Press, 2000); Karen Armstrong, *The Battle for God* (New York: Knopf, 2000).

20. Max Weber, *The Sociology of Religion* (Boston: Beacon Press, 1922).

21. Donald E. Smith, *India As a Secular State* (Princeton, N.J.: Princeton University Press, 1963).

8 *Taking Exception to American Exceptionalism*

1. S. M. Lipset, *American Exceptionalism: A Double-Edged Sword* (New York: W. W. Norton, 1996).
2. Alexis de Tocqueville, *Democracy in America*, trans. George Lawrence, ed. J. P. Mayer (1835; reprint, New York: Harper and Row, 1966); Max Weber, *The Sociology of Religion*, trans. and ed. Ephraim Fischoff (1922; reprint, Boston: Beacon Press, 1963).
3. Ronald Ingelhart, *Modernization and Postmodernization: Cultural, Economic, and Political Change in 43 Societies* (Princeton, N.J.: Princeton University Press, 1997).
4. Roger Finke and Rodney Stark, "Religious Economies and Sacred Canopies," *American Sociological Review* 53 (February 1988):41–49; Judith R Blau, Kent Redding, and Kenneth C. Land, "Ethnocultural Cleavages and the Growth of Church Membership in the United States, 1860–1930," in *Sacred Companies: Organizational Aspects of Religion and Religious Aspects of Organizations*, ed. N. J. Demerath III, Peter D. Hall, Terry Schmitt, and Rhys H. Williams (New York: Oxford University Press, 1997).
5. N. J. Demerath III and Richard Levinson, "Baiting the Dissident Hook: Some Effects of Bias on Measuring Religious Belief," *Sociometry* 34 (fall 1971):346–359.
6. C. Kirk Hadaway, Penny Long Marler, and Mark Chaves, "What the Polls Don't Show: A Closer Look at U.S. Church Attendance," *American Sociological Review* 58 (December 1993):741–752.
7. N. J. Demerath III and Yonghe Yang, "What American 'Culture War'? A View from the Trenches As Opposed to the Command Posts and the Press Corps," in *Culture Wars in American Politics: Critical Views of a Popular Thesis*, ed. Rhys Williams (Chicago: Aldine de Gruyter, 1997).
8. J. Milton Yinger, *Ethnicity: Source of Strength? Source of Conflict?* (Albany, N.Y.: SUNY Press, 1994).
9. William R. Hutchison, *From Diversity to Pluralism in American Religion* (New Haven, Conn.: Yale University Press, 2001).
10. Wade Clark Roof and William McKinney, *American Mainline Religion: Its Changing Shape and Future* (New Brunswick, N.J.: Rutgers University Press, 1987); Phillip E. Hammond, *Religion and Personal Autonomy: The Third Disestablishment in America* (Columbia: University of South Carolina Press, 1992).
11. N. J. Demerath III, "Snatching Defeat from Victory in the Decline of Liberal Protestantism: Culture and Structure in Institutional Analysis," in Demerath et al., *Sacred Companies*.
12. Charles Kurzman, ed., *Liberal Islam: A Sourcebook* (New York: Oxford University Press, 1994).
13. Eileen Barker, James A. Beckford, and Karel Dobbelaere, eds., *Secularization, Rationalism, and Sectarianism* (Oxford: Clarendon Press, 1993); Rodney Stark, "Secularization, R.I.P.," *Sociology of Religion* 60 (fall 1999):249–274.
14. Thomas C. Reeves, *The Empty Church: Does Organized Religion Matter Anymore?* (New York: Simon and Schuster, 1996).
15. N. J. Demerath III and Rhys H. Williams, *A Bridging of Faiths: Religion and Politics in a New England City* (Princeton, N.J.: Princeton University Press, 1992).

16. T. N. Madan, *Modern Myths, Locked Minds* (Delhi: Oxford University Press, 1998).

17. Martin Riesebrodt, *Pious Passion: The Emergence of Modern Fundamentalism in the United States and Iran* (Berkeley: University of California Press, 1990); Bruce B. Lawrence, *Defenders of God: The Fundamentalist Revolt against the Modern Age* (London: I. B. Tauris, 1990); Martin E. Marty and R. Scott Appleby, eds., *Fundamentalism Observed*, 5 vols. (Chicago: University of Chicago Press, 1991–1995); Mark Juergensmeyer, *The New Cold War: Religious Nationalism Confronts the Secular State* (Berkeley: University of California Press, 1993); Mark Juergensmeyer, *Terror in the Mind of God: The Global Rise of Religious Violence* (Berkeley: University of California Press, 2000); Jose Casanova, *Public Religions in the Modern World* (Chicago: University of Chicago Press, 1994); Lester R. Kurtz, *Gods in the Global Village* (Thousand Oaks, Calif.: Pine Forge Press, 1995); R. Scott Appleby, *The Ambivalence of the Sacred: Religion Violence and Reconciliation* (Lanham, Md.: Rowman and Littlefield, 2000); Karen Armstrong, *The Battle for God* (New York: Knopf, 2000).

18. Nulafer Gole, *The Forbidden Modern: Civilization and Veiling* (Amsterdam: University of Amsterdam Press, 1996).

19. Jean-Jacques Rousseau, "Of Civil Religion," in *Social Contract*, ed. Ernest Barker (1770; reprint, London: Oxford University Press, 1960).

20. Emile Durkheim, *The Elementary Forms of the Religious Life*, trans. Karen Fields (1912; reprint, New York: Free Press, 1995).

21. N. J. Demerath III and Rhys Williams, "Civil Religion in an Uncivil Society," in *The Annals* 480 (July 1985):154–166.

22. Robert N. Bellah, *The Broken Covenant: American Civil Religion in a Time of Trial* (New York: Seabury Press, 1975).

23. Robert Wuthnow, *The Restructuring of American Religion: Society and Faith since World War II* (Princeton, N.J.: Princeton University Press, 1988).

24. Peter L. Berger, *The Sacred Canopy* (Garden City, N.Y.: Doubleday Anchor, 1969).

25. Robert Bellah and Phillip E. Hammond, eds., *Varieties of Civil Religion* (New York: Harper and Row, 1980).

26. Roland Robertson, *Globalization: Social Theory and Global Culture* (Los Angeles: Sage, 1992); Peter F. Beyer, *Religion and Globalization* (Los Angeles: Sage, 1994).

27. Adam B. Seligman, *The Idea of Civil Society* (New York: Free Press, 1992).

28. Rodney Stark, *The Rise of Christianity: A Sociologist Reconsiders History* (Princeton, N.J.: Princeton University Press, 1996).

29. Doug McAdam, John D. McCarthy, and Mayer Zald, eds., *Comparative Perspectives in Social Movements* (New York: Cambridge University Press, 1996).

30. Edward W. Said, *Orientalism* (New York: Random House, 1978).

31. James Carrier, ed., *Occidentalism: Images of the West* (Oxford: Clarendon Press, 1995).

32. Samuel Huntington, *The Clash of Civilizations and the Remaking of World Order* (New York: Simon and Schuster, 1996).

33. Benjamin Barber, *Jihad versus McWorld* (New York: Ballantine Books, 1995).

Appendix

1. Clifford Geertz, *Local Knowledge* (New York: Basic Books, 1983).

Index

democracy, 199ff.; Hindus vs. Christians, 199; Hindus vs. Muslims, 199; India, communal violence in, 198ff.; Indian constitution, 198ff.; "new" religious movements, 200–201; politicians vs. state officials, and vice versa, 198, 202ff.; religious extremism, 198; reservations policy, 199; secularism, 198; Sikhs vs. Hindus, 199; state as religiously neutral, 199; Tamil rebels vs. Buddhists, 199

secular states and secular politics, 195–196: Communism, as quasi-religion, 196; Enlightenment, 195; religion, revitalization of, 195; religious disestablishment, 195; religious vs. sacred, 196; Western Europe association with, 195; Western ideology, 196

secularization, 6–7, 59, 90, 123, 125, 155, 180, 195, 228–230, 244, 246: "all to nothing," 229; Enlightenment, 229; evolutionists, 229; "middle range," 229; postmodernity, 229–230; power, 230; cultural, 230; religion, revitalization of, 229; vs. the sacred, 229; sacralization, 229ff.; secularism, 228ff.; as state ideology, 230; secularity, 228ff.; statistics, 230

secularization and secularism, 210–212: "Communist conspiracy," 211; marginality, 211–212; mobilization, 211; politicization of religion, 212; power as powerlessness and vice versa, 212; religious extremists, 211; religious movements, 211, 212; "religiously neutral" constitution, 212; sacralization as precondition for revitalization, 211; secularists, 211; U.S. religious right, 211

separation of church and state, xi,

1, 34–35, 37, 55, 58, 141, 145, 184ff., 202, 220, 246: and First Amendment, 4. *See also* church-state separation, cultural vs. structural; religion, separation from politics vs. the state

Serrano, Jorge, 27, 30, 31
Seventh-Day Adventists, 150
Sharkansky, Ira, 103
Shanghai, China, 252
Sharif, Nawaz, 83, 84
Shinto, 138–147, 157
Sikhism, 3, 92, 114ff., 117, 120, 125, 173, 174, 175, 180, 224: *kara,* 115; *kesh,* 115; Khalistan, 115; *khanga,* 115; *kirpan,* 115; *kucha,* 115; Punjab, 115
Singh, Gobind, 114
Sinn Fein, 46, 47, 48, 52
Smith, Donald, 213
Social Democratic and Labour Party, 47
Solidarity labor movement (Poland), 37, 38, 42, 171, 205, 217, 231, 237
Solomon (biblical figure), 93
South Africa, 117: Truth and Reconciliation Commission, 33
South Asia, 79
South East Asia, 139
South Sumatra, 90
Soviet Republics, former, 249
Soviet Union, 74, 240
Spain, 25, 26, 33, 251
Spencer, Herbert, 229
Sri Lanka (Ceylon), 122, 130, 131–132, 199, 210
state religion vs. religious state, 4, 184–214
Stormont, Northern Ireland, 47
Straight, Karen, 249
Sub-Saharan Africa,
Sudan, 249
Suharto, M., 85, 87, 88–89, 169, 178, 197, 205
Sukarno, Achmad, 85, 86, 99
Sukarnoputri, Megawati, 88
Suksamran, Samboon, 135

About the Author

N. J. Demerath III is professor of sociology at the University of Massachusetts at Amherst and author of eight books, among them *Sacred Companies: Organizational Aspects of Religion and Religious Aspects of Organization* and *A Bridging of Faiths: Religion and Politics in New England City*. He is the current president of the Society for the Scientific Study of Religion.

different relations to politics versus the state, and the fluidity of individual religious identity, Demerath exposes the fallacies underlying many of our views on religion and politics worldwide.

Finally, Demerath places within a comparative context the commonly held view that America is the world's most religious nation and argues that our country is not "more religious" but "differently religious." He concludes that the United States represents a unique combination of congregational religion, religious pluralism, and civil religion.

N. J. Demerath III is a professor of sociology at the University of Massachusetts at Amherst and the author of ten books, among them *Sacred Companies: Organizational Aspects of Religion and Religious Aspects of Organizations* and *A Bridging of Faiths: Religion and Politics in a New England City*. He is the immediate past president of the Society for the Scientific Study of Religion.